Civility and Its Development

"A small step in showing consideration for others is a big step toward civility."
Civility campaign poster in Beijing. Photo by the author.

Civility and Its Development

The Experiences of China and Taiwan

David C. Schak

Hong Kong University Press
The University of Hong Kong
Pokfulam Road
Hong Kong
www.hkupress.hku.hk

© 2018 Hong Kong University Press

ISBN 978-988-8455-97-3 (*Hardback*)

All rights reserved. No portion of this publication may be reproduced or transmitted in any form or by any means, electronic or mechanical, including photocopying, recording, or any information storage or retrieval system, without prior permission in writing from the publisher.

British Library Cataloguing-in-Publication Data
A catalogue record for this book is available from the British Library.

10 9 8 7 6 5 4 3 2 1

Printed and bound by Paramount Printing Co. Ltd., Hong Kong, China

Contents

Preface	vi
1. Introduction	1
2. Civility	11
3. Comparability of China and Taiwan	29
4. Civility in China	70
5. Civility in Taiwan	112
6. Discussion: What Social Conditions Are Needed for a Society to Develop Civility?	136
Glossary	159
References	165
Index	196
About the Author	200

Preface

Soon after arriving in Taiwan in 1969 to begin research for my PhD dissertation, I heard about an issue that had remained on people's minds six years after it had become public. A foreign student at National Taiwan University had written an essay that was published in the official ruling Nationalist Party (Kuomintang, or KMT) newspaper saying that while *renqingwei* (the human touch) was found in abundance in Chinese society, *gongdexin* (public morality) was conspicuous by its absence. Having spent more than two years in Taiwan in the early 1960s, this was quite familiar. Nothing had changed in the interim. I made a mental note of the public morality issue and continued the research I had set out to do. Over the next two decades of research on other projects, I was from time to time reminded of the issue and noted the lack of improvement. The initial essay had set off a campaign in Taiwan's universities and middle schools that petered out within a couple of years. From time to time the government initiated other campaigns to correct some of Taiwan's public morality and other social order problems, but these suffered a similar "tiger's head, snake's tail" fate, beginning with a loud fanfare but quickly forgotten. Like so many previous KMT government campaigns, being seen to be doing something or to be concerned seemed more important than actual enforcement or results. Another part of the problem was that the socioeconomic conditions needed for people to regard public morality as important in their lives had not yet developed.

Then, from the early 1990s, civility began to take hold in Taiwan. Some improvements appeared gradually, such as smokers becoming considerate of nonsmokers and cognizant of regulations prohibiting smoking in various places. Others came about through strong top-down enforcement—for example, much more conscientious policing of traffic rules produced significant improvement in driver behavior in Taibei and gradually spread throughout the island. Overall, the change in civility over the previous decades was remarkable.

An invitation in 1996 to a round table on public morality at Melbourne University's Department of Philosophy provided an incentive to put together some thoughts on what I had observed and learned over the years. Over the next decade, though engaged in other research projects in Taiwan and China, I noted more observations and published a paper on the development of civility in Taiwan (Schak 2009b). Soon afterward, a grant from the Chiang Ching-kuo Foundation enabled me to carry out dedicated comparative research and write this book, which represents observations and research that span my career as an anthropologist studying society in Taiwan and China.

Civility's significance is conspicuous in its absence, for example, when South Carolina congressman, Rep. Joe Wilson, yelled out, "You lie!" during President Barack Obama's 2009 State of the Union address to Congress (CBS 2009) or throughout almost the entirety of the recent 2016 US presidential campaign. However, civility is more than merely a matter of decorum, of politeness or rudeness. It is also important because a society in which people treat each other civilly is a more pleasant society, and a more pleasant society can create its own virtuous cycle since people who are treated with a modicum of decency will be happier, feel more positive and less resentful, be less vulnerable to stress, and will likely treat others civilly in return. This, in turn, may foster health and longevity. Wilkinson and Pickett show a positive correlation between stress and increased morbidity (2009), and I would argue that the anger and tension arising from unpleasant encounters with rude drivers and impolite or inconsiderate people may have a similar effect.

I would also argue that a society in which people are civil to each other is easier to govern, especially when the public's encounters with public servants, police, and other authority figures are part of that civility. Civility acts as a sort of moral economy or social insurance for people who slip and fall or are knocked down in the street. People in Taiwan, and especially in China, also regard it as important. Every time I have explained what I am researching to persons from China, they have remarked that it is vitally needed in their society, which many there say is undergoing a moral crisis.

My aim in this book is to examine the development of civility in Taiwan and compare it with the development of civility in China. My purpose is not to show which society has gone further in this direction. That would be no contest. Few Chinese who have spent more than a short guided tourist holiday in Taiwan would argue that civility is more developed in China than in Taiwan. My aim is, by studying two societies that share a cultural heritage and have had similar political histories since separating, to shed light on what conditions in society facilitate or hinder its development. My research shows that attempts to impose civility top-down from the state are ineffective. The KMT government made such an effort in the 1930s in China and did so again in Taiwan from the 1960s until the end of the 1980s when Taiwan began to democratize. Civility appeared in Taiwan only *after* state efforts to impose it ceased. The Chinese government has conducted civility campaigns since 1980, with only limited success. This book analyzes the factors that move people to become more civil.

Conventions

I use Hanyu pinyin for personal and place names except for a small number of names and terms that have well-established alternative spellings. For person's names, I follow the conventional Chinese practice of listing the surname before the given name. Translations from cited Chinese texts are my own.

Acknowledgments

I owe a great debt of gratitude to a Chiang Ching-kuo Foundation grant, RG008-P-09, "The Development of Civility in Chinese Society," for providing funding for this research. In addition, a short field trip to China was funded by a Hanban (Office of Chinese Language Council International) travel grant through the Chinese Consulate in Brisbane.

Hill Gates, Miao Ying, Gene Anderson, Mark Moskowitz, and Morrie Fred all read the manuscript and made helpful suggestions. Any shortcomings in the book are, of course, my responsibility alone.

Griffith University's Department of International Business and Asian Studies provided me with adjunct status while working on the book, and the Griffith Asia Institute provided a space for me to work and congenial company. Griffith University techies kept my computers going.

In Taiwan, the Institute of Sociology at Academia Sinica welcomed me as a visiting scholar on numerous visits to Taiwan. I also benefited from helpful discussions with Sociology Institute scholars (Chang Mau-kuei, Chen Chih-jou, Chiu Hei-yuan Hsin-huang, Michael Hsiao, Hsiau A-chin, Ka Chih-ming, Shieh Guo-Shyong, Wang Fu-chang, Wang Horng Luen, and Yang Wen-Shan) and with Institute of Ethnology researchers (Hu Tai-li, Huang Shu-min, Yeh Kuang-hui, and Yu Guang-hong). Tu Hsin-fei and Luo Zhao-kuang were able research assistants. In China I enjoyed hospitality and visiting scholar status from the Department of Anthropology at Xiamen University on several occasions. My thanks to Chairman Zhang Xianqing, Lin Hong, Song Ping, Sheng Jia, and Liu Tingyu. In addition, two students from the department, Lin Huanhuan and Yang Jieqiong, were first-rate research assistants.

Thanks also go to the three anonymous reviewers of the manuscript, Ketty Chen, C. L. Chiou, J. Michael Cole, Larry Crissman, Feng Hui, Feng Lei, John Fitzgerald, He Kai, Hou Xiaohui, Julia Howell, Fraser Howie, Huang Xiaotong, Wayne Hudson, Paul Ivory, J. Bruce Jacobs, Jia Xijin, David Kelly, Leong Liew, Lung Ying-tai, Russ Moses, Frank Muyard, Sidney Rittenberg, Sang Ye, Doug Smith, Sue Trevaskes, Michael Turton, and Xie Tao.

Finally, a special expression of gratitude to those at HKU Press who guided this project along, Susie Han, Clara Ho, and copyeditor Miki Alexandra Caputo.

1
Introduction

On May 18, 1963, an opinion piece appeared in the supplementary pages of the *Central Daily News* (*Zhongyang Ribao*), the official Kuomintang (KMT) newspaper. The author of the piece identified himself as Di Renhua, but he was in fact an American graduate student from Yale named Don Baron who was studying Chinese history and philosophy at National Taiwan University. Baron entitled the piece "*Renqingwei yu Gongdexin*" (The human touch and public morality). He wrote that *renqingwei*, i.e., treating others with consideration and generosity as befitting a warm relationship, was ubiquitous in Chinese society, but such treatment was limited to one's own social circle. Strangers, by contrast, were ignored, and people gave no consideration to the effects of their actions on those outside their social circle. The human touch also clashed with the rule of law in society, hindering democratization and assisting corruption.

Baron listed many obvious examples of the lack of public morality: not queuing and cutting in line, cheating on exams, nonstudents using a student's bus pass, ignoring No Smoking signs, being self-centered and disregarding others, distorting the law to help one's friends, turning a blind eye to what was going on around oneself and not regarding this as bad because one was inured to improper or illegal behavior. These sorts of actions, some of which were of limited significance in and of themselves, created serious problems such as a lack of public morality and knowledge of what is good and proper behavior. Given such patterns of behavior, Baron asked, how can people, in particular university students, the future leaders of the nation, be expected to obey the law and maintain public order? Taiwanese, he wrote, are selfish, envious and indifferent. Taiwan society is corrupt, "mocking the poor but not the prostitute."[1] Votes are bought at election times with packs of MSG and toothpaste; to find a job one needs to "go by the back door"; and there is a culture of bribing officials. If people do not act correctly in small matters, they certainly won't do so in important ones, and this will inevitably harm the nation and the society (Jou 1996; Lin 1992).

Baron's critique was by no means exaggerated. Littering and spitting were commonplace. Smokers smoked wherever they liked, disregarding No Smoking signs

---
1. A common Chinese saying, *xiao pin bu xiao chang*.

and smoking's effects on others. Students hid books they were reading in the library to "reserve" them for themselves, and some even cut out sections that they needed to read, depriving other students access to them. People failed to apologize for bumping into others in the public space, and crowds routinely walked by anyone who had slipped or fallen or had come off a bicycle or motorbike. Drivers drove with scant regard for pedestrians. Despite a well-publicized rule of pedestrian right-of-way in crosswalks, motorists frequently drove through them as if they were not there. Autos would exit from small alleyways across sidewalks into larger roads with no precautions to avoid pedestrians other than perhaps a blast of the horn. When I mentioned such behavior to locals, they simply accepted it, reasoning that cars were bigger than people, and therefore people had to yield to them; that's the way drivers were, and nothing was going to change them. Car drivers, in fact, had to maintain a similar wariness around trucks and buses on highways.

Shops, hawkers, and department stores routinely appropriated sections of the sidewalk to display goods. Construction sites were even worse, often blocking the entire walkway with equipment and forcing pedestrians to step out into the street. Motorcycle shops were the same,[2] routinely taking up most of the footpath in front of their shops to expand their repair areas, leaving only a narrow passageway over grease-stained tiles littered with parts and tools.

Another problem was the massive increase in small factories that, in the absence of zoning laws, could be located anywhere, even in residential areas. In the heady days of the early export-oriented industrialization period, the government urged people to "turn their front rooms into factories" (*keting ji gongchang*). In many cases this meant performing value-added work such as assembling Christmas tree lights, making sweaters on knitting machines, or gluing wigs on dolls' heads. Some of these processes were unobjectionable, but others produced pollutants in the form of smoke, fumes, noise, or sawdust. Complaints to neighbors, factory owners, or the local authorities usually went unheeded.[3]

Hawkers were a more complex problem. Especially in downtown areas where pedestrian traffic was heavy, they regularly occupied half or more of the sidewalk, including those in pedestrian underpasses and on overpasses. In such areas, they were sometimes arrested, moved on, or frightened away by police, but elsewhere they were usually tolerated by the authorities as well as local merchants and residents and were, in fact, well patronized. Those who operated at night markets were even welcomed, night market shopping being a popular form of recreation in

---

2. Such shops were commonplace at the time because of the high motorcycle-to-population ratio. All these problems were made worse by the very high population density in Taiwan, especially in Taibei.
3. A woman reported that the occupant in the bottom story of the apartment block in which she lived made products on wood lathes, sending fine sawdust into the air that exacerbated her son's asthma. Getting no satisfaction talking with the factory owner or local government officials, her architect husband got some construction workers to visit the factory owner to convince him to move elsewhere; in this case, one incivility resolved another.

Taiwan. Though hawking was illegal, the police did little to eliminate it, regarding it as a means of livelihood for the vendors.

The lack of queuing was a manifestation of public space as a space without rules. This was especially true in train stations, shops, and bus stops. In post offices, which also functioned as savings banks, there were no queues. Patrons simply crowded around a service window and placed their letters or savings passbooks onto the counter, some putting theirs in front of those of others in order to be served first. Clerks paid little attention to whose turn it was, and because the idea of "first come, first served" had not been adopted, patrons were reluctant to complain. Queuing at bus stops was difficult because one could not know when their bus would arrive or exactly where it would stop. Buses did not run on a strict schedule but, for example, every four to six minutes, or every eight to ten minutes, and stops usually served more than one bus route. Thus, if a bus for one route was at the stop, an incoming bus would have to stop in front of or behind it, forcing passengers to run to where it was waiting. Crowding while boarding was common, especially by older men, anxious to get a seat for themselves, or by older women, many of whom would rush to a seat and then yield it to an adult son. Primary school students were taught that they should queue, but my son, who attended a Taibei primary school during one fieldwork period, said that they did so only if a teacher was there to supervise.

In contrast to the KMT government's 1934 New Life Movement while still governing China and its 1966 Cultural Renaissance Movement in Taiwan,[4] Baron's op-ed, given the strong approval implied by its appearance in the party/state paper, had an immediate effect. Within two days, the article had provoked a self-awareness campaign at National Taiwan University, whose president called on students "to engage in self-examination, build up a sense of public morality and carry out their responsibility to the nation" (Chen 1996). Other universities quickly followed suit, and two days after the publication of Baron's op-ed, two university students, Chen Zhenguo and Xu Xitu, announced the formation of China Youth Self-Awareness Promotion Movement, a group dedicated to enhancing public morality and whose slogan was "we will not be judged by history as selfish or decadent." The Movement attracted support from middle school and tertiary level students throughout Taiwan as well as a wide variety of citizens, and it set out to perform philanthropic services. Volunteers, wearing movement armbands, monitored bus stops and stoplight intersections to ensure orderly queues, prevent crossing against the light, direct traffic, and help the disabled cross safely. They observed theater entrances to ensure that patrons queued while buying tickets and entered the theaters in an orderly fashion, and they picked up rubbish left on the ground. The movement also sent cadres throughout Taiwan to speak at schools about the moral goals of the organization.

The movement published a booklet listing violations of public morality. Those pertaining particularly to students included

---

4. Discussed in Chapter 3.

- cheating on exams;
- nonstudents using a student's bus pass;
- smoking where prohibited;
- breaking rules;
- allowing nonresidents to stay in student dorms;
- taking up a desk in the library when not using it;
- cutting out portions of library books or magazines; and
- not paying for stamps at the Taiwan University Post Office's trial stamp dispenser.

The booklet also listed examples of good public morality:

- Bus drivers accelerating and braking smoothly
- Drivers obeying traffic rules
- Buying goods from shops that give receipts[5]
- Shop clerks and bus attendants being polite and friendly to customers
- Bus passengers accompanying small children removing the children's shoes and covering the seat with plastic bags to keep it clean
- Cheerfully helping persons asking directions
- Protecting public property (Yan 1972, 3; cited in Chen 2005, 17–18)

Although the movement enjoyed some success, one of the organizers, Xu Xitu, also organized what he called the Unity Foundation, a group recruiting young people that aimed to unify Taiwan and China and was critical of both the KMT and the Chinese Communist Party (CCP) governments. However, early in 1969, the movement was disbanded, and later that year five of its leaders, including Xu, were arrested, tried, sentenced to prison terms of up to fifteen years, and stripped of their civil liberties for an additional ten years (Lin 1992; Zijue Yundong).[6]

The trials took place in June. When I began my PhD thesis field research in September, I learned of the human touch–public morality dichotomy, which was a matter of public discourse, but not of the trials. Moreover, whatever success the movement might have had in changing people's habits, I saw little effect of the public order that volunteers for the movement had tried to promote. Between 1969 and 1979 I spent a total of four and a half years in Taiwan during which I saw no effective efforts to promote public morality or evidence of its becoming more established. It was much the same in the two and a half years I spent there in the 1980s. Throughout these two decades, people continued to disregard the above-mentioned enjoinments to observe public morality. Occasional short-lived

---

5. The government introduced receipts (*tongyi fapiao*) in order to stop bargaining and cash transactions, the former to save time and be "modern," the latter to facilitate tax collection.
6. Their sentences were reduced following President Chiang Kai-shek's death in 1975. After the lifting of martial law in 1987 and the beginning of Taiwan's democratization, the case was reopened, and the verdict was overturned.

government campaigns and primary school moral education courses that included civil comportment instructions were also ineffective.

Then, in the early 1990s, Taiwan began to change. People not only became more polite, but the general level of concern was perceptibly higher. Smokers became more considerate of nonsmokers and nonsmoking venues. People queued, and they littered less. After a sustained campaign by the Taibei City Government to enforce traffic laws in the mid-1990s, driver behavior also improved. This does not mean that incivility did not occur; indeed, it did. But through the 1990s it decreased to the extent that civility became the norm, and incivility went from being so commonplace that it usually went unnoticed and unremarked upon to being generally unacceptable to the public and even attracted reprimands.

These changes coincided with democratization and the cessation of government campaigns to promote public morality. In a previous paper (Schak 2009) I identified democratization as one of a number of factors that plausibly aided or hindered the development of public morality or, as I call it in this book, civility. I will further explore the relationship between these factors and the development of civility in the final chapter.

This Book

The purpose of this book is to better understand the social conditions needed to establish civility in a society. I do this by comparing Taiwan's experience with efforts to develop civility in China, two societies that are similar in the most salient features—cultural heritage, a history of autocratic governance, ideas about significant others and strangers, the treatment of public space and public facilities, and, until a few decades ago, general values. Note that in the book "China" is formally the People's Republic of China; "Taiwan" is formally the Republic of China. I will refer to them as China and Taiwan throughout the book for the sake of simplicity but, most important, because my reference to them is as *societies*. No political intent should be implied.

Both Taiwan and China have run civilizing campaigns, as did the KMT government when it governed China before the victory of Mao Zedong and the CCP in 1949, and as did successive dynastic governments at least from the Ming Dynasty through the end of the imperial era. Ethnically, aside from the Malayo-Polynesian first peoples (about 2 percent of the population), the majority of the people in Taiwan are Han whose ancestors migrated from China. Those arriving before 1945 came mainly from Fujian and Guangdong Provinces and make up the Taiwanese. Those arriving after World War II came from all parts of China and are referred to as Mainlanders. Some quite noticeable cultural differences have arisen between the people in Taiwan and those in China since 1949, and especially since 1975, but the root causes of their historic incivility are the same in both societies. Moreover, from what I observed in my several visits and periods of residence in Taiwan beginning in 1959 and in China beginning in 1983, the sorts of uncivil actions people engaged in and the kinds of behavioral changes the governments of each have enjoined their citizens to adopt are also the same. I will explicate these points in subsequent chapters.

Developing civility is important for several reasons. In the eyes of the governments of the societies studied in this book, a civil population is a mark of a civilized nation, one whose peoples cannot be derided as coarse and uncultured as the Chinese were in the century preceding the Communist revolution. Anagnost reports that in the early 1920s China's elites echoed these criticisms, condemning the "low quality" of the population, including what they regarded as their uncivil habits, as the root cause of China's lagged development (1997, 77–79, 194). In a democratic society, where people have differences of opinion on sometimes sensitive social, political, or moral issues, civility means toleration of others' views, agreement to disagree. A lack of civility, the demonization of those with whom one disagrees, can rend a society, weaken democracy, and give rise to conflict. Civility, in the sense of not littering, spitting, defacing public facilities or stealing public property, provides clean and hygienic public spaces and reduces the costs of maintaining public facilities, businesses frequented by the public such as shopping complexes, theaters, sporting venues, and public recreation areas. Civility by motor vehicle operators means safer roads and fewer frayed tempers. Finally, civility toward others makes life more pleasant and society more harmonious, an oft-stated goal in China.

Civility

A search on the subject of civility reveals hundreds of books, but other than the few that look at its development in the West or its practice in a particular country, the vast majority examine it in the United States or other modern Western societies. Moreover, most of these deal with the importance of civility in maintaining democracy or in a particular social or occupational realm, lament its decline, or prescribe sets of rules of civil behavior. To my knowledge, although some social scientists and political philosophers write about civility, none has defined it as an analytical tool, and few have applied it to a non-Western society. An exception is Weller's excellent book comparing Taiwan and China. However, although titled *Alternate Civilities*, the book focuses on civil society rather than civility (Weller 1999a). Below I will briefly define civility for operational purposes and describe the sources of the data used in the book.

By civility I refer to the behavior, and the attitudes which shape that behavior, that are referred to in Taiwan as *gongdexin* (public morality) and in China as *wenming*,[7] which can be translated as civilized, civility or civilization, depending on

---

7. Both *gongde* and *wenming* were coined in Meiji Japan and borrowed by China late in the nineteenth century. *Wenming* is broader in meaning. In the phrase *jiang wenming* it means to emphasize civility. *Gongde* means "public morality" or "civility"; *xin in gongdexin* refers to an attitude or way of thinking.

the English context. At its most basic, civility refers to consideration of and respect for others, especially strangers, even in banal ways. This essentially means recognizing others as fellow beings with whom one shares humanness, assuming that, in general, they have no ill intent toward others, affording them a modicum of courtesy, and treating them in the spirit of the Confucian version of the Golden Rule, *ji suo bu yu wu shi yu ren*, do not do to others what you would not want them to do to you. Civil treatment of others extends to the public space and to public facilities. Everyone is a stakeholder in the public space and public facilities, which exist for the use and enjoyment of all. Thus, any despoliation of either is an uncivil act in the same category as harm to another's private property.

Being civil toward strangers means avoiding collisions with others while walking in a public place or stepping on another's toes on a crowded bus, and apologizing if either does occur. It means assisting someone who asks directions or who looks lost. It means queuing and letting people get out of an elevator or a subway car before trying to enter or board. It means aiding someone who appears to be in distress—as one would hope that others would do if one were in a similar situation. It could also mean returning a greeting or a smile when encountering a stranger while walking in a park. But it does not mean that one needs to put oneself in jeopardy, make great sacrifices for others, or go about looking for persons to greet or assist.

The European origins of civility raise the question of whether examining civility in China or Taiwan is imposing Western notions of propriety on those societies. The answer is yes—but. Westerners in China in the late nineteenth and early twentieth centuries, largely western Europeans, Americans, and Australians, were highly critical of the Chinese for all sorts of reasons, including their lack of hygiene and their appearance and behavior in public. However, since the KMT imposed the New Life Movement in the early 1930s, which reflected these criticisms (see Chapter 3), this imposition has been from Chinese governments themselves, largely independent of Western influence. And while one possible explanation is that the leaders of the once proud, but humbled since the Opium War, Chinese imposed rules of civility in order to bring the Chinese public up to a standard where they were beyond Western ridicule and thus no longer a cause of lost national face, it has been governments in the Republic of China in China up to 1949 and in Taiwan to 1988, and the Chinese government since 1980, that have imposed these standards. Moreover, there is nothing in the statements of any of these governments that even hints at seeing civility as a Western imposition. China's government certainly went out of its way to eliminate any potential cause of ridicule before the 2008 Beijing Olympic Games, including eliminating Chinglish from signs, menus, and the like. In short, civility has now become as indigenized in China as tea drinking has in the West, and the behavior that I have singled out as indications of civility or incivility is the behavior that KMT governments in China and Taiwan and the CCP government in China themselves have, very publicly, tried to change. Thus, the comparisons of civil behavior—civility—in Chapters 4 and 5 reflect the aims set forth in the civility-promotion campaigns run by their respective governments.

Data for this project come from a variety of sources: observations, conversations and interviews, secondary accounts, government documents and the use of quantitative data as indirect social indicators of civility. The observations I made and recorded were of those behaviors listed above that manifest the presence or absence of civility. In China and, before the 1990s in Taiwan, after which civility palpably began to increase there, I was more likely to observe negative examples than positive ones. This reflects the nature of observing civility in that breaches are much more conspicuous than compliance. Indeed, Chen Ruoshui observes that in Taiwan public morality is phrased negatively, in lists of "do nots" (2005, 19).

My observations began when I first went to Taiwan in 1959 for a stay of about thirty months, though at this time they were very unsystematic, just the sort of things that someone from a different cultural background might observe when in a foreign society. I returned in 1969 to carry out field research for my PhD dissertation, which is when I heard about the public discourse on the lack of public morality in Taiwan, and although I did not focus on that as a research topic until many years later, it stayed in my mind, and I began to take note of civil and uncivil behavior. I continued to do this during the dozen years I spent in Taiwan over the next four decades. I spent most of that time in Taibei, but have also lived for various periods in Miaoli, Xinzhu (Hsinchu), Tainan, Hualian (Hualien), and Gaoxiong (Kaohsiung) in addition to short visits to many other places. Residence in these places varied, one month in Miaoli, fifteen months in Xinzhu, and several years in Taibei. My first visit to China was in 1983 when I spent a week in Guangzhou. I made regular visits from 1995 to 2000 to major cities and to the Pearl River Delta Region where I carried out a study of Taiwanese entrepreneurs. From 2009 to 2015 I made yearly visits in which I spent about six months each in Beijing and Xiamen, with shorter periods in Shanghai and several places each in Anhui, Guangxi, Jiangsu, Hubei, and Zhejiang. The relevant sorts of behavior I have observed in China are very similar to what I saw in Taiwan between 1960 and 1990.

While traveling I had occasion to note behavior in rural areas and smaller towns, but most China observations were of behavior in the more cosmopolitan and well-off urban areas where the levels of civility, as well as levels of education and economic development, are higher than in areas further inland or in the countryside. It should be noted, however, that when I write that, for example, violations of no smoking rules are common in China, I am not making a blanket statement about all Chinese smokers, merely that it is common to see people smoking in restaurants and to smell smoke in public toilets, elevators, and other places where it is formally prohibited. The majority of Taiwan observations were in Taibei, but because of its much smaller size, its higher and more uniform level of education and income, and its more even level of economic development, the regional differences in civility are fewer than in China. I have also had many conversations with local people and with foreigners who had spent periods of time living in Taiwan or China and mixing with locals, asking them whether they thought that what I observed was commonplace, whether they had had similar experiences, and how they interpreted or felt about those incidents. In addition, I gathered information from secondary sources: news reports, op-ed pieces and short essays, and from official sources such as civility campaign announcements. Regarding the latter, when official sources admonish people not to act in a particular way it is certain that such behavior is common and that the authorities regard such actions as undesirable and in need of correction. Furthermore, I have looked at various indirect indicators of the level of civility including levels of social trust, donations to charity, volunteerism, voluntary blood donations, and philanthropic activities, particularly those aimed at alleviating suffering or social disadvantage.

I also analyzed four sets of primary school moral education textbooks, two each from Taiwan and China, one set used in the 1980s and another used in 2011, in order to learn the extent to which the two societies define civility in the same ways and regard the same behaviors as uncivil. Both Taiwan and China have undergone significant shifts in ideology since the establishment of the latter in 1949, and these ideological shifts are very evident in the texts. The early Taiwan set strongly reflects the New Life Movement, which was revived in 1966 in the Cultural Renaissance Movement (*Zhonghua wenhua fuxing yundong*). The 2011 set reflects a general humanist life perspective, advocating values, outlooks, and actions that would fit comfortably in a modern Western society. The early Chinese set contains elements of Marxism such as lessons on the valorization of labor and the gratitude all should show toward the products of workers' toil by not wasting. The 2011 set reflects the changes brought about by economic development and urbanization in China, for example a lesson on consumer awareness and another on the need for worldwide environmental consciousness. However, despite the almost thirty years of rejecting traditional values under Mao, the civil behaviors taught in the 1988 edition of China texts did not differ from those in the 2011 set or in either of the Taiwan sets.

The structure of the chapters is as follows:

Chapter 2 analyzes civility, tracing its origins to Europe where, as states grew in size, rulers began demanding that lesser feudal lords and knights behave civilly when visiting court. This expected manner of deportment eventually spread to the rising bourgeoisie and to other commoners. It next explores how various scholars and authors have understood and used civility and what it means in the present study. It then examines and refutes the idea that notions of civility have existed in China since the time of the early Confucian philosophers. Finally, it looks at comments on the state of civility in late imperial and early twentieth-century China by prominent Chinese and foreign writers.

Chapter 3 examines the comparability of Taiwan and China, two societies, I argue, that are as similar to each other in the areas relevant to the issue discussed in this book as any other two societies are. Aside from the shared history of the two societies until the Qing government ceded Taiwan in perpetuity to Japan in 1895 as a part of the settlement following the Sino-Japanese War of 1894–1895, the ROC government in China and Taiwan and the government in China since 1949 have engaged in campaigns to "civilize" their citizens. This chapter also includes the above-mentioned analysis of primary school moral education textbooks and shows that, although they use different Chinese terms to express it, there is no difference in the kinds of behavior that the Taiwan and Chinese governments see as constituting civility.

Chapters 4 and 5 analyze the level of civility in the two societies under question, China and Taiwan. A convenient starting point is 1950, by which time the Chinese government was established, almost all of the Mainlanders who would leave China and go to Taiwan had arrived there, and the ROC government had settled in Taiwan and begun to implement its programs. Chapter 4 examines the state of civility in China and some of the underlying factors and forces that affect it—the high level of inequality, the divisions in the population, and the condescension of some sectors of Chinese society toward others.

Chapter 5 first assesses the state of civility in present-day Taiwan. It then investigates the evolution of Taiwan from a place peopled by four ethnically separate groups that were further divided into many small, disparate communities, what I call a "society in itself," to a "society for itself," one that encompasses the whole of Taiwan and in which a strong majority of the population form a moral community based on civil nationalism. With that transition, Taiwan became a civil place. Both the level of civility and the strength of the moral community have continued to increase.

Chapter 6 discusses various factors germane to the development of civility. It deals first with differences between Taiwan and China relevant to Taiwan's having become a civil society and China's greater difficulties in doing so: differences in area, population, population composition, and integration; Taiwan's economic development beginning thirty years earlier and also being uninterrupted by internal factors; Taiwan's greater income and wealth equality; differences in social unity and in governance, especially elections in Taiwan and the KMT government's noninterference with the existing social organization; and the differential levels of trust in the two societies. It next assesses, in light of the information in previous chapters, the set of conditions that I list in Chapter 2 as likely either to facilitate or hinder civil development. It finishes by examining the links between civility and postindustrial values, becoming a "society for itself," and democracy.

2
Civility

Civility, as it is known in Europe and the Anglophone world, evolved in the West. While it may have been practiced among elites in a small number of societies—for example, among citizens in Athens or Rome, its practice was limited to a small proportion of the population. These exceptions aside, civility was not found in the ancient or the preindustrial societies of Europe, the Islamic world, India, or China (Hall 2013, 34). Accounts of medieval Europe describe it as highly decentralized, made up of hundreds of small territories ruled by warrior knights, many of whom were illiterate. They were the strongmen of the era, and they delighted in violence, which was their main tool of rule and survival. Most lived both by and for the sword. Moreover, in society as a whole, violence by the warrior class—killing, rapine or wreaking violence on others, often for its own sake—was common, as were feuds through which people administered their own justice. Among the common people, violent spectacles were a popular form of entertainment (Elias 2000, 161–68; Pinker 2011, 17–18). Yi-Fu Tuan writes that such conditions lasted until at least the seventeenth century in Europe, as family feuds, magnate rivalries, and strong-arm tactics used by vagabonds and robbers were the rule of the day. According to Tuan, "the greatest threat to life, limb and property came from other people in the local neighborhood, whether urban or rural" (1979, 132).

Violence was not the only incivility of the time. Not only did people give vent to emotions such as anger and vengeance but exercise of self-restraint in general was very weak, whether in terms of aggression, ablutions, speech, bodily functions, sexual behavior, or how one partook of food. In short, medieval Europe was not a civil place.

Change began to take place in the High Middle Ages. People devised defensive means to make incursions by Vikings and other marauders much more costly, bringing relative peace and a revival of both commerce and urban life, and this, combined with improved farming techniques, contributed to population increases. The number of smaller manors ruled by warrior knights declined as some feudal lords were able to consolidate their power and expand their territories. They found it in their interest to reduce violence and the economic loss it brought, so acts of violence became criminalized offences against the crown rather than torts between two parties. Knights then offered their services to kings, and they thus had to learn courtly behavior (Pinker 2011, 75–77). The elites were stratified into kings, high-ranking and titled nobles, and ordinary knights, and they competed with each other and with the rising bourgeoisie for status (Davetian 2009, 67–68, Chap. 5; Keane 1998, 115).

Whereas in previous times status had been ascribed at birth or achieved through winning battlefield victories, with the 1530 publication of Erasmus's *Handbook on Good Manners for Children* (*De civilitate morum puerilium*), status gradually became determined by knowing how to behave properly. Nominally addressed to Henry of Burgundy, the 11-year-old son of Prince Adolph of Veere, as instructions on how to behave in the company of adults, Erasmus's book was embraced by a more general audience. While not the first book published on proper behavior, it took Europe by storm, with more than 130 editions published, a tenth of these as late as the eighteenth century (Elias 2000, 55).

Erasmus's book detailed how people should comport themselves in society, in particular regarding "outward bodily propriety." This included how one looked at others and carried one's body; one's gestures, dress, and facial expressions; keeping one's nose clean and wiping it with a cloth while turned away from others rather than with the hand or one's clothing; and trying not to break wind or vomit in the presence of others (Elias 2000, 47–55). The sorts of instructions in the text also paint a picture of the general behavior of persons associated with the courts of the time. As reported by Elias, specific rules include the following:

- Don't dip bread in the soup after you've taken a bite.
- Don't gnaw on a bone and put it back onto the common plate.
- Don't slurp soup from the same spoon as another.
- Don't clear your throat, blow your nose, or wipe your nose with your hand at the table.
- Don't make noises while eating.
- Don't scratch yourself while eating (food was taken from common dishes with the hands).
- Wash before eating (there was no soap, but a servant poured water over diners' hands).
- Don't loosen your belt or fall asleep at the table.
- Don't clean your teeth with your knife or with the tablecloth. (Elias 2000, 55–57)

The book appeared in a transitional period during which restraint of emotions became important and as the reigning lords increasingly monopolized both power and the right to legitimately use force. In addition to refraining from violence and concealing bodily functions such as sexual behavior, relieving oneself or breaking wind, this included using more refined and polite language. This was also a time when people of different social strata such as nobles, writers and artists, bourgeois intellectuals and the bourgeoisie in general increasingly found themselves in each other's company. Aside from establishing boundary-maintaining mechanisms between the various strata, the developing code of behavior also reflected a desire not to give offense by exercising consideration toward others as well as self-reflexivity. Demanding *courtoisie*—proper court behavior—enabled the kings and higher nobles "to compel people to exercise restraint" (Elias 2000, 61, 169; see also Keane 1998, 122–23). Thus, if the lesser nobles and the rising bourgeoisie wanted to attend court, they had to conform to the kinds of behavior that Erasmus prescribed, and gently correcting someone for a breach of proper behavior itself became a sign of civility (Elias 2000, 55, 70).

Reflecting the centralization of Europe around kingdoms and the corresponding decline in political importance of smaller feudal principalities, Calhoun, citing Marvin Becker, states that civility in its early conception also referred to "the individual as someone not primarily defined by his loyalty to local lordships." It instead reflected a notion of the public good based on the country as a whole rather than on one's local society, thus an early meaning of civility was fitness for a civil postfeudal society (Calhoun 2000, 252; Becker 1988).

Elias states that religion itself never played a civilizing role, it "being exactly as 'civilized' as the society or class which upholds it" (2000, 169), but Davetian refutes this. He writes that codes of civility began to be adopted around the time that the Church was trying to assert itself into the politics of Europe. Bishops and popes made increasingly strong claims of political authority, putting them over any secular ruler or force. This also injected the rules of monastic restraint and self-discipline into court life, thus contrasting the courteous noble with the brutish, crude, heartless peasant. Clerics also attributed virtue to the nobility, one work describing the monarch as a capable, courageous, wise and benevolent leader who possesses an impeccable sense of honor. Such depictions seem to be a part of status reinforcement, bestowing on the nobility the necessary traits to make them worthy of their exalted status. Among these traits were that they must assume the role of protector of the poor (whom they had pillaged in the past). The Church also added to the character traits of the nobility piety, the love of God, and the willingness to do battle to defend the Church and Christians. This gave the knights a code of chivalry and civility to live up to if they were to be accepted by the noble, his family, and the ladies of the court (Davetian 2009, 30–44).

Hall, too, argues that religion played a part in developing civility. He writes that European rulers finally decided, following the long periods of war brought on by the Protestant Reformation, that they could no longer enforce *cuius regio, eius religio*, and that toleration of different faiths was preferable to warfare (1998).

According to Davetian Protestantism also contributed to the adoption of civility. Contrary to motives in the medieval church to please God, those in the Renaissance were to get on with one's fellows, a secular rather than a spiritual goal. Moreover, Calvinism declared that all have callings determined by God, and being determined by God, all callings were equal, none more or less important than others. This implied that people in general were also equal, which extended civility to all, not just to one's peers, as was the case when civility was the code only of the nobility. Furthermore, in Protestantism, the attitude of the doer of a deed was more important than the deed itself, therefore civil behavior had to be sincere, not mere form. As in any relationship in which God is a participant, one needed to please God and find his favor in all things (Davetian 2009, 68, 88–89).

Briefly summarizing the development of civility in the later Middle Ages and early Renaissance periods, on the surface civility denoted manners, etiquette or decorum, but underlying this was consideration of the feelings of others, not committing acts that might disgust or give offense. Works on decorum reflected these notions in the ensuing centuries, for example, in George Washington's "Rules of Civility & Decent Behavior in Company and Conversation." In addition, undoubtedly reflecting the times, Washington's rules also recognized social hierarchy and stipulated deference behavior and displays of humility toward one's social superiors (1971). According to Walzer, civility "once had to do more directly with the political virtues of citizenship: one of its obsolescent meanings is 'civil righteousness.'" But it has increasingly come to denote only social virtues: "orderliness, politeness, seemliness are the synonyms the dictionary suggests" (1974, 597). Even today, civility can refer to displays of good manners or being nice to others, whether superficially or sincerely proffered (Carter 1998; Caldwell 1999).

However, some scholars interested in politics, civil society, or liberal democracy define civility more as an attitude or a moral virtue underlying particular forms of thought or behavior. Calhoun and Shils both distinguish it from merely being civil (Calhoun 2000, 253–55; Shils 1991, 12–13). Shils and other twentieth-century political philosophers see civility as the mark of a good citizen and a civil virtue, as universalistic and transcending the personal in modern society (1992). He cites Ferdinand Mount, who wrote that civility inferred "inclusion in the same moral universe" (1991, 12; Mount 1973, 12), and that moral universe consists of the entire society, even the whole of humankind, rather than merely the local community in which one lives or the primordial community of which one is a member (Shils 1997a, 17). Elsewhere Shils states that civility reflects the recognition of a public that includes the complete society and that despite other inequalities, all are equal as citizens:

> Civility is an attitude and a pattern of conduct. It is approximately the same as what Montesquieu called virtue. Montesquieu said, "Virtue, in a republic, is a very simple thing: it is love of the republic. . . . Love of the republic in a democracy is love of democracy."
>
> Civility is an appreciation of or attachment to the institutions which constitute civil society. It is an attitude of attachment to the whole society, to all its strata and sections. It is an attitude of concern for the good of the entire society. . . . It is solicitous of the well-being of the whole, or the larger interest.

More fundamentally, civility is the conduct of a person whose individual self-consciousness has been partly superseded by his collective self-consciousness, the society as a whole and the institutions of civil society being the referents of his collective self-consciousness. (Shils 1991, 11–12)

To Margalit, civility denotes decency. He writes, "A DECENT society is a society that does not humiliate. More precisely, it is a society whose institutions do not humiliate people who depend on them" (1997, 147, emphasis in original; 1996). Rorty qualifies this, stating that civility must also include economic security, and that if institutions, despite formal policies of cosmopolitanism, discriminate against particular groups, there will be no civility or decency (1997).

In the liberal democracy literature, civility is often associated with tolerance, not in any condescending way but genuinely accepting values and political preferences different from one's own as valid in such a political system (Shils 1997b). Schonsheck notes the presence of "rasp," "the friction of jostling of political, moral, religious and ethnic groups that is inevitable in any multicultural liberal democracy" (2004, 169). Walzer states that much of the literature on civility over the past three decades is on its importance to maintaining liberal democracies, but he also argues that, because activists hold strong positions, political activism is at odds with civility (1974, 602). However, Kesler writes, "When citizens are civil to one another, despite their political disagreement, they reveal that these disagreements are less important than their resolution to remain fellow citizens" (1992, 57).

Orwin takes civility out of the political arena and places it in the wider society in which individuals interact less intensely. Contrasting the heavy obligations of civility and civic duty in Pericles's Athens, where the latter was a public virtue, with the comparatively light obligation of the citizen in a modern society, where it is a private virtue, he sees civility as "the bond uniting honest men busy minding their own affairs. . . . [It] resembles neither friendship nor any sort of intense attachment" and is more like "neighborliness" (1991, 560; see also Shils 1997c, 71–72). Joan McGregor sees civility as even less intense, being about "our treatment of strangers; it is an ethic for relating to strangers. Civility requires in some basic sense that we exhibit respect toward them," treat them "as if they matter. . . . Treating strangers as if they matter means that when they are in distress one ought to help them, at least if one can do so without threatening one's own life or welfare" (2004, 26).

Finally, Shils recognizes that not all are civil all the time. In no society will all have a high degree of civility. It is important that those in particular roles—"the higher judiciary, senior civil servants, leading legislators, eminent academics, prominent businessmen, influential journalists, and others like them"—display it in a way that is visible to the public. "There must also be a scatter of persons of moderate degrees of civility throughout society. There must be at least small degrees of civility in most citizens" (1991, 18). Civility displayed radiates through society.

In this study, civility refers to an attitude that includes a recognition that all, strangers as well as acquaintances, are fellow human beings deserving of a modicum of consideration, respect and decency, not mere "objects" in the physical environment. It also includes a recognition that public facilities and the physical public space belong to all and that all have a stake in their respect and care. Littering or vandalizing thus not only harms the public space itself but is also inconsiderate toward others and encroaches on their "property rights." Civility, while likely coexisting to some extent with civil society, differs from it in being attitudinal rather than structural or organizational.

I will argue that for a society to be civil it must exist not only objectively—that is, as a territory with a population and a government, but it must exist subjectively, "for itself," in the minds of its members. In other words, in their "imagined community" (Anderson 2006), people must recognize that others in society are their consociates, people with whom they share at least one thread of identity as fellow members of that society, however weak that thread may be. I also argue that civility can exist on a broad-scale level only if a "public," as described by Habermas in the public sphere, exists. "Public" here refers to a group of people who have a conscious common interest on which they can act (Habermas 1989). Having a notion of the public is important because for people to be civil to strangers, they must recognize some sort of connection with them. "Public" also implies the existence of a realm, space or facilities that are open to all, not just to the members of a royal court or of a particular kinship group. This means that simply being members of the society in which they live gives people the right to use or enjoy them, which also means that others have the same right and thus have a common link that creates a relationship, even though it may be a very weak one. For example, the creation of Beijing's Zhongyang Park, the earliest public park established by a Chinese government, facilitated the creation of a public in China for the first time in its history. Visitors to the park were able to get together and discuss matters of mutual interest much in the fashion of the denizens of the salons and coffee houses Habermas cites (Smith 2006, 214, 222–24). Yang and Calhoun also note the creation of "publics" through interaction on the internet (2007). This means that they must have a "right" to interact. They must be citizens, not subjects, as subjects have no such right. I will trace the transformation of Taiwan into such a society in Chapter 5 and further discuss the importance of a society for itself for the development of civility in Chapter 6.

For their societies to be societies with civility, citizens in Taiwan and China must regard all their countrymen and women, whether family, acquaintances or strangers, as fellow citizens, as consociates who deserve decent treatment and consideration of their feelings, sensibilities and their right to feel comfortable in public spaces. They must respect the physical public space and public facilities and recognize their own responsibility in maintaining them. To include strangers, persons well outside the primordial community, as moral equivalents and members of the same moral universe, and to regard public property as something to be protected are profound changes for societies that have a Chinese cultural heritage.

The necessary links between members in a society may be created through primordial, kinship or community ties or as a collectivity that comes about through the development of a civil collective self-consciousness (Shils 1997c, 71–72), that is, one based on particularistic or universalistic ties. I argue that the existence or nonexistence of civility depends on the nature of peoples' links to others. If they perceive all but *zijiren*, "insiders,"[1] as simply other human beings but of no significance to them, they are unlikely to treat them with civility. However, feeling a bond with fellow citizens, a bond that confers something meaningful in common with them, increases the chance that they will behave civilly toward each other.

The development of civility in Taiwan illustrates this. In 1950 Taiwan society could be described by the phrase *yi pan san sha* (a plate of loose sand) used initially by Liang Qichao and later by Sun Yat-sen—in other words, lacking cohesion. It was made up of four ethnic groups—the indigenous peoples, Hoklo Taiwanese, Hakka Taiwanese, and Mainlanders—which each consisted of many small communities in the form of tribes, villages, factions, or workplaces. Civility was conspicuously absent. However, as I will show in Chapter 5, over the next four decades a civil collective self-consciousness developed as identity with Taiwan intensified through a series of social and political struggles. Taiwan became a civil society rather than merely a congeries of small inward-looking communities with scant interest in or recognition of others.

In a paper on Taiwan's becoming a society with civility, I posited a number of conditions that would likely either facilitate or hinder its development (Schak 2009b). Looking first at facilitating conditions, most important is that people must trust that their civility will be met with civility from others. As long as people fear discourtesy or being preyed upon or cheated by strangers, they are likely to avoid involvement with others that may put them in a vulnerable position. Someone hindered when alighting from a subway by strangers in a rush to board and get a seat may well act in a similar fashion when boarding the next time. Such an experience may also reinforce the stereotype of the discourteous stranger. Another important condition is that people generally feel personally secure enough not to fear being harmed, materially secure enough not to feel that others are their direct economic competitors or that society is a zero-sum game (see Rorty 1997, 113). A generally optimistic view of the future, that things will improve over the medium term, is also helpful, as is being generally satisfied with society.

Civility will also be enhanced in societies in which people or groups show concern for others by volunteering or being active in philanthropy or in which they obey road rules and drive courteously rather than in an aggressive "me first" manner toward other drivers. An example of driver courtesy is a place in the city in which I live where traffic from three separate roads merge into a single lane to get onto an expressway. During the morning rush hour drivers from the three lanes of traffic

---

1. Literally, "one's own people." I will render *zijiren* below as "insiders" or as "social circle" where the referent is clear. In other cases, I will use *zijiren*.

"take turns," ignoring the rule to yield to the vehicle on the right, and let a car from each of the other two lanes in before proceeding. This merge point is not supervised, nor are there signs instructing drivers to behave in this way, but drivers can see this pattern of behavior before their turn comes, which probably explains why they conform. From what could be a difficult intersection, traffic proceeds smoothly and as rapidly as could be expected given the number of vehicles.

Governments might also play a role in the development of civility, enhancing the general level of cheerfulness and satisfaction if they are regarded as benign and not oppressive, if they are seen as making efforts to meet public expectations, if they are viewed as clean, honest, responsive, and fair, and if citizen interactions with public servants are handled with courtesy, helpfulness, and efficiency. If, however, there is a culture of putting on airs at the points of service, as there was in Taiwan before the 1990s, people will feel negatively toward the government, which may affect their moods in general public encounters.

Civility in terms of caring for the physical public space is improved if people identify with and have a positive attitude toward it. A potential factor in identifying with where one lives is domestic tourism, as it provides opportunities to appreciate attractive or interesting features of one's country. The existence of public places that people enjoy, religious pilgrimages, or places such as parks, malls, nature reserves, scenic drives, mountain trails, water recreation areas, hot springs, historic spots, and natural wonders may engender positive feelings toward the homeland. Domestic tourism is limited until people have a modicum of economic comfort, but as their economic conditions improve and they can visit attractive spots, they may become more environmentally conscious and less willing to sacrifice either the natural or the built environment for economic growth or to despoil it by littering. Public education campaigns can assist in this, reminding people not to litter, as can the provision of public waste disposal facilities and enforcement of antilittering and antivandalism regulations. Also important is keeping the public space clean and in good repair, a sort of "no broken windows" policy (Pinker 2011, 142; see also Kelling and Wilson 1982). In many cities in Taiwan and China, sanitation workers sweep the streets early in the morning so that they are clean at the beginning of the day.

Civility is unlikely to develop if people do not or cannot trust each other, e.g., in a police state, particularly one in which there are large numbers of citizen informers, as was the case in the former East Germany or in China during the Cultural Revolution, because no one can be trusted (e.g., see Spülbeck 1996; Vogel 1965, 46). However, even without the fear of being informed on, if one distrusts strangers, one will not likely be inclined to treat them with civility or to lend assistance if they need help. Trust in or interaction with strangers will be affected if people feel that society is unsafe or feel threatened by crime. Civility will also be hindered if there are ethnic or religious rifts in society that create out-groups "undeserving" of civil treatment or if there are large disparities of income or wealth, especially if these are accompanied by condescension toward the poorer by the wealthier, or if there are people who hold a born to rule or born to privilege attitude (Hall 2013, 251; Rorty 1997).

I reconsider these propositions in Chapter 6 based on evidence presented in Chapters 4 and 5.

Was There a Chinese Tradition of Civility?

Aside from the lack of civility in Europe until relatively recent times, I would argue that the same was true for China and probably for all preindustrial societies based on smallholder agriculture. Such societies were made up of myriad small villages inhabited by peasant farmers who rarely traveled very far from home. These peasants were parochial in their outlooks (Almond and Verba 1963), and their social networks and identities were limited to their own villages, to nearby villages in which kin lived, and more tenuously to those they had dealings with in the local market town area. Others in the country or principality in which they lived were strangers, and the anxiety toward and fear and distrust of strangers was a common phenomenon not only in peasant societies but continues to be, to a lesser extent, in modern societies (Tuan 1979, 155–60).[2] Curfews were instituted not only to deal with fire but also with strangers, and the notion that strangers to an area should be gone by sundown was not at all uncommon. Under such conditions, it is difficult to see how civility toward strangers could have existed.

However, there were concepts well over two millennia ago in China that superficially resembled a code of civility. A key notion in China's classic philosophical literature was *li*, the polite, ceremonious behavior that *junzi* (gentlemen; i.e., those of noble character) should employ when interacting with each other. *Junzi* was initially a term denoting aristocrats, but Confucius and his followers recognized that all had the capacity for education and self-improvement through study of the classics and the moral principles they contained, followed by reflection and self-rectification (*xiushen*). Those who did so seriously would learn to behave and interact properly toward others, and they became *junzi*, gentleman. Those who failed to do so remained *xiaoren* (petty people, or commoners). The redefinition of *junzi* from hereditary aristocrats to the achieved status of those whose conduct was exemplary and who knew how to treat others properly made it imperative for those in high office to claim to be moral paragons, even if they were not, as justification for the positions they held.

However, despite the high moral level of the classical virtues and the polite interactive behavior they prescribed, their existence was not evidence of a society

---

2. Tuan writes that the "we/they" dichotomy is reduced in modern societies because we frequently deal with strangers and with faceless institutions (1979, 213). The incapacity or unwillingness to extend the protection of law to segments of the population, whether in pre-industrial or modern societies, also builds distrust of strangers.

with civility. First, even within the *junzi* elite, people were of different rank and status, and what *li* referred to were *guiju* (rules), regulations on how to act with proper deference to superiors, rather than *limao* (manners) to be applied to all. And although some, in their deferential behavior, may have expressed genuine respect toward their superiors, *guiju* were essentially status confirming and maintaining devices that were more easily judged in the performance than in knowledge of the intent. Second, in practice, few besides aristocrats had the necessary resources—the wealth needed to hire tutors or to free one's sons from direct material production—to achieve the necessary level of literacy and erudition to master the classics and become *junzi*.

Shils writes that there are Confucian concepts that could potentially contribute to a civil society. Moreover, Buddhism contributed the important virtues of compassion and charity. However, Shils continues, "This does not mean that Confucius thereby envisaged a civil society in either the narrow or the broad sense. A civil society is one in which individuals pursue ends in the public or civic sphere which they themselves choose and it is the obligation of the government to maintain such a situation" (1996, 46–47). Kim concurs: "*Li* can be reinvented as the generic foundation of Confucian civilities, and . . . self-restraining Confucian civilities can provide a great bulwark for a viable democracy" (2014, 59). However, such conditions did not exist in dynastic China.

The Xiangyue Institution[3]

The classics contained a moral philosophy, an ideal of how people should behave toward one another, but they were not descriptions of how people actually behaved. They did, however, establish an obligation of the *junzi* to help the benighted *xiaoren* to become refined by teaching, writing, and especially by setting a good example. In the *Analects*, Confucius frequently used models of exemplary behavior in answering queries from his students as to what they should do in particular circumstances. His follower, Mencius, stated that people were inherently good, and if those around them behaved properly, showing them the correct path, they would naturally follow it.

This use of models eventually inspired a rural community-action and mutual-aid institution called *xiangyue* (village compact). Devised by Confucian scholar Lü Heshu in 1076 CE, it was also intended to educate and to promote morality. Lü's intention was that the village compacts should be locally organized and run rather than imposed by government, but governments soon put their own stamp on them. The compacts went through various iterations in succeeding dynasties, and when the Qing adopted them, it did so as a means of thought control, ignoring their other functions. The emperor ordered that exposition pavilions (*shengming ting*)

---

3. This account is based on Hsiao 1960, 184–206; and Alitto 1979, 206–7.

be built in each village at which degree holders or upstanding commoners would give lectures. The initial text on which the lectures were based, the Six Maxims of a Hortatory Edict (*Liu Yu*), was written by the first Qing emperor, Shunzhi (r. 1643–1661 CE). It contained sayings enjoining proper filial and familial behavior, harmonious relationships with neighbors, how to educate and discipline children, proper economic behavior, avoiding unlawful actions, and maintaining peace and order. Later emperors wrote more detailed texts, sometimes adding subjects of concern, e.g., enjoinments against millenarian groups such as the White Lotus sect or heterodox thought such as Catholicism. Lectures by members of the gentry were held on the first and fifteenth of each lunar calendar month, the lecturer also discussing the good and bad deeds done in the neighborhood. Offenses by villagers against filiality or fraternal duties were posted in the local pavilion and left there until offenders changed their ways. All villagers were expected to attend under threat of punishment.

The emperors took this institution very seriously and wanted it to be successful, but despite positive reports from officials, accounts from retired officials and foreign missionaries, persons who had no reason not to be objective, stated that attendance was poor and lectures were ineffective—poorly delivered, sometimes in formal written language or in a dialect foreign to the locals, and sometimes not delivered at all. According to Hsiao Kung-chuan,

> For every claim that it operated well . . . there were many that it did not. Allowing for the likelihood of official exaggeration in both directions, it is difficult to entertain any optimistic view of the effectiveness of the lecture system in the face of the predominant number of unfavorable statements concerning its operations. (1960, 195)

The major reasons for the failure were the ineptitude of scholars, trained to write rather than orate, in delivering the lectures, the opportunity costs for degree holders to use their time in a such a poorly remunerated activity, and the "unsatisfactory condition under which the bulk of the Chinese peasantry was condemned to live. The dire want and glaring inequities that were the lot of many villagers silently but indisputably controverted almost every one of the injunctions of imperial Confucianism" (Hsiao 1960, 199). By the nineteenth century, bandits and antigovernment groups were using these inequities as rallying points to recruit supporters.

Commoners also had rules of propriety within their social circles that included deference to those of different statuses, generally to males and those superior in age or generation. In his model of traditional Chinese social relationships, *cixu geju* (differential modes of association), anthropologist Fei Xiaotong used the image of the set of concentric circles that result from dropping a stone into a pond. The innermost circle is one's immediate family, the next other agnatic kin, followed, in descending order, by other kin, neighbors and friends. Those outside the circles, with whom one lacks an established relationship, are strangers (Fei 1948). Those within them are insiders. As in other preindustrial peasant societies, insiders were a narrow range of persons who lived close by, within the range of one's travels, and seldom further than the nearest market town.

As expressed in the phrase *ren chi ren de shijie* (people eat people world), the world outside the village, especially outside the market town area, was regarded with unease, perhaps even with foreboding. People in neighboring villages or from different lineages were rivals for scarce goods such as land or irrigation water. In the market towns, peasants were fearful of merchants cheating them. In some areas, e.g., the environs of Guangzhou and the tea-growing areas in the mountains west of Xiamen, there were feuds among different lineages or ethnic groups or dangers from bandits such that people had to build fortifications to maintain their safety. In short, people had rights in and obligations toward their insiders differing according to the structural or emotional closeness of the relationship. However, those outside one's social circle were strangers with whom one avoided contact and who, if not regarded with suspicion, were at least owed nothing.[4]

Richard Wilson wrote that this insider-outsider view was still reflected in 1960s and 1970s Taiwan child socialization patterns in which the moral equivalence of other human beings was limited to members of the family and others within the social circle. He observes, "In societies where right thinking and conduct rigidly define group membership [such as Chinese society], individuals who are outside this realm of group orientation are often regarded as of lower moral worth on this account" (1981, 11–12). Living with a Chinese family during my first period of field research, I sometimes heard parents tell their children things like, "It's okay for you to act that way here at home, but if you do that outside, people will laugh at you/dislike you." Although this reflects the indulgence of Chinese child socialization, it also creates an inside-outside social dichotomy and an image of the outside world—the world of strangers—as harsh and hostile. Historian Chen Ruoshui, noting that present-day Chinese lack respect toward strangers and are indifferent toward harming them, writes,

> comparing this sort of very common attitude with traditional Chinese ethics we can't but say that the low level of Chinese public morality and our traditional culture's lack of emphasis on everyday people-to-people relations are very closely linked to each other. (2005, 30–31)

In short, civility, as the term is commonly used today and as defined in this book, was not commonly practiced in any society having Chinese heritage and Chinese rulers until the 1990s in Taiwan.

Preindustrial Chinese society, in fact, may have been even more parochial and family-centered than other peasant societies because of the strength of the

---

4. Luigi Tomba reports a homeowner activist in Beijing saying, "The Chinese already know how to get along with their leaders, how to get along with friends and relatives; what they don't know is how to mix with strangers, and this is the reason that we haven't had communities yet" (2014, 12).

patrilineal principle in its kinship system. A son's sacred duty was to continue his family line by adding another generation to ensure that sacrifices would be made to his ancestors and parents after their deaths. To do this, the family property, which in principle was owned by the descent line with the principal adult male at the time only its steward, needed to be maintained and, if possible, increased. Any loss of resources to persons outside the descent line was contrary to family interests, as was illustrated by the idea popular in Taiwan that educating a daughter was a "capital-losing transaction" because daughters married into families of a different patronymic, which meant that their talents and their productive and reproductive capabilities were lost to their natal families. The strength of this agnatic principle differentiates preindustrial Chinese society from peasant societies that had bilateral kinship systems—that is, those in which recognition of matrilateral and patrilateral kin was more equal.

Lin Yutang notes the result of this very strong agnatic principle:

> The Chinese are a nation of individualists. They are family-minded, not social-minded, and the family mind is only a form of magnified selfishness. It is curious that the word "society" does not exist as an idea in Chinese thought.[5] . . . "Public spirit" is a new term, so is "civil consciousness," and so is "social service." There are no such commodities in China. (1939, 172–73)

Lin argues that while Westerners are involved in a variety of extrafamilial activities and groups such as sports and church communities, Chinese are not. Because of the devotion people should have to their own families, being involved in society, far from being praiseworthy, is discouraged. Social work is interfering in other's business.

> The best modern educated Chinese still cannot understand why Western women should organize a "Society for the Prevention of Cruelty to Animals." Why bother about the dogs, and why do they not stay at home and nurse their babies? (1939, 174–75)

An additional reason Lin finds for the neglect of society is the Confucian Five Relationships: ruler–subject, father–son, husband–wife, elder brother–younger brother, and friend–friend. Missing, Lin writes, is "man's social obligations toward the stranger, and great and catastrophic was the omission" (Lin 1939, 180). The result is that

> Samaritan virtue was unknown and practically discouraged. . . . The family, with its friends, became a walled castle, with the greatest communistic cooperation and mutual help within, but coldly indifferent toward, and fortified against, the world without. In the end, as it worked out, the family became a walled castle outside which everything was legitimate loot. (1939, 180; see also Luo 1985)

---

5. The Chinese term for society, *shehui*, was one of a number of neologisms introduced from Japan in the latter half of the nineteenth century.

That society consisted of "walled castles" containing family and friends reemphasizes the point that public-spiritedness and the notion of a public consisting of all the people in society were absent in preindustrial China. The character *gong* is now commonly used in much the same way that "public" is used in English, but this meaning, and the concept's existence in Chinese, is a relatively recent phenomenon. The original meaning of gong was simply "that which does not contain that which is private" [*wu si ye*] (Shu et al. 1948, 224). According to Chen Ruoshui, there were five traditional Chinese views of behavior and affairs to which *gong* refers. The earliest reference was to the rulers, the government, or the aristocracy. During the Spring and Autumn period (771–476 BCE), it took on a meaning of public interest or welfare of the people. This meaning is found in Confucian writings and elsewhere, and by the end of Warring States period (475–221 BCE) the purpose of government was regarded as ensuring general welfare and the fairness of sacrifices of individual interests for those of the whole. It later took on meanings of the people, the charitable giving of alms, and neighborhoods and counties acting neighborly. However strongly held, these ideas "lacked a clear idea of scope [i.e., what and who "public" included and what was private]." Moreover, in contrast to Japan and the West, gong had no reference to place in China, leaving unclear which objects are public and which are private (Chen 2005, 33, 65–66). At some point, *gong* also developed the meaning of "public," implying the common weal, juxtaposing it with *si* (private), which implies selfishness and antisocial behavior (see, e.g., Jones 1987, 19, 38).

The modern meaning of "public" came from Liang Qichao, who introduced it in the term *gongde* (public morality), which he took from the writings of Japanese scholar, author, journalist, and founder of Keio University Fukuzawa Yūkichi. Liang regarded public morality as fundamental to the human ability to form society, a sentiment later echoed by Liang Shuming who said that public morality was the sine qua non for the existence of social life (Liang 1949, 70, cited in Chen 2005, 6). Whereas some said that private morality or the friend–friend relationship of Confucian ethics was sufficient, Liang Qichao argued that it was an incomplete social ethic, that morality demands that people be altruistic, and that public morality benefits all members of society. However, in the early twentieth century, public morality rarely had such political connotations as advocating social solidarity or love of country but instead was used to criticize the lack of it. A ditty in a 1906 school textbook on ethics in which half the pages were about public morality reads, "Public roads are filthy, people cut down public flora [for their own use], people crowd when boarding public transport and businesses commit fraud on their customers."[6] A 1930s Shanghai publication outlined positive manifestations of public morality: benefiting others and benefiting the self, public welfare, following public order, conserving time, carrying out responsibilities, fraternity, proper recreation, not taking

---

6. A folk saying depicting the unkempt nature of the public space goes, "Public buildings leak, public horses are thin, and the public hall stinks of chicken feces" (*guan fang lou, guan ma shou, guanzhong tangwu ji shi chou*).

advantage of others, and the existence of self-governing groups and localities (Chen 2005, 5–16).

In a chapter in *Chinese Characteristics* entitled "The Absence of Public Spirit," Arthur Smith, a missionary who worked for fifty-four years in Shandong, avers that neither the government nor the common people had any notion of or commitment to the commonweal. The government, he writes, "although patriarchal, is much more occupied in looking after the Patriarch, than in caring for the Patriarch's family.... The people recognize distinctly that the prospective loss of taxes is the motive force in government efforts to mitigate disasters such as the continual outbreaks of irrepressible rivers" (1900, 107–8). Moreover, in its 250 years of rule the Qing government (1644–1911) had not bothered to repair roads that were once well constructed, "paved with stone and bordered with trees," that Smith surmised had been in disrepair since the end of the Ming (1368–1644), which it succeeded (1900, 108).

Smith further states that the government's attitude is reflected in those of the people in that neither cares about "what is done with the public property so long as he personally is not the loser. In fact, the very conception that a road, or anything, belongs to "the public" is totally alien to the Chinese mind" (1900, 108–9). Most roads, in fact, actually belonged to one farm or another:

> It is evidently in the interest of the farmer to restrict the roads as much as he can, which he does by an extended system of ditches and banks designed to make it difficult for anyone to traverse any other than the narrow strip of land which is indispensable for communication.... A man who wishes to load or to unload his cart leaves it in the middle of the roadway while the process is going on, and whoever wishes to use the road must wait until the process is completed. If a farmer has occasion to fell a tree he allows it to fall across the road, and travellers can tarry until the trunk is chopped up and removed. (1900, 109–10)

Moreover, no one would do anything in a public-spirited way to benefit others, and any object in the public space was fair game to anyone wanting to take it:

> No one individual, even if he were disposed to repair a road (which would never happen), has the time or the material wherewith to do it, and for many persons to combine for this purpose would be totally out of the question, for each would be in deep anxiety lest he should do more of the work, and receive less of the benefit, than some other person.... Not only do the Chinese feel no interest in that which belongs to the "public," but all such property, if unprotected and available, is a mark for theft. Paving-stones are carried off for private use, and square rods for the brick facing to city walls, gradually disappear. A wall enclosing a foreign cemetery in one of the ports of China was carried away till not a single brick remained, as soon as it was discovered that the place was in the charge of no one in particular. (1900, 111)

Chen Ruoshui echoes Smith's observations: "Chinese are quite confused about public benefit or strangers. In their behavior, they frequently appropriate public goods or do injury to strangers in order to advantage themselves. To put it dramatically, many Chinese seem to have an inherent conflict relationship with the public interest" (2005, 20). He also notes a passage from Liang Qichao's 1916 *Guomin qianxun*,

> There is no public forest that is not cut down, no public road that is not blocked and impassable, no public field that has not been invaded and occupied, no public garden that has not been ruined. Westerners feel that they have an interest in public goods so they protect and maintain them in order to continue to enjoy them. A Chinese will take that share that he regards as his so that he alone can enjoy it, then he will take advantage of those who are unaware [of their shares] or are unable to protect them and seize them as his own. (2005, 21–22)

Liang's overriding concern was China's weakness and its need to be strengthened in order to defend itself against the West. He attributed its weakness to two factors. First was the atomization of the population because of the Confucian overemphasis on family ties that resulted in the relative neglect of relationships to the state or society (H. Chang 1971, 153), and to the emphasis in Song Confucianism on self-cultivation. Self-cultivation was a practice that should have been aimed at preparing scholars to provide ethical governance, but it became an individual-oriented practice aimed at self-refinement rather than improving state and society (H. Chang 1971, 176). Both of these fed into the "plate of loose sand" nature of the Chinese population.

Second was Liang's view of the political status of China vis-à-vis surrounding countries. In Europe states bordered on other states, creating clear political identities in the peoples of each polity. China, by contrast, following its initial unification at the end of the Warring States period, existed as *tianxia* (all under heaven), a moral community extending to surrounding regions rather than as a state among states. As a result, there was no sense of national consciousness among Chinese; their loyalty was to a court rather than to a country (Levenson 1959, 111–12; H. Chang 1971, 297–98). Moreover, the rulers of that court were Manchus who, at the time, were regarded by the Han majority as foreigners. Pointing to the character for family (*jia*) in the word for country (*guojia*), Liang argued that China was not like a country but like a big family with an emperor as its head.

Thus, according to Liang, the most pressing need for China, was cohesion, which he expressed as *qun* (collectivity or grouping). The notion of *qun* originally came from his mentor, Kang Youwei, but over the years, it evolved in Liang's mind "from the Confucian cultural ideal of moral gemeinschaft toward an incipient idea of national community" maintained through voluntarism (*li*) and dynamism (*dong*), as opposed to inactivity and apathy (H. Chang 1971, 100, 178). These were antidotes to what Liang saw as endemic fatalism, manifested in passivity and resignation, in the traditional Chinese mind. Without cohesion, China would be unable to defend itself.

Crucial to grouping is morality, which Liang dichotomized into public and private. Both are important for groups, public morality (*gongde*) to promote group cohesion, and private morality (*side*) so that group members can achieve the moral perfection for their groups to function properly (Chen 2005, 9; H. Chang 1971, 151). Fukuzawa, from whom Liang borrowed these notions, wrote, "In traditional Japan and China, virtue almost always referred to the private virtue of the individual and his narrow surrounding circle" (Chen 2005, 9).

Lu Xun took the lack of a notion of public and the indifference toward strangers further, coining the phrase *kanke wenhua* (gawker culture) to describe the coldness Chinese showed when seeing prisoners marched off to be executed or to suffer some other injustice. He made this observation when he went to Japan to study medicine. Occasionally one of his teachers would show slides, and on one particular day one of the slides was of a Chinese person about to be beheaded by Japanese soldiers for assisting the Russians during the Russo-Japanese War while a group of Chinese gathered around to watch the event. This made a deep impression on him: a war by two foreign imperialist powers being fought on Chinese soil and a Chinese being beheaded while other Chinese simply looked on with indifference. He deeply felt the sorrow of the nation, and the cheering of his Japanese classmates at the site was a further blow to his dignity. His writing is steeped in a critique of the Chinese mentality as he saw it. He described his compatriots as narrow-minded, selfish, and numbed. Beheadings were a spectacle to be enjoyed, and people were ill-treated according to a pecking order of strong to weak to weaker (Lu 1990, x–xi, Wu H. 2012).[7]

More recently, Bill Purves and Peter Hessler have noted the problem of taking public goods for private use. Purves became the manager of a joint venture company in Gaozhou, Guangdong Province, in the 1980s. When he arrived at the company, he noticed that one couple, employees of the Chinese firm, did not come to work unless it was to take supplies from the warehouse to use in their own private business (1991). Hessler, in his travels in the early 2000s, noted the theft of bricks from the Great Wall, some of which were taken centuries ago but others as recently as the latter half of the twentieth century (2010). Moreover, the Chinese government regarded such behavior as significant enough to include a story about it in a grade-five moral education textbook. Little Wang, a lumber mill worker, sees another worker and his son taking a log from the lumberyard for their private use at home. He tries to stop them but his coworker rebuffs him, "It isn't yours, so mind your own business." The coworker and his son then proceed to take the log home. Wang reports them the next day, and the coworker has to return the log, but he then cuts down Wang's saplings in revenge. Justice prevails, however; the coworker is jailed for five days and has to compensate Wang (RMP 1988, 52–54).

---

7. See his stories, *Yao, A-Q zhengzhuan, Zhufu, Kong Yiji*.

When I began doing field research on business and management culture among Taiwanese factory owners in the Pearl River Delta Region in the mid-1990s, I often heard Taiwanese say that the Cultural Revolution had destroyed traditional Chinese morality. Many from China have told me the same thing. However, despite the very different roles of tradition in the governance of Taiwan and China after 1949—the Taiwan government self-consciously preserving it in part to appeal to the Overseas Chinese, the Chinese government strongly attacking it—how each government has defined civility, the actions each regards as civil or uncivil, remains remarkably similar.

In the next chapter I examine the efforts of the KMT and CCP governments to "civilize" their citizens and will also examine the comparability Taiwan and China for a study such as this one.

3
Comparability of China and Taiwan

Comparing societies can be problematic because the number of cultural differences between them makes it difficult to identify the factors on which to base clear comparisons. However, China and Taiwan share a number of similarities that are particularly relevant to comparing how and to what extent each has developed civility. These include a population largely originating in China and thus a shared cultural heritage, having the same central government for approximately two centuries up to 1895, and top-down attempts to impose civil behavior by Leninist governments in the twentieth century (Dickson 1997, 3; Taylor 201109, 411, 442). In this chapter I will examine the comparability of China and Taiwan and aspects of their cultural heritage that are germane to their development of civility. Following this is a review of attempts by their governments to "civilize" the masses.[1] In addition, mindful of the assault on traditional morality by the Chinese government under Mao Zedong, I also analyze primary school moral education textbooks from China and Taiwan, one set from each used in the late 1980s and another from each used in 2011, to learn how the two societies define and teach civility. The late 1980s date is appropriate for China because the government began its civilizing campaigns in 1980, after Mao's death. A possible challenge to this claim of cultural similarity is that in the 1960s and 1970s, some asserted that Taiwan was not a valid place to study Chinese society because it had been culturally "tainted" by its fifty years as a Japanese colony. I refute this in Chapter 5 below.

Cultural Heritage

Although both have undergone much social and cultural change since 1949, Taiwan and China share a cultural heritage. The majority populations of both are predominantly from the Han ethnicity. Non-Han people constitute approximately 2 percent of Taiwan's population and 6 percent of China's. Before the early seventeenth century, almost the entire population of Taiwan was Austronesian. Han fishermen and traders occasionally visited from China to trade, stock up, or take respite

---

1. "Civilize" denotes precisely what Chinese governments have consciously attempted to do to their people.

from storms, but there was no migration or settlement to speak of. Beginning with Dutch attempts to establish plantation agriculture in southern Taiwan from 1624, various events attracted Hoklo[2] migrants from the Zhangzhou and Quanzhou areas of Fujian province, across the Taiwan Straits from Taiwan. By 1684, when much of western Taiwan came under the control of the Qing Dynasty, the Han population had reached 100,000, outnumbering the indigenous population (J. Jacobs 2012, 19–22; Knapp 2007, 9–10). Migration continued over the next two centuries, despite Qing government efforts to stop it, and included Hakka migrants from northeastern Guangdong province. In 1895, the Qing government ceded Taiwan to Japan in perpetuity as part of the settlement after its loss in the 1894–1895 Sino-Japanese War. Migration from China to Taiwan nominally stopped at that time, which greatly restricted communication between those who had migrated to Taiwan and their ancestral areas in China. In 1905 the first Japanese census in Taiwan found the Han population had reached 2,492,784, with the indigenous population numbering 82,795 (Knapp 2007, 10). Cultural differences between Taiwan and China at this time were minimal, manifestations of regional cultural differences that are present throughout China.

China and Taiwan began to diverge in 1895 as Taiwan went under Japanese colonial rule for the next half century. Both the colonial government in Taiwan and the post–Republican revolution governments in China made efforts to modernize, but they were less effective in China and affected a far smaller proportion of its people owing to its vastly greater size and population and the ineffectiveness of the post-Qing warlord and Republican governments. Taiwan, however, was Japan's first colony,[3] and it wanted to make it a model to show other colonial powers that it could be a better one. After quelling local resistance, it set about to develop Taiwan's agricultural sector, road and rail transport system, communications, banking and finance, health and hygiene, and education. China remained largely under the control of Chinese governments with the exceptions of various treaty-port concession areas and the areas Japan occupied following its incursion into Manchuria in the 1930s and during World War II. It had a succession of warlord rulers until Chiang Kai-shek nominally unified it in 1928, but even then various warlords had de facto control of large parts of the country. This meant that governance from the center did not penetrate very deeply into the hinterland, hampering modernization projects. Such projects were much more successful in Taiwan under its strict, modern, and efficient Japanese rulers. However, China did produce a small elite of well educated, sophisticated, well-off, and influential people who had a high level of exposure to Western and Japanese ideas and lifestyles. Taiwan also produced a small educated elite, their cultural exposure being to Japan.

---

2. Hoklo refers to Minnan speakers. The other Han group is the Hakka. Their languages are mutually unintelligible.
3. Some would argue that Okinawa was the first colony, but it was brought into Japan as a prefecture in 1879, not as colony, though it also experienced assimilation pressure (Rabson 1996).

The colonial government in Taiwan took gradual steps, mostly in the latter part of its rule, to Nipponize the Taiwanese. It established primary schools within its first decade and used teaching materials based on the Imperial Rescript on Education in order to transform the Taiwanese into Japanese subjects (Tsurumi 1977, 10–11; 133–45). In 1919 the Taiwan governor established an assimilation policy under which Taiwan would become an extension of the home islands of Japan, which encouraged Taiwanese to use Japanese as an everyday language. A stronger attempt to assimilate the Taiwanese began in 1937 under the *kōminka* (literally "transform into imperial subjects") policy when the government increased pressure to use the Japanese language, called for people to adopt Japanese dress, housing styles and names, and formally outlawed indigenous religion in favor of Shinto.

However, the cultural effect of these attempts was limited. Some Taiwanese did assimilate. For example, at a Taibei wedding I attended in 1974, the groom's businessman father, who lived with his Japanese wife, was fluent in Japanese and English but spoke no Mandarin and gave his speech at the wedding banquet in halting Hoklo. However, for most Taiwanese, the assimilation effects were shallow. Few became Nipponized to this extent, mainly some of those who achieved elite status during the colonial period. Not only were most Taiwanese rural villagers, on whom urban change had little effect, but there were also various forms of discrimination against them, e.g., limits on education, restrictions on occupational choice,[4] and residential segregation. Moreover, the more intensely assimilative period of kōminka was simply too short—eight years—to effect anything other than superficial cultural changes (see Ching 2001).

It is true that many Taiwanese, particularly those in urban areas, did learn Japanese, but it is likely that the majority did not. Even in 1944, when primary school attendance was at its highest level, the enrolment rate was still only 71.31 percent (Tsurumi 1977, 148), and although the language of instruction was Japanese, the number who would have retained it is open to question. Students in urban areas would have had their Japanese reinforced through usage and exposure to Japanese cultural products and government, but most rural students would have returned after school to homes, villages, and neighborhoods in which people spoke Hoklo or Hakka. After finishing primary school, most boys would have helped their fathers in the fields or become apprentices in local shops, and most girls would have helped out at home for a few years until they married. These students would likely have lost their facility in Japanese from disuse, having only used it in the past during school hours.[5] Chang notes that most, even up to World War II, were illiterate, a factor that later made it difficult for Taiwanese elites to mobilize them (2003, 43).

Thus, with the exception of a small Taiwanese elite who quite markedly assimilated, the effect on Taiwanese culture during the fifty years of Japanese colonial rule

---

4. The main high-status occupation open to Taiwanese was medicine.
5. I base this on a similar phenomenon I encountered in the early 1960s. Many teens from rural areas I met had learned Mandarin in primary school but had largely forgotten it through disuse and lack of reinforcement.

was superficial. Taiwanese, even most of the elite, maintained their customs and, according to Wang, "never denied their Chinese inheritance." Japanese censuses counted them as Taiwanese, and after retrocession to the Chinese government in 1945, they "strongly resented the accusation of Taiwanese Nipponization by the Chinese officials of the KMT regime" (2013, 161; see also Chang 2003). They have maintained their customs since 1945. Li Yih-yuan, Taiwan's foremost anthropologist at the time, stated when interviewed by Alan Wachman:

> At a basic level Taiwanese are like Chinese from elsewhere in that they abide by the same notions of the temporal, supernatural, spatial, and cosmological dimensions as manifested in such common practices as fortune-telling (*suan-ming*) and geomancy (*feng-shui*). Their attitudes toward interpersonal relations—in the family, the community, and the state—are the same as Chinese elsewhere, as are their attitudes toward food and health. (Wachman 1994, 101–2)

Wang Fu-chang writes, "To this date, most Taiwanese people still carve the names of their ancestral homes, typically the name of a county of a province in the Chinese Mainland, on their tombstones to show their family lineage if they are buried in the traditional way" (2013, 161; see also Shih 2000). DPP politicians Yao Chia-wen and former President Chen Shui-bian both identified themselves as *huaren* (ethnic Chinese), indicating recognition of their Chinese cultural heritage (Wachman 1994, 81; CNA 2000).

In the nearly four years I spent in Taiwan from 1959 to 1962 and 1969 to 1970, theaters showed Japanese films, I heard Japanese popular music as well as Hoklo popular music that was melodically influenced by Japanese *enka*. Many rural and poorer urban Taiwanese wore wooden clogs (*geta*, *muji*). The Hoklo language has some Japanese loan words for items introduced after colonization. One occasionally heard older Taiwanese reminisce about the Japanese period, sometimes because they resented their treatment by the KMT government, sometimes because of the more orderly society they remembered the Japanese as having run. Later in the 1970s, Japanese-style coffee shops began to open.

However, these are superficial cultural items that are no more evidence of significant cultural assimilation than Westerners owning a tamagotchi or enjoying ragas played by Ravi Shankar. I saw no evidence of cultural changes in the Taiwanese that differentiated them from the general Han Chinese patterns their ancestors had practiced when still ruled by the Qing, other than those attributable to modernization. The basic cultural institutions, kinship and religion, showed no Japanese influence. Moreover, although some Mainlanders were quite free in criticizing or looking down on the Taiwanese, I never heard anyone even hint that the Taiwanese were any less "Chinese" than they were.[6]

---

6. Early KMT government suspicions were based on the Taiwanese having fought against KMT forces in the war, their being educated in Japanese, and their unwillingness to accept the mode of governance dictated to them by KMT officials. However, Phillips states that the Taiwanese initially welcomed KMT officials and were happy

Most important for this study, in areas of culture relevant to civility such as familism or disregard of strangers or of the public space, there were no significant cultural differences between Taiwanese and Mainlanders, which also means that in terms of key cultural institutions Taiwan and China were essentially the same. Extrapolating from the behavior of Mainlanders in Taiwan, Taiwan and China were at similar levels of civility in the late 1940s when the bulk of the Mainlander population went to Taiwan. That population was by no means uniform. It contained people who were well educated, sophisticated, and affluent, many "middle-class" people such as teachers and public servants, and a large number of soldiers, who were mostly from rural areas in China and, to the extent that they were educated, had received local private schooling (*sishu*) rather than formal public education. Some middle-aged and older Mainlander men behaved less civilly than others, pushing their way to an empty seat on a bus or jumping the queue at a post office service window, but, as Baron's 1963 op-ed piece indicated, in general, neither Taiwanese nor Mainlanders were very civil.

Cultural divergence between China and Taiwan began as the governments of each began to implement their development and political consolidation policies, the Taiwan government beginning a few decades earlier. With the Japanese surrender at the end of World War II in 1945, the KMT government took control of Taiwan. Although the Taiwanese initially welcomed the replacement of Japanese rule by a Chinese administration, their relations with the new government soon deteriorated due to high-handed and corrupt misrule and misunderstandings caused by different sets of expectations toward each other by Chiang Kai-shek and the KMT on one hand and the Taiwanese elites and public on the other (Phillips 2003). Taiwanese disappointment and resentment culminated in a massacre by KMT soldiers following the 1947 "February 28 Incident" (228, *ererba shijian*) and the ensuing "White Terror" (*baise kongbu*) over the next four decades. Government efforts to reverse whatever Nipponization it believed had been imposed on the Taiwanese during the colonial period and to "re-Sinify" the Taiwanese exacerbated the resulting enmity. The government mandated Mandarin as the language of instruction in schools and fined Taiwanese children for using their home languages. The curriculum emphasized Confucianism and traditional Chinese culture and history, with scant mention of Taiwan. Moreover, in order to ward off what they feared was a rejection of the government and the "Chineseness" that it represented,[7] officials also suppressed expressions of Taiwanese identity and discriminated against them in areas of government employment, teaching, and the military. In addition to these official practices, there was widespread condescension toward Taiwanese by Mainlanders.

Through the efforts of tens of thousands of initially labor-intensive, then technology-intensive, export-oriented small and medium enterprises characterized

---

to see the Japanese leave (2003).
7. In the early 1960s some privately claimed, "I'm Taiwanese, not Chinese." However, this statement was political rather than cultural.

by high levels of entrepreneurship, Taiwan's market-based economy developed rapidly from the late 1950s and created an environment of economic opportunity.[8] People became materially better off while society remained relatively egalitarian. Although initially authoritarian and repressive, Taiwan's politics eventually democratized in both structure and culture, the impetus mainly coming from grassroots pressure.[9] Democratization also ended the suppression of Taiwanese ethnic consciousness. Moreover, although the education system stressed Chinese culture and values, Taiwanese were also exposed to a good deal of foreign influences, especially American, through study and living abroad and cultural products such as films, TV, music and reading materials. Compared to those in China, Taiwanese are overall better educated and generally better off economically. They have also embraced the principles of liberal democracy and have a high level of civility.

In China the first thirty years of CCP rule saw attacks, some quite violent, on traditional ideas, social organization, and human relations through a suite of campaigns aimed at changing the economy, social structure, and culture and consolidating first the government's power and then that of the Maoist faction. According to acquaintances from China and Taiwanese manufacturers in China, some of these campaigns did great damage to the Chinese social fabric (see Gold 1982). The socialized economy led initially to relative equality but an equality of poverty. The authorities kept tight control of what people were able to hear or read. Until the Reform and Opening Up (*gaige kaifang*) policy of the 1980s, there was little in the way of foreign influence or entrepreneurial activity. The 1980s saw some liberalization as the government began to open the economy to market forces and society to foreign ideas. However, it also tried at times to limit foreign influences to those that had economic utility while limiting exposure to outside concepts of law, politics, art, or other notions that officials found objectionable, labeling them "spiritually polluting" (Hughes 2006, Chap. 1).

Since Reform and Opening Up, China has adopted a mixed-market economy in which state firms still play a large role and success still frequently depends on *guanxi*. Politically, there have been fewer changes. China is still an authoritarian party/state, the only semblance of democracy being at the village level, where in some places there are relatively freely contested elections. The government expends less effort controlling people's lives and generally leaves them alone if they do nothing it sees as a potential threat, but it monitors communication and tries, with partial success, to control information.

Despite the divergent paths Taiwan and China have taken since 1949 and the different worldviews they have created, in some areas they have changed in

---

8. Taiwan's economy was also mixed, the party/state having taken over the firms established by the Japanese in 1945, but the growth in the economy that brought about Taiwan's spectacular development from the 1960s came largely from the myriad SMEs of the private sector.
9. Huntington states that Taiwan's democratization was top-down (1991). It is true that in the end, Chiang Ching-kuo decided not to block the formation of opposition parties, but that was at the very end. Grassroots pressure had been building for well over a decade by then. See J. Jacobs 2012.

the same direction. Both have experienced massive urbanization and a shift from family-based farming, a collective activity, to industrial or service-based employment, which is carried out and remunerated individually. This affects the authority and interaction patterns in kinship relations, especially the relative independence of children from parents (see Harrell 1982, Yan 2009) and wives from their husbands. Three-generation households are less common, in rural areas because the middle generation has largely left to work in the cities, in the cities because of the lack of space in the kind of housing that most migrants can afford to accommodate a third generation. Other reasons are (1) the relative bargaining power and lesser willingness to live with parents-in-law after marriage that young women have as a result of being income earners, and their relative scarcity because of fetal sex selection, which has resulted in an abundance of males,[10] and (2) the increase in young people finding work in cities other than those in which their parents live. Spouse choice has shifted to the bride and groom themselves, though parents still control some levers because parental approval of a child's prospective spouse remains culturally important and because the bride's parents insist that the prospective groom owns an apartment before consenting to a marriage, something few young men can afford without help from their parents.[11]

Some things have remained the same. In the mid-1990s I studied Taiwanese business owners operating in the Pearl River Delta Region who lived in their factories. Having experienced predemocratization business conditions in Taiwan, they felt they had an advantage over other non-Chinese entrepreneurs because they understood the local drinking and business entertainment culture and its accompanying gift giving as well as how officials behaved and how bribery worked.

However, it is the differences in behavior and outlook that are most noticeable. As I will show in more detail in the next chapters, civility is far better established in Taiwan. Chinese visitors to Taiwan are highly impressed with the gentle society they find there, people queuing, saying "sorry," "excuse me," "please," and "thank you," and being helpful and showing genuine concern for others.[12] They feel that Taiwanese have preserved aspects of Chinese culture that the political paroxysms of the Maoist period destroyed.[13] Taiwanese, by contrast, feel themselves culturally distant from Chinese citizens because of the littering, spitting, crowding, and the like that they encounter from short-term Chinese tourists in Taiwan or when visiting China themselves (Rowan 2016). People in Taiwan also understand democracy, both as

---

10. Taiwan's sex ratio at birth imbalance began to rise in 1985. At present the sex ratio in the 15–29-year-old marriage age population is 107:100, which means that over half a million men will be unable to find a local bride (Poston and Yang 2014; Interior Ministry 2014). The reason for the increases is that many women do not want more than one child, and if they are going to limit births to one, a son is generally preferred.
11. It is quite possible that parents' willingness to help their sons is a way to ensure that they have at least a moral claim to spend their senior years in the homes they've helped them buy.
12. A blogger who had studied Chinese in both Beijing and Taibei wrote that Taiwan is "like China but everyone in Taiwan stands in line and says please and thank you" (Birdabroad).
13. There is no question that the upheavals of the Maoist period had a deleterious effect on moral behavior, but the notion that before this period Chinese were civil is a nostalgic myth.

a political system and in their acceptance of different opinions and the choices of voters. They better understand the principles and workings of a market economy and are more exposed and have unhindered access to foreign ideas and cultures. Moreover, the nationalism found in Taiwan is more civic than ethnic. Although these are relatively recent developments, manifesting since the 1990s, University of Toronto political science professor Joseph Wong has stated that Chinese students who go to study in Taiwan "tend to experience Taiwan as a fundamentally different place," which is "unlikely to become one" with China (Rovnick 2012).

Civilizing Campaigns as a Tool of Governance

Both the CCP and the KMT governments, before the latter's democratization, used education and propaganda campaigns to "civilize" the masses and to try to mold them into an idealized form of human being. To the KMT, this idealized person was a "proper" Chinese who adhered to the hoary tenets of Confucian culture; to the CCP, it was initially the new socialist man (Chen 1969). Campaigns by these governments often had political aims as well, in particular increasing loyalty to country and government and, in China, willingness to follow Party directions.

Republican/KMT government civilizing campaigns

In the late nineteenth and early twentieth centuries, China was at its nadir. Western forces, and even more galling, its former tributary state, Japan, took advantage of China's immature state of industrialization and its lack of a modern fighting force to defeat it in several wars. Meanwhile, the number of foreigners in the country—missionaries, educators, adventurers, merchants, and administrators in foreign concessions in the treaty ports—was growing, and they were often highly critical of China's weakness and backwardness and the behavior and habits of its people. They disparaged China on a variety of issues, from foot binding and female infanticide, to the general unsanitary conditions of city and country, to the behavior and habits of the peasants and the urban poor. They even labeled China "the sick man of Asia." Unsurprisingly, this caused a great loss of face to the Chinese, especially the elites, and challenged their ingrained belief that theirs was the superior civilization. It also stirred a desire to revive the nation.[14]

However, two of China's leaders, Sun Yat-sen and Chiang Kai-shek, who had both spent time abroad,[15] gave the Western critique some credence. In a 1924

---

14. I was in Taibei in 1973 when the Bruce Lee film, *Enter the Dragon* opened in local theaters. Newspapers advertised the film by stating, "No one will ever call China the sick man of Asia again!"
15. Sun spent much of his teenage years in Honolulu and Hong Kong and later traveled extensively in the United States and England raising funds and support for the anti-Qing revolution. Chiang spent six years, from age 18 to 24, in Japan at a military academy and served in the Imperial Japanese Army. Thus, both had experienced more modernized societies.

speech on the Three People's Principles, Sun criticized the Chinese people for their lack of concern about their appearance and manners, the basis on which foreigners disdained them. He also linked gaining the respect of foreigners with foreign acceptance of the right of the Chinese to govern themselves free of foreign occupation (Brady 2003, 26). Chiang was even more critical, describing the Chinese as selfish, undisciplined, and dissolute. In a speech attributed to him, he stated that "the general psychology of our people today can be described as spiritless. The people fail to distinguish good from evil, and officials the difference between public and private and use public funds for private purposes." As a result, officials tend to be dishonest and avaricious, the masses are undisciplined and calloused, youths become degraded and intemperate, adults are corrupt and ignorant, the rich become extravagant and luxurious, and the poor become mean and disorderly (de Bary 2008, 695).

New Life Movement (*Xinshenghuo yundong*)

In 1934, Chiang Kai-shek, the de facto leader of the ROC, instituted the first civilizing campaign of the post-dynastic era, the New Life Movement (NLM). To some extent, this campaign was a reaction to foreign criticisms of the Chinese and their manners, their personal hygiene habits, appearance, decorum, and general lack of sanitation. However, another aim was to instill discipline, even military discipline, into the Chinese people in order to strengthen China and put it on the road to recovering its past greatness.

The NLM was ideologically based on Chiang Kai-shek's four favorite Confucian virtues, decorum or discipline, right conduct, having a clear notion of right and wrong, and being self-conscious enough to know shame (*li*, *yi*, *lian*, and *chi*). For the masses, these virtues were to be realized through a long and wide-ranging list of ninety-six do-and-don't rules that included various aspects of public health and orderly behavior. Examples include the following: take frequent cold showers; wear simple, clean, utilitarian clothing; keep the top button on the tunic buttoned; eat clean food and wash utensils after meals; sit and stand straight, and don't slouch; no spitting, drinking, gambling, or whoring; no smoking in public; don't interrupt when others are talking or quarrel with others; be courteous; don't talk loudly or eat noisily; be kind to neighbors and considerate of others; help the old and the weak and respect elders; keep the streets clean; use the left side of the roads; don't shuffle about the streets, stop in the middle of the road, gape about, or block the traffic; spend less on weddings and funerals; use native commodities; lead a regular life; and treasure public goods and facilities. Adherence to these rules was aimed at disciplining people and changing their inner selves. That, in turn would produce desired qualities such as obedience, strictness, cleanliness, accuracy, diligence, secrecy and a willingness to sacrifice for group and nation through the militarization of the population (Eastman 1974, 67–68; Dirlik 1975, 976; Wikipedia, "Xinshenghuo

Yundong"). There was also a dress code for women requiring that necks, arms, and legs be "decently covered" (to the elbow and below the knee); hats were to be worn straight, not cocked at an angle; slippers, hairnets, and eyeshades were for indoor wear only; hair should be straight, not curled; and bound breasts and high heeled shoes were prohibited (Finanne 2008, 171–72).

We see in these rules a mixture of civility in the sense of being considerate of and avoiding offence to others as well as in the sense of personal manners, decorum, and hygiene that Elias noted in sixteenth-century Europe. However, aside from reforming these aspects of citizen behavior, the NLM had other purposes. First, it was launched as a countermeasure to the appeals of the Communist movement, although according to many scholars (see Dirlik 1975; Schoppa 2000, 84; Culp 2006), it was not very effective or appealing. Second, it was basically about discipline and order. At this time, Chiang was enamored with fascism, understandable given that Italy had lifted itself out of the sort of deep hole that China was in by a leader following this ideology. To Chiang, a military man from his early days, the discipline and militarization of society must have seemed to be the answer:

> In fascism the organization, the spirit, and the activities must all be militarized. . . . In the home, the factory, and the government office, everyone's activities must be the same as in the army. . . . In other words, there must be obedience, sacrifice, strictness, cleanliness, accuracy, diligence, secrecy. . . . And everyone together must firmly and bravely sacrifice for the group and the nation. (Iwai 1937, 37–38; quoted in Eastman 1974, 202)

Second, Chiang saw disciplining and militarizing the population as necessary for the salvation of China and of the Chinese as a people.

The NLM kicked off in Nanchang in 1934 and spread to other cities. One issue in implementation was whether to use moral suasion, as championed by Wang Jingwei, China's then premier, or the proposal of Chiang Kai-shek, then chairman of the National Military Council, that the rules should be treated as laws and enforced by police. They reached a compromise, though it leaned heavily toward enforcement rather than voluntary adherence. People's homes were searched to ensure that they were clean and orderly, and violators of any of the public behavior rules were to be remonstrated against (Liu 2013). The NLM was to be led by officials, who were to present themselves as exemplars of the movement. Students were also recruited as monitors.

However, the NLM was ineffective. Many officials paid it only lip service or ignored it altogether; Eastman notes that even the president's wife, Madame Chiang, ignored the NLM smoking ban in the Officers' Moral Endeavor Corps (1974, 275, 370)! Three years after its launch, Chiang declared that it had only been "a temporary and superficial renovation without attaining a fundamental reform." Officials had made speeches and coined slogans but did little to actually implement it (Eastman,

1974, 14). However, the spirit and many of the rules of deportment of the NLM were later revived during the Chinese Cultural Renaissance Movement (CCRM).

Chinese Cultural Renaissance Movement (*Zhonghua wenhua fuxing yundong*)

The CCRM began in Taiwan in 1966 under the direction of Chiang Kai-shek, then president of the Republic of China, in reaction to China's Cultural Revolution, which had been launched earlier that year. Chiang's government inaugurated the CCRM to position itself as the protector and savior of Chinese culture and by doing so hoped to win the hearts and minds of Overseas Chinese communities, whose support was important for investment purposes as well as in its propaganda war against the Communists. However, the CCRM provided other opportunities, such as for the government to strengthen its efforts to Sinicize the Taiwanese and put off any push toward nativization;[16] to reemphasize Chinese culture and tradition to the youth who were perceived as becoming Westernized; and to tighten its control. Its first item was "Be loyal to the national leader; a patriot of the nation; faithful and obedient to parents; respectful to teachers and the aged; kindly and helpful to the poor and distressed" (Tozer 1970, 86; Lin n.d.).

As a widely publicized movement, the CCRM was not long lasting, but it had sustained effects on youths and the arts and in the form of recycled NLM rules included in the primary and secondary school curriculum. Texts contained instructions on how to eat and dress properly and behave toward one's family and in public (Tozer 1970, 86). Primary school moral education texts, for example, remained virtually unchanged throughout the 1970s and most of the 1980s, a new edition coming shortly before democratization began (Schak 2012). Police raided and closed some "unhealthy" venues frequented by youths and forced young males with long hair who caught their attention to get haircuts. Among the censorship targets was Peking opera, which was supported by military officials because of its popularity among Mainlander soldiers. Although its stories are moralistic and stress Confucian virtues and behavior, the Cultural Bureau updated old scripts and censored racier bits or parts that did not conform to Cultural Renaissance Confucian moralistic emphases. This formed a mold for other forms of art, stifling creativity and reality in favor of morality plays (Tozer 1970, 87). Despite this, the early 1970s saw the birth of Taiwan's rural-based social realist literature, *xiangtu wenxue*, which painted a more accurate picture of rural life than that which government publications offered (see Chapter 5).

Although the Cultural Renaissance paid at least lip service to the acceptance of science, technology, and democratization, according to Winckler, it was another

---

16. This was a reaction not to suspected Nipponization of the Taiwanese but to their rejection of and enmity toward the KMT government for its ill treatment of them.

decade before science was decently funded in Taiwan (1994, 34), and another two decades before Taiwan took major steps toward democratization. According to Tozer, even in its early stages, the CCRM did not strike a chord with the public:

> The populace is either apathetic, or, as in the case of the native Taiwanese, suspicious of the movement because it is sponsored by the Nationalist Government. Intellectuals and students, too, are indifferent, or alienated by the government's abuse of the Cultural Renaissance. The latter show little interest in Chinese tradition or in its preservation. (1970, 98–99)

The predemocratization, authoritarian Kuomintang government in Taiwan mounted other civility-related campaigns, generally directed at single issues such as buying local goods, clearing busy pedestrian walkways of hawkers, or urging drivers to be courteous and follow road rules. It was also enamored with slogans, which were written on walls and on all sorts of consumer goods packaging. Some were political, such as "expose Communist spies, recover the mainland, develop Taiwan," some exhortative, prodding people to be frugal, law abiding, and not to waste time. However, these campaigns were very short-lived, commencing with loud announcements but petering out within a few weeks. Moreover, unlike the CCRM, there was at best only sporadic enforcement, and that only in the few days that a campaign was in the news. After the death of Chiang Ching-kuo in 1988, with three exceptions, all successful, governments in Taiwan ceased to carry out civility campaigns.

Two of the exceptions occurred in the early 1990s, both in the Taibei Municipality at the direction of then-mayor Chen Shui-bian, who represented the opposition Democratic Progressive Party. Chen was the first directly elected Taibei mayor in close to thirty years, and he knew that he had to be able to show accomplishments if he were to be reelected.[17] One campaign aimed at improving road-user behavior, mainly drivers, but pedestrians as well. Chen ordered that all traffic police be on duty during morning and evening rush hour with orders to strictly enforce the traffic code, especially regarding parking, red lights, turning at intersections, and respecting pedestrian right of way. To ensure compliance, he also ordered public servants onto the streets to monitor police actions. This campaign was sustained for several months. Cab drivers said that people initially thought that this one, like similar campaigns in the past, would soon fizzle out, and when it did not, there was a lot of complaining, but after several months, people got used to abiding by traffic regulations and realized the benefits in doing so. As an example of the campaign's effectiveness, prior to it, when pedestrians crossed at an intersection, they would never assume that motorists wanting to make a right turn would stop; afterwards, they could assume that they would.

The other was a reform of the behavior of clerks and others in the District Offices who interacted directly with the public when citizens had business to

---

17. Taibei mayors were appointed by the central government in those three decades.

conduct with the city government. Before democratization clerks often acted officiously and condescendingly toward the public, especially those who appeared to be poor or not well educated.[18] Chen ordered that citizens be treated as guests in one's home. Before the reform, after members of the public found their way to the correct window, they had to stand and wait in line until their turn came, and then they had to transact their business with a clerk who was sitting at a desk behind the window while they stood. After the reform when they arrived at the District Office, a volunteer greeted them and directed them to the correct floor to transact their business. When they got there, another volunteer asked if they needed help filling in forms or other assistance and then asked them to take a number, be seated, and wait till their number was called. Waiting areas were furnished with chairs, sofas and tables, magazines and newspapers, a TV, a photocopy machine, a play area for small children, and pairs of reading glasses for visitors to borrow if needed. When their number was called they went not to a window but to a desk and sat down, face to face with the clerk on the other side. On the public servant's side was the clerk's name plaque and phone number. If a follow-up was needed or there was a complaint, the client could phone the clerk directly. Procedures were simplified so that clients could transact their business more quickly, and public servants would visit the less mobile in their homes.

At the beginning of this campaign, some department heads objected to these procedures, saying that the changes would undermine their authority, but they were converted after implementation when they saw that the public responded to their courtesy with civility and gratitude. To ensure compliance, departments monitored service levels, each month asking a proportion of clients to evaluate the service they had received. Departments then used the evaluations in employee appraisals.

The success of these two campaigns is still evident. It is doubtless thanks in no small measure to the persistence of the campaigns rather than the sort of "lots of thunder but no rain" campaigns of the authoritarian past. However, by the time Chen became mayor in 1994, civility was already improving in Taiwan. Moreover, whereas the earlier campaigns came top-down from an authoritarian government of which few were enthusiastic supporters, Taiwan was then on its way to becoming a democracy, and Chen was a popularly elected mayor in a genuinely contested election.

The third campaign was run by the Transport Ministry when Taibei's Mass Rapid Transit (MRT; *jieyun*) system was initiated. Six months before the MRT's opening, the ministry began an education campaign about the service itself—how to queue, the prohibition on smoking, eating, drinking or chewing gum on the platform or the trains, and on passenger courtesy. After the service opened, there were monitors at all stations ensuring that passengers followed the rules. This was

---

18. Chinese officials were notorious for acting officiously (*bai jiazi*; *da guan qiang*), but in Taiwan it is likely that this behavior was exacerbated by the Mainlander-Taiwanese relationship, public servants tending to be Mainlanders.

also a highly successful campaign (Lee 2007), particularly given that it socialized the public into a completely different behavioral regime than that which they had previously followed on urban public transport. A measure of its success is that the passengers, themselves, remind rule breakers of the proper behavior when using the system.

Chinese Communist Party / People's Republic of China campaigns

The CCP has spawned far more campaigns than the KMT, thirty-nine since 1930 (Wikipedia, "CCP Campaigns"). Campaigns were an important tool of governing in the Maoist period, and some, such as Land Reform, the Great Leap Forward, and the Cultural Revolution, were very disruptive to society. Since 1976, the year of Mao's death, there have been twelve campaigns, most of which have been exhortative rather than aimed at mobilization, and thus more peaceful. With the exception of the 1963 Learning from Lei Feng campaign, those with a civility theme have come from the post-Mao period.

Whereas only two KMT-instigated campaigns were named, Chinese government campaigns have been more formal, and they began almost two decades before the CCP assumed power in China. They have generally had political aims, if not as the marquee goal of the campaign itself, at least as a subgoal. For example, the Land Reform redistributed land to the tiller, an economic goal, but it also decimated the landlord class, getting rid of the only sector of the rural population that could possibly resist the government. The Three-Anti and Five-Anti campaigns were aimed at eliminating corruption from the bureaucracy and the business community, respectively, but in addition they eliminated all doubt in the minds of the targeted groups that the CCP was in charge and that things would be different in the future. There were also campaigns aimed at particular elements in society such as the many antirevisionist or reeducation campaigns directed mainly at government or party officials or at various "enemies of the people" such as counterrevolutionaries, landlords, or former elites. The Cultural Revolution, despite its name, was essentially a power struggle between Mao's forces and those who opposed him, and the campaigns that took place in the few years after Mao died were power struggles between Maoist and anti-Maoist forces. Since 1978, there have been at least two campaigns ostensibly aimed at combating Western influences, though they were also struggles between forces wanting to maintain socialism and those who promoted a greater role for markets, "socialism with Chinese characteristics." The post-Reform and Opening Up campaigns have been much less strident than those of the Maoist era.

Learning from Lei Feng (*Xue Lei Feng*)

The earliest campaign to advocate what could be called civility was Learning from Lei Feng. In contrast to the broad themes of other campaigns, it was built around a model individual. According to Mei Zhang, the Communists have used models for a long time to "prescribe proper socialist attitudes, to create peer pressure to conform to acceptable norms, and to accomplish its frequent campaign goals—whether they be political, economic, or educational." During the revolutionary war, the heroes were brave fighters and martyrs. Those coming afterward were models of socialist morality. Under Mao, they were promulgated by virtually all media, including loudspeakers set up in the streets of towns and villages (1999, 111–12).

Lei Feng was born in Hunan in 1940 but was orphaned as a youth and raised by the Communist Party. He came to people's attention posthumously through what was said to be his diary. He became a member of the Communist Youth Corps as a youngster, and at age twenty, he joined the People's Liberation Army, where he served in a transport unit. He died in an accident two years later in 1962, hit by an electricity pole knocked over by a reversing truck. Up to that point, few had heard of him, but a campaign built around him was launched in 1963 based on the diary in which he had recorded his deeds and declared his dedication to Chairman Mao and the CCP. The diary, written in flowery language, was illustrated and contained over 200,000 words. It was published and widely distributed with the urging to "learn from Lei Feng"—that is, emulate his selflessness, willingness to help others, and dedication to the Communist state and Party.

There are three images of Lei Feng: (1) his "nail-like spirit" (*dingzi jingshen*), "nailing himself" to the study of Mao's works; (2) his service to the people (*wei renmin fuwu*), a "boy scout" always looking for people, including strangers, for whom he could do good deeds because Chairman Mao wanted him to; and (3) his function as an "eternally rust-proof screw" (*yongbushengxiu de luosiding*), a term taken from his diary referring to his making indispensable contributions while remaining anonymous and being always reliable (Zhang 1999, 113–14). Mei Zhang writes, "Lei Feng symbolized devotion to the Party, collectivism, sacrifice and altruism—with politics and Mao's teaching as the hub of all activities" (1999, 115). A *People's Daily* editorial from March 5, 1993, states:

> When Lei Feng died in the line of duty, he was only 22, but his short life gives concentrated expression to the noble ideals of a new people, nurtured with the communist spirit, and to the noble moral integrity and values of the Chinese people in the new period. These are firm faith in communist ideals, political warm heartedness for the party and the socialist cause, the revolutionary will to work arduously for self-improvement, the moral quality and self-cultivation of showing fraternal unity and taking pleasure in assisting others, the heroic spirit of being ready to take up cudgels for a just cause without caring for his own safety, the attitude of seeking advancement and studying hard, and the genuine spirit of matching words with deeds and enthusiastically carrying out one's duties.

There is no question that the Lei Feng model, which has been revived several times, has made an impact on China. There is a Lei Feng Commemoration Day, March 5, on which teachers tell students about the deeds he did and encourage them to follow his example. A teacher from Liaoning recalled that when asked what they did on that day, students said they returned lost wallets, volunteered in their neighborhoods to help the elderly clean their houses, or carried luggage for passengers at railway stations (Xinhua 2003). However, other good deeds, such as cutting people's hair or fixing broken appliances, raised objections from workers in these trades because it cost them business. One can describe a selfless individual as a "living Lei Feng [*huo Lei Feng*]" (Fowler 2008).[19] A China.org.cn[20] article lists a number of such individuals who say that Lei Feng inspired them to do their good deeds. In Harbin there is a Lei Feng Taxi Squad, a company with three hundred cabs and seven thousand volunteer drivers. One of its drivers found a suitcase left in his cab containing the passenger's passport and other documents. He searched out the passenger to return the lost items and commented, "No matter how poor I myself am, I only feel relieved when I try every means to return the property left in my taxi" (Xinhua 2008). A *People's Daily* story claimed that many who volunteer or donate money, blood or organs are inspired by Lei Feng to do so.

However, it would be wrong to assume from this that the Lei Feng campaign was an immediate success. First, although learning from Lei Feng became part of the school curriculum in 1963, schools were shut down a few years later during the Cultural Revolution and remained closed for several years (Meng and Gregory 2002), though other available outlets enabled the government to get the Lei Feng message out. However, the struggles of the Cultural Revolution were not at all conducive to the practice of civility, which would have blunted the message of service to others. Second, since the 1980s the Chinese government has seen the need to initiate several other campaigns to instill a spirit of civility into the population, implying that not all were inspired to follow the Lei Feng message.

Third, remembering and emulating Lei Feng is far from universal. A recent report in a local newspaper in Henan Province said nearly half of the 100 interviewed pupils in two primary schools in Zhengzhou, the provincial capital, said they did not know Lei Feng at all. But they were much excited when talking about famous Hong Kong stars such as Andy Lau. (Xinhua 2008)

Fourth, Lei Feng was "updated" in 2012 as a young lad who liked poetry and dancing and had a girlfriend, but that version of him did not capture the public imagination as much as the Lei Feng antihero created by two Beijing Film Academy students.[21] They created him as a "Clark Kent" persona who worked as a street cleaner but kept being beaten up by people who rejected his help (Ng 2011; Hu 2013). A video game about his life turned out to be a dud. On the 50th anniversary celebration of Learn from Lei Feng Day, Weibo was filled with mocking comments, some of which poked holes in the Lei Feng story, and three films made about his life

---

19. This follows the term "living Buddha" (*huo pusa*) for a very moral person.
20. A website of Xinhua, China's official news agency.
21. This is available on Youku, http://v.youku.com/v_show/id_XMjkxNTgxMDU2.html

and released for the 2013 annual Lei Feng Day all flopped, some theatres selling no tickets at all (Ng 2011; J. Jacobs 2012; Levin 2013a).

However, despite the apparently lack of appeal of Lei Feng to younger people, the Central Publicity Department[22] continues to mount Learn from Lei Feng campaigns to promote the spirit of serving others. A new one began in 2013; soon afterward I saw a large billboard just outside the Xiamen airport featuring the classic Lei Feng picture and exhorting all to serve the people. Moreover, the blood bank where residents went to donate blood following a factory explosion in Kunshan in 2014 is called the "Study Lei Feng" voluntary service branch (Fauna 2014). According to a *South China Morning Post* editorial, officials see Lei Feng as a less threatening choice vis-à-vis stability than charity drives by religious groups (SCMP 2012).

Five Stresses, Four Beauties, Three Fervent Loves (*Wu jiang si mei san reai*)

Although Lei Feng was meant to symbolize selflessness, that selflessness was limited by the prevailing political reality. Especially during the Cultural Revolution, a primary theme was class struggle, which drew a line between "the people" and "class enemies," the latter seen as undeserving of consideration or civil treatment. When Deng Xiaoping assumed power, he formally set aside class struggle to concentrate on what he regarded as China's most important problem, poor economic productivity, and he chose to develop the economy by opening it up to market forces. That decision, formalized in December 1978, at the Third Plenum of the Eleventh Central Committee of the Communist Party, was meant to reassure a populace both weary and leery of politically motivated campaigns that pitted one category of people against another. One consequence, however, though it took several years to manifest, was increased inequality, and although this was both condoned—"some will get rich before others"—and lauded—"ten thousand yuan households"—it created popular discontent and a potential threat to CCP legitimacy (Dirlik 2005, 151–59).

The government took two steps to counter this discontent; it created "socialism with Chinese characteristics," which allowed it to redefine socialism, and it began a series of campaigns focused on culture and civilization. Each centered on a particular term, in reverse order, *hexie* (harmony), *suzhi* (quality), and *wenming* (civilization)—though not just any *wenming* but *shehui zhuyi wenming* (socialist civilization), features of which the *People's Daily* listed as "love of public property, respect for the group, [support] for labor and for science, and love for the Communist Party which led us to the socialist road" (Niu 1979; cited in Lin 2009, 112).

Wenming was first mentioned in 1978 at the Third Plenum of the Eleventh Central Committee of the Communist Party at which the leadership decided to

---

22. This was formerly the Ministry for Propaganda; the Chinese word *xuanchuan* can be translated either way. The Chinese government changed the English name in 1998.

promote socialist spiritual morality. Along with egalitarianism, it was a key plank of Marxist ideology. Deng Xiaoping used the term in an address on April 4, 1979, in which he said that creating the new socialist person went hand in hand with economic development—that is, it referred to both material as well as spiritual civilization. The stated reason for promoting it had nothing to do with legitimacy or inequality. According to the *Worker's Daily*, it was to repair the damage to China's morality code that had existed before the ten calamitous years when Lin Biao and the Gang of Four had turned right and wrong on their heads (WDIED 1982, 2) and to raise the skills, attitudes and dedication of the labor force to enable China to compete in the world marketplace (Lin 2009, 86–89).

Preparation for the civilization-based campaigns began in late December 1980, with the study of documents. It was the most intense campaign up to that time under post-Mao leaders, and it even revived Cultural Revolution themes such as "Learn from Lei Feng," another Cultural Revolution hero, Wang Jie,[23] and one of Mao's favorites, "The Foolish Old Man Removed the Mountains." Other themes included the struggle against Japan and the selfless service and sacrifice of the Yan'an spirit (Dirlik 1982, 365–66). Then, on February 28, 1981, the Party Central Committee and the Ministries of Education, Culture, Public Health, and Public Security issued the "Circular on Fostering Civil Manners" (Dirlik 1982, 360–61), out of which the first major civilizing campaign, Five Stresses[24] and Four Beauties (*wu jiang si mei*), emerged (Baike).

The Five Stresses and Four Beauties campaign was announced on February 25, 1981. It was an omnibus movement aimed at improving not only public decorum but also the performance of factories, commercial enterprises, services, public health and sanitation, education, public transport, the military, cadres, science and technology (Murthy 1983, 10). A year later, Three Fervent Loves were added. In addition, a National Civility and Good Manners Month and a campaign to use five polite phrases were established.

The Five Stresses are to stress—be particular about—being civilized, mannerly, hygienic, orderly, and moral. Murthy describes them as being about removing "dirt, disorder and lack," lack referring to the lack of good service (1983, 6). The Four Beauties are to be beautiful in spirit, speech, and behavior, and to keep the environment beautiful. The Three Loves are to love the motherland, socialism, and the Party, though with the linking of the stresses and beauties to the Party and its ideology (see below), the addition of the loves seems superfluous. A handbook on the stresses and beauties states that "taking up the Five Stresses in a big way, the entire

---

23. Wang Jie was a PLA platoon leader who, during a training session, threw himself on dynamite that was about to explode. He saved his platoon from harm but sacrificed his life in the process.
24. *Stresses* is the standard translation, but *jiang* is more clearly translated as "to pay particular attention to" or "to be particular about."

country, especially the youth, will achieve the Four Beauties" (WDIED 1982, 3).[25] The handbook's explanation of the beauties illustrates the breadth of the movement.

> Being beautiful in spirit means focusing on ideology, moral character and noble thoughts; safeguarding the Party's leadership and the socialist system; being patriotic, upright and sincere; doing nothing to dishonor the integrity of the nation or another person; not harming others to benefit oneself; and not resorting to deceit or committing fraud.
> Beautiful language is using and popularizing polite language, being amicable, elegant and modest, and avoiding coarse or dirty language, irrational arguments and using evil words to harm others.
> Beautiful behavior refers to being someone whose actions benefit other people and society as a whole, being hard-working, kind-hearted and disciplined, and doing nothing to harm the collective, public goods or social order.
> Beautiful environment means putting oneself in order, managing the environment well around the family and the workplace, maintaining public sanitation, being hygienic, clean and green; and not spitting, littering or damaging [public] plants and flowers. (WDIED 1982, 3)

The handbook then corrects two "misunderstandings" by the public: that speaking crudely and roughly is the natural disposition of simple and straightforward manual workers and that having good manners is the hypocritical style of the bourgeoisie (WDIED 1982, 4). It then examines various issues in vignettes: What should I do if a comrade is having difficulties; if someone curses me; if a beautiful woman flits by and I can no longer be faithful; if the toilet hasn't been cleaned; if the teacher makes a mistake? The answers are essentially morality tales with one character inevitably carrying out the advice of the stresses and beauties as an object lesson to others.

In promoting the campaign, the leadership divided civilization into material and spiritual, though in practice they overlapped. Much of the effort in promoting socialist spiritual civilization was to change the attitudes and dedication of workers, to raise their consciousness and dedication to work harder and more efficiently, and to keep their workplaces clean (Murthy 1983, 5). Dirlik notes that a report on a meeting in January 1981 instructed youth organizations to uphold Communist thought, ideals and morals; castigated those who put personal interest and gain over all else; and called on youth organizations to "launch activities stressing civility, politeness, order, morality and hygiene, and to advocate the beauty of the spirit, language, behavior and environment. Youth needed to continue to "learn from Lei Feng and build a new style" (Dirlik 1982, 367). In support, in a 1982 speech Deng Liqun stated that although the normal workday is eight hours, "instances are not lacking where many among our workers, cadres, intellectuals and soldiers have

---

25. The handbook is a compilation of short discussions of the stresses and beauties done the previous year; thus, it does not include the loves.

worked for more than 8 hours. Those of us who worked overtime, have we fussed about it? No" (Deng 1982; cited in Murthy 1983, 4).

The stresses, beauties, and loves campaign had a variety of goals, civility being just one, but one aspect of it was a relatively straightforward effort aimed precisely at being civil. This was the promotion of "five polite phrases" (*wu ge limao de ci*): hello, please, sorry, thank you, and goodbye.[26] The Chinese terms to express these are relatively new, derived from terms in Western languages that Chinese became aware of through their interactions with outsiders in the treaty ports. In pre-twentieth-century China, the sentiments expressed by these phrases were used toward a more restricted set of people than the modern-day expressions; for example, one would not have thanked a shop clerk[27] and one would not even have spoken to a stranger. The traditional terms reflected the hierarchical social relationships in society and carried status implication differentials between speaker and hearer. Because of Chinese claims of being an egalitarian society, the traditional phrases fell out of favor after it was established. However, the newly recommended substitutes for these phrases, because they came from the West, were status neutral and could be used when speaking to anyone, whether familiar to one or not. The campaign urged people to use them when speaking to strangers or others with whom they had only a fleeting relationship in order to create a friendlier society. In addition to using the above phrases, the campaign enjoined people not to speak crudely and to avoid *tamade*, the *guoma* or "national curse" (Erbaugh 2008).

In the early stages, the stresses, beauties, and loves campaign saw some positive results (People 2008). A commentator wrote that as a youngster in the 1980s,

> We took the Stresses, Beauties and Loves as the most direct, commonplace and lucid instructions on quality [*suzhi*; see below]. We not only shouted them, we also were fervent in carrying them out. Every day we would see who killed the most flies, whose clothing had spots of dirt; we took aim at those who used dirty language and reported it to the teacher right away. (Civil 2008)

Murthy reports that, in the spirit of the stresses, beauties, and loves, medical students in Beijing treated people with minor complaints at the railway station, saving them the time and trouble of having to wait for long periods in local hospitals, and other students helped the aged and other needy passengers carry their luggage (1983, 8). However, such tasks are often assigned by teachers or other educational authorities, rather than being strictly voluntary, and, given that campaigns with very similar goals have continued to the present day, it is unlikely that these tasks resulted in long-lasting change.

---

26. In order, *nihao, qing, duibuqi, xiexie,* and *zaijian.*
27. Nor would one thank one's parents. One thanked people for doing something they were not obligated to do. Parents are obligated to do things for their children. Thanking them would be tantamount to denying the parent-child relationship. For similar reasons, one would not thank close friends, schoolmates, etc. Doing so would be *shengfen,* to act distantly toward those to whom one should be close.

Quality / education for quality (*Suzhi* / *suzhi jiaoyu*)

The stresses, beauties, and loves campaign ran through the 1980s and into the mid-1990s when a new campaign was launched, this one based on *suzhi* (quality)—the quality, for example, of individuals, of the Chinese population, of the level of civility the people practiced, and of education. This usage of suzhi is rather odd. It was originally used in the *Erya* to refer to the white color of a bird,[28] and it seems to have had the meaning of the purity of plainness (Lin 2009, 38–39). In the early twentieth century it was used to express "nature" in discussions of nature and nurture and initially referred to intrinsic characteristics, nurture being expressed as *suyang*, and qualities of things that can be improved as their *zhiliang* (Murphy 2004, 2; Kipnis 2006, 297–98). Until the 1980s, suzhi was rarely used in academic article titles, but its usage has increased rapidly, from only 14 times before 1980 to 2,589 in the 1980s, just under 30,000 in the 1990s, and 64,000 between 2000 and 2007 (Jacka 2009, 533). Its common use also increased, e.g., criticizing a person by saying that he or she *mei suzhi* ("is uncultured"; literally, "lacks quality"). Lin cites an example of a note left on the wall of a Beijing apartment building calling the person who left rubbish in the elevator a beast and saying that those "with no suzhi do not deserve to live here" (2009, 4).

Unlike the stresses, beauties and loves, the suzhi project was not announced from the government, though there were official mentions of it early on (Bi 1981). Instead, various aspects of suzhi were mentioned in the *People's Daily*, which, especially in the early 1980s, published discussions of *renkou suzhi*, population quality. From there, academics took their cue and began applying the term to other areas. In 1985 Deng Xiaoping gave a speech on education in which he applied suzhi to human capital. Soon afterward it was applied to education as "education for quality" (*suzhi jiaoyu*), the idea that primary school education should not be about learning for examinations but oriented toward socialist citizenship. In 1996, education for quality became official education policy. It was meant to replace the emphasis on rote memorization, especially in middle school where the stress is on doing well in examinations (*yingshi jiaoyu*) and advancing up the educational ladder (*shengxue jiaoyu*) (Kipnis 2006, 298, Murphy 2004, 4; Woronov 2003). There was also criticism of the narrowness of the curriculum and the neglect of the "all-round development" (*quanmian fazhan*) of students (Lin 2009, 163).

Although the government did "open up discussion" on *suzhi jiaoyu* it shut it down quite quickly when criticisms began mounting. Clearly, it had an agenda, socialist civilization, and nothing else was to be tolerated (Lin 2009, 170–73). However, it did result in a new approach to teaching, at least at the primary level. A comparison of primary school moral education text books published in 1988 with those published in 2007 shows a clear change from a teacher-centered to a student-centered pedagogy in which student participation begins on the first day of

---

28. The *Erya* is the oldest extant Chinese dictionary, dating from the third century BCE.

class in grade one, and there are lessons aimed at developing student individuality (Schak 2012).[29] However, at the middle school level, education for quality merely added some non-examination subjects such as music, art, and Chinese poetry to an already crowded curriculum, in effect increasing the burden on the students, because they still had to master the more traditional material tested in the university entrance examination (*gaokao*), which did not include these subjects. The *People's Daily* reported in 2000 that education for quality was an unprecedented success; by 2005 it and other papers said the policy had largely failed (Lin 2009, 137).

However, the overall goal of the suzhi campaign was "civilizing and cultivating citizens for socialist nation building" (Lin 2009, 85). Like the stresses, beauties, and loves, the suzhi campaign was very broad and covered much the same ground: modernization, nation building, increasing political commitment, nationalism, and civil behavior. As with the stresses, beauties, and loves, the government wanted (1) to raise the skills, competence, and commitment of the work force so that the Chinese economy could develop rapidly and catch up with those of advanced nations; (2) to strengthen the commitment of the citizenry to the official ideology and to upholding the rule of the CCP; (3) to bolster nationalism to inoculate against enticement by products of Western "spiritual pollution"; and (4) to increase levels of civility, culture, and politeness in order to raise the prestige of and respect for China and the Chinese people in the eyes of the world. Lin provides a list of sixty-eight varieties of suzhi terms. These include ideological, psychological, cultural, moral, professional, student, industrial, occupational, population, nationality, librarians, parents, people's representatives, and cadres. She further states that the number of such terms is virtually infinite as new terms can always be coined (2009, 46–47), an example being ecological suzhi, found in a recent paper (Zheng et al. 2012).

As mentioned in Chapter 2, self-improvement or self-refinement is a very old notion in China. The suzhi project is based superficially on it, but it differs in that, in the past, although the government regarded one of its missions as educating the masses and unifying their thinking, it lacked the administrative infrastructure and the commitment from the educators to be effective. This was true even of the NLM under the Kuomintang government. The Chinese government, however, has both. Comparing the NLM with the socialist ethics and courtesy campaigns, Dirlik says that they differ in that the present regime is "serious in its commitment to achieving social justice and equality—if only out of a sense of self-preservation—though how and when those goals might be achieved remains problematic" (2005, 374).

Another difference is that self-refinement, as presented in the Confucian classics, was a personal goal whereas the ostensible purpose of the suzhi campaign is to refine the individual as human capital for the benefit of the state. As the state is no stronger than its citizens, if China is weak or poor it is because the quality of its citizens is too low. The suzhi project is about making individuals more competent

---

29. This is based on the texts themselves; what actually happens in the classroom could be something else entirely.

and useful citizens. However, the state also uses it as a means of fostering dependency; sending the message that the masses are inadequate makes them dependent on the state for guidance (Lin 2009, 13–14), as only the state can decide whether one's suzhi is adequate. Similar to what Hu Yaobang said about spiritual civilization in the stresses, beauties, and loves campaign, it is a means of control (Dirlik 2005, 159–60).

Another negative aspect of the suzhi project is that it provides a justification for disdain. As Jacka puts it, "Suzhi is not just a normative goal or substance, supposedly attainable by all. It is also a value coding used to differentiate and highlight gaps between, for example, good and bad, rich and poor, civilized and uncivilized" (2009, 525). This is apparent in the government's civilizing projects aimed at national minorities (Harrell 1995), its condescension toward the rural population (Murphy 2004, 14–15), or its civilizing campaign against Hui'an County women because of their distinctive head dress and unorthodox postmarital residency practices (Friedman 2004). It is also apparent in those who discriminate against others on the basis of educational level, rural origin, social class or even such innate qualities as being short or near-sighted (Kipnis 2001, 11; 2006, 297).

An extension of the stresses, beauties, and loves and the suzhi campaigns is the "five-good household" (*wuhao jiating*) program. Although the program began in the 1950s, it fell into disuse but was revived in the 1980s along with the civilization campaign under All-China Women's Federation sponsorship. It was renamed the "five-good civilized households" (*wuhao wenming jiating*) in 1996. The "goods" have also shifted from time to time, and they vary from place to place, depending on what local officials see as important. But they include following government ideology; working and producing well; having a harmonious family; being respectful to the elderly and loving the young; educating sons and daughters; practicing family planning; loving the country and observing the law; being enthusiastic in public affairs; achieving gender equality, good household management and sanitation; and protecting the environment (Murthy 1983, Baike).

Another manifestation of this campaign is a project aimed at civilizing those in rural township and village areas called "ten star civilized households" (*shi xingji wenming hu*). The stars each represent a particular virtue, and, again, they appear to be locally chosen as they differ from place to place. In Anning Township (Sichuan) the stars are for manifesting the five loves (the motherland, the people, labor, science, public property), rules and discipline, science and education, planned births, hygiene, neighborliness, duty, greening, prosperity and following new customs. A campaign in Tucheng County (Liaoning) differs in including industriousness and solidarity but omitting greening and neighborliness. Families deemed to be adhering to these virtues are awarded a plaque that they can place outside their homes. The plaques differ only in the virtues chosen by the local authorities and the place identification.

An example of such a civility campaign is that of Xiao Heba Village,[30] a rural township in Jiangsu not far from Zhangjiagang. The village committee, consisting of government and Party authorities, has enjoined residents to obey all laws and directives from the cadres, be enthusiastic workers in the fields, refrain from indulging in bad habits, uncooperativeness, or selfishness, have a well-behaved family and a neat-as-a-pin home, have completed schooling and military service if required, be active and participative in village events and affairs, and love the group and the Party. It laid down sets of rules in the form of numerical mnemonic devices, some like the ninety-six NLM rules on personal and environmental hygiene and cleanliness and others as an effort to change how people think:

- The Five Regulars (*wu qin*): regularly wash, change clothing, sun clothing and bedding, get haircuts, and trim one's nails.
- The Seven Don'ts (*qi bu*): don't clean the commode at the side of the well or on the river embankment; don't carelessly throw away melon seed hulls, fruit pits, paper or other miscellaneous items; don't spit on the ground; don't urinate just anywhere; don't carelessly toss garbage away; don't carelessly toss out dirty water; and don't smoke in public places.
- The Five Loves (*wu ai*): love the motherland, the people, labor, science, and socialism.
- The Four Haves (*si you*): have ideals, morality, civility, and discipline.
- The Three Kinds of Morality (*san de*): social and public, occupational, and familial.

The committee also set standards for qualifying as an enlightened household, a good mother-in-law and a good daughter-in-law, and it judged households and women accordingly. These standards are much more specific and plentiful than the more general ones included in the stresses, beauties, and loves or the suzhi campaigns, and they are almost certainly an accurate reflection of the state of behavior in the village.

Members of enlightened households:

- love the country and the collective, follow through on all duties and procedures, and pay water and electricity bills on time;
- lead in discipline and obey the law, don't read or pass on obscene things, and don't gamble or steal, even very small amounts;
- voluntarily follow the "Civilized Citizen Handbook," and don't commit uncivil or immoral acts;
- voluntarily see to the hygiene of the home and its surrounds; be active in combatting the four harms, put rubbish in bags and dispose of it properly; don't pile things up outside the house or hook the home up to the electricity grid without permission;

---

30. This account taken from the village gazetteer (Fang 1998, 204–12).

- abandon old customs and steer clear of superstitious activities;
- get along with neighbors, showing them solidarity and friendship; refrain from fighting or arguing with them, inciting quarrels, or infringing on others' rights;
- create a harmonious household with love between the spouses, good treatment of the elderly and no quarrelling between husband and wife;
- voluntarily follow the Marriage Law and the Family Planning Regulations and eschew out-of-plan and out-of-wedlock pregnancies, induced labor, early courtship or marriage, and premarital or illegal cohabitation;
- strictly uphold the land management laws; do not occupy land illegally or build unauthorized buildings, and if in a household under the responsibility system, plant and harvest in a timely manner
- voluntarily uphold the Compulsory Education Law and the Military Service Law; do not drop out of school or evade military service;
- take the initiative in participating in village organization activities and carry out work arranged in the village seriously; complete all responsibilities at a high standard and quality and without conflict or negativity;
- maintain a high-quality family; closely follow the three *li* (manners, etiquette, courtesy) and the four virtues (individual moral character, social morality, family virtue, occupational morality); do not engage in actions that violate discipline, the law, good manners, or virtuous conduct;
- keep family goods neatly stored and the home neat, clean, and decorated appropriate to one's level of prosperity; leave no unkempt spots;
- steadfastly uphold justice and righteousness, follow new customs, dare to struggle against those whose words or actions are crude, and do not speak nonsense or make mischief; and
- strive to achieve prosperity and initiate civility, eschewing laziness, gluttony, and seeking personal gain through currying favor.

The good mother-in-law:

- resolutely supports and carries out the Village Committee's program and actively participates in all its public welfare activities;
- is at one with her family and lives in harmonious coexistence with and respects her neighbors;
- understands and supports the younger generation in all their upright pursuits;
- correctly leads the younger generation to become civil individuals who undertake civilized activities;
- regards her daughter-in-law as her newly born daughter and shows appropriate concern for and looks after her and refrains from contending with her over small matters but instead thinks of the group and the overall situation; and

- liberates her thinking, renews her ideas, goes ahead at the appropriate time, actively advocating the new enlightened trend of thinking, and dares to struggle against those whose customs are twisted and evil.

The good daughter-in-law:

- resolutely supports and carries out the Village Committee's program and actively participates in all its public welfare activities;
- works hard to achieve prosperity, is disciplined and law-abiding and strives for the "four haves";
- respects the elderly and shows concern for them, loves the young, and is friendly toward and in unison with neighbors in all matters;
- establishes a correct worldview and correct values, strives to learn about technology, culture, and common knowledge (*changshi*), and spreads modern cultural information;
- treasures and shows respect toward her husband as he should toward her; [they] show each other mutual respect, love and forgiveness, and help each other and learn together to develop mutual beliefs;
- does not just raise her own quality as a person but bravely struggles against gambling, feudal superstition, and similar stupid or evil acts; and
- does not sow discord, gossip or shirk labor but struggles to be a civilized person who performs many civil deeds (Fang 1998, 200–11).

To stimulate the villagers to carry out this project, the committee wrote two songs, one with three-character lines with instructions for being civil, the other with five-character lines for producing a virtuous family. To educate the villagers, the committee leaders personally gave lessons to the villagers and contracted law enforcement leaders to do the same. This program started in 1995, and by 1996 there were twelve periods of classes providing instructions to a thousand people, over 95 percent of the residents. The gazetteer writers judged the lessons to be effective in raising the moral quality of the villagers.

Be civilized (*Jiang wenming*)

The phrase *jiang wenming* dates back to the early 1980s, originally associated with the stresses, beauties, and loves. It took on a life of its own in 1997, after the Central Civilization Committee (*zhongyang wenming weiyuanhui*) was established following then President Jiang Zemin's direction to implement fully a Fourteenth Central Committee decision from the Sixth Plenum to found a spiritual civilization activity. Since then it has sometimes been followed by *shu xin feng*, "adopt new habits." The Central Civilization Committee launched "Stress Civility, Adopt New Habits" as a theme, and on July 15, 1997, it held a teleconference to kick it off. The stress civility, adopt new habits combination is still seen on billboards and walls, usually followed by a phrase beginning with *ying* (welcome) and the name of an occasion.

The government has used this combination of slogans to launch a variety of undertakings. In 2008 the Olympics were welcomed; in 2009 it was National Day for the sixtieth anniversary of the People's Republic of China; and in 2010 and 2012 it was World Expos in Shanghai. Aims of all such activities include promoting public morality, civility aspects of *wenming* such as being courteous and considerate, not shunning strangers, and refraining from spitting and littering. They also endorse other goals such as raising the quality of service in commercial establishments and government offices, improving road user behavior, and raising support for political goals such as increasing patriotism, nationalism, and support for the regime and its official ideology, socialism. Although these slogans are sometimes just that, phrases on a billboard, they can also be linked to specific programs that direct people such as cadres, officials, or neighborhood volunteers to carry out plans of action to make improvements according to a program's specific goals. Below I will examine two campaigns run under this banner, Welcome the Olympics in 2008 and Welcome National Day in 2009.

The Welcome the Olympics project began several years before the actual games in 2008. The Olympics were to be China's showcase, and, always mindful of foreigners disparaging Chinese behavior, the government wanted its citizens to comport themselves with civility and behave flawlessly—not only to give foreign visitors the impression that they were courteous, sophisticated, polite, and gracious, but also to give no grounds on which anyone could find fault with or criticize China. There was even a campaign to ensure that signs, notices and advertisements in English were translated correctly and contained no Chinglish.

Welcome the Olympics was also a backdrop for the introduction of President Hu Jintao's Eight Honors and Eight Shames,[31] which called for people to avoid breaches of civil behavior, use polite language, treat others politely and obey the law in order to ensure the success of the Olympics (Xichengdudao 2006). The government provided instructions on how wide to smile to foreigners, proper spectator behavior, and the importance of polite and attentive service and maintaining a clean environment. It provided monitors at public transport stops and increased efforts in traffic management. A poster enumerated what not to ask foreigners: do not ask about income or spending, age, love or marriage, health, home address, past experiences, religious or political beliefs, or what they are busy doing (Murdoch 2008).

In addition, the government provided citizens with General Principles of Protocol in Dealing with Foreigners:

---

31. Eight Honors Eight Shames was announced on March 4, 2006, as a set of maxims by which to measure the work, conduct, and attitude of Party officials: (1) Love the country; do it no harm. (2) Serve the people; never betray them. (3) Follow science; discard superstition. (4) Be diligent, not indolent. (5) Be united and help each other; make no gains at others' expense. (6) Be honest and trustworthy; do not sacrifice ethics for profit. (7) Be disciplined and law-abiding, not chaotic and lawless. (8) Live plainly and work hard; don't wallow in luxuries and pleasures.

1. In appearance and manner, one should be graceful and elegant.
2. Be neither too humble nor too flattering; be calm.
3. Seek common ground, be reasonable and display moral integrity.
4. Follow local customs and respect ethical teachings.
5. Abide by agreements and keep promises.
6. Be appropriately enthusiastic and treat outsiders properly.
7. Be appropriately modest, but be sure of yourself.
8. Don't ask about private matters; follow convention.
9. Ladies first; behave in a gentlemanly manner.
10. Be noble, of a high standard, and act harmoniously toward others.

The Welcome the Olympics campaign was aimed mainly at instructing those living in the cities in which Olympics events would take place how to interact with foreigners and generally how to behave civilly in public (e.g., queue and don't spit or litter). It was an event to showcase China to the world and to give it face.

The following year's National Day celebrations were completely different, aimed at shoring up patriotism, nationalism, and support for the regime and the official ideology. Although some foreign dignitaries were present on the reviewing podium for the parade, the ceremony was aimed mainly at Party and government officials. The masses were not allowed to be present at the parade, or even view it from their windows or balconies, but could only watch it at home on TV.

The masses' duty was to participate in various schemes to improve the physical appearance of their local areas and the personal hygiene, behavior, provision of service, and manners of residents. As part of the preparation for the 2009 National Day, the Establish Spiritual Civilization Guidance Committee Central Office issued the "Implementation Plan for the Broad Scale Launch of 'Welcome National Day, Stress Civility, Adopt New Habits.'" Individual local governments drew up plans to improve the physical attributes of their jurisdictions and pay tribute to the nation. An example is the very broad improvement plan drawn up by the local Wenming Ban (Civility Office) for Dongcheng, a district in central Beijing.[32] The Dongcheng plan consisted of thirty projects encompassing everything from improving civility and the local environment to regulating traffic, improving window service (*chuangkou fuwu*) and food safety, removing dangerous items from the area, organizing a service for travelers, and holding performance activities and activities aimed at youths. These projects were to be carried out over varying periods in the latter half of 2009 with different units completing specific projects in their areas of responsibility. As well as civility, political goals infused these projects, which were replete with messages and activities to promote love of country, the Party, and socialism.

Organizers were to employ emotively powerful cultural and personal appeals to spark the residents' enthusiasm, pride in being Chinese, and partaking in its "excellent culture" and "beautiful virtues" (which confer this excellence and beauty

---

32. The account to follow is taken from the Wenming Ban plan.

on the participants themselves); pride in being a resident of Dongcheng with its *hutong* (a type of residential construction) culture and its two culturally significant sites, Tiananmen Square and the Temple of Heaven; and the symbolism of popular holidays and the foods associated with them. Organizers were instructed to use traditional holidays—Duanwu, Double Seven, Mid-Autumn, and Double Nine[33]— ensuring that their origins, cultural content, customs associated with them, and morality and courtesies contained within them enter deep into people's hearts. They were also

- to conduct cultural seminars, traditional knowledge competitions, song recitations and discussions of calligraphy;
- to launch a "heavy in emotion depiction of Duanwu, the fragrance of *zongzi* filling Dongcheng";
- to hold Chinese poetry recitations, a family maxim contest, an "under the same moon, dreaming the same dream" Mid-Autumn activity,
- to organize a neighborhood cultural festival and educational activity to remind all of China's moral precept of honoring the elderly; and
- to promote China's excellent traditional culture and pass on its great people's spirit.

Projects aimed to improve the general levels of civility, manners, courtesy, concern for others and spiritual civilization in Dongcheng. Specifically mentioned were the "five goods" (*wu hao*)—hygiene, language use, appearance, obedience to traffic rules, and pet management—and the "five noes" (*wu bu*)—do not spit or litter, obstruct others by suddenly stopping and traversing as you please on roads or footpaths, use coarse language, go out in public without a shirt, or relieve oneself in public.[34] Residents were enjoined to adopt the attitude "[civility] starts with me, it starts from youth, and begins with small actions" so that others might follow public morality as a matter of course and not shy away from stopping others from committing uncivil actions. "If everyone takes a further step toward renewing courteous behavior, acting civilly, understanding manners, and obeying laws and rules, society will be harmonious."

Three projects aimed at improving the manners and attitudes of window service personnel in government offices and commercial establishments. Window service employees were criticized as cold, impolite, slow (e.g., in providing refunds), or for completely ignoring customers.[35] The plan stated that these employees should

---

33. These are all ancient lunar calendar festivals. Duanwu or Dragon Boat Festival occurs on the fifth day of the fifth lunar month (5/5, Gregorian May to June) during which stuffed glutinous rice dumplings (*zongzi*) are eaten. Double Seven, Qixi Jie (7/7), is a sort of Chinese Valentine's Day; Mid-Autumn, Zhongqiu Jie (15/8), celebrates the moon at its fullest for the year. And Double Nine, Chongyang Jie (9/9), is a very positive, or *yang*, date now celebrated as Senior's Day.
34. Another version calls for consideration toward the elderly and disabled and acting warmly toward others.
35. "We'll get back to you," but they never do, or being left on hold. These are expressed in Mandarin as *leng, ying, tuo*, and *ka*.

"present a gift" to the nation in honor of National Day by improving their language use, appearance, behavior, service, and the tidiness of their stations.

Several projects focused on improving social order. Of specific mention were queuing, littering, spitting, violating building regulations, safeguarding public property, civil behavior in public parks, and traffic order, which included both driver and pedestrian behavior as well as the use of pedal-driven three-wheeled carts.[36] One project specifically targeted public transport. Passengers were reminded of the importance of queuing, not crowding, and yielding seats to those in need. Monitors were called on to instill this into the passengers so that they need not be reminded. Volunteer groups were also asked to set up a travelers' aid service.

Another project targeted commercial establishments regarding the sale of bogus and counterfeit products and providing honest service. Yet another focused on the food industry, calling for better service, better trained workers, and guarantees of safe products. Echoing then President Hu Jintao's Eight Glories and Eight Shames it states, "being honest and keeping one's word is glorious; seeking profit and ignoring honesty is shameful."

Other projects were designed to clean up and beautify the district as a part of keeping Beijing clean and ensuring the five protections—the blue skies, the green trees, the emerald water, family courtyards, and streets and alleys. Specific projects included residents growing flowers and cleaning up public toilets, parks, hospitals, and unsightly or unsanitary areas where sickness could spread; providing public information to help control smoking and reduce emissions; holding seminars on the environment and the promotion of energy-saving products and measures; reporting dangerous products; and implementing measures to control dust from factories and refuse from vehicles and outdoor cooking. Authorities were to enforce rubbish management and separation, maintain sanitation and clean public toilets, and protect public facilities. They were also to establish neighborhood competitions.

The National Day theme was interwoven into the projects, which were presented as ways to show one's appreciation for the nation by carrying them out in honor of National Day (dedication of the individual to the nation is a constant theme of the civilizing campaigns). One project specifically aimed at ensuring security for the celebration. Being the sixtieth anniversary, a round number, it took on a special significance, and the smooth running of the events of the day would symbolize the efficacy and legitimacy of the government. Thus, any contradictions and disputes in the district needed to be resolved in order to create a peaceful National Day. Authorities and a neighborhood watch were to investigate all hidden dangers to security in the area, including rental properties, in order to safeguard stability and order and give the people a feeling of safety. They were to use concern and love in examining and resolving hidden dangers and implement all necessary preventative

---

36. Although not specifically mentioned, this includes not picking flowers, taking plants, ignoring signs not to walk on the grass, and carving one's name into trees.

management procedures to guarantee the smooth progress of the 60-year-old "new China."

The entwined National Day theme also heralded the infusion of patriotism, nationalism, and other themes in what seems to have been an attempt to appeal to self-identity. One project was to launch a "love the motherland, love Beijing, love Dongcheng" educational activity and to host a "Sing Red Songs" mass festival: "Include all ethnic groups as the cultural backbone and sing one hundred common patriotic songs. Make prominent that this is a Dongcheng activity and push the fashion city and imperial city attractiveness angles." Another called for holding a talent show in Tiananmen Square and the Temple of Heaven Park featuring local performers and focusing on being proud of the motherland.

A third highlighted Dongcheng's special characteristic—Beijing's *hutong* culture. "Launch the first Famous Streets in Chinese Cultural History Competition with awards. Publicize Chinese cultural studies and promote traditional culture. Love the flag, the country, the county's will, and the national, Party, military and Olympic flags. Enhance local tourism." And a fourth project celebrated "Our Holidays," the tasks including editing a handbook on holiday celebrations to show their origins, associated customs, cultural content, moral message, and etiquette so that "this information penetrates deep into the heart of the residents." This project included traditional knowledge competitions, song recitations, calligraphy and any other activities appropriate to each of the holidays. A neighborhood cultural festival to respect the elderly and honor their "beautiful morality" received special mention.

Four additional projects focused on youths, especially at enhancing their patriotism and purity of thought. Crucial to the latter were to prevent youths from getting access to pornographic,[37] lewd, violent, superstitious, or nonscientific materials, and to ensure that the environs of schools were morally healthy milieus. To bolster their patriotism a series of get-togethers and discussions between youths and five categories of the elderly—old teachers, cadres, Party members, PLA soldiers, and moral models—were organized. A separate project aimed at studying moral models and included singing songs praising the CCP and socialism, the motherland, occupational morality, family virtues, and good individual character. By studying models, residents will understand shame and practice civility, thus advancing an era of harmony (Wenming Ban).

In addition to special, targeted projects like those above, various local government authorities have published *wenming liyi shouce*, "civil etiquette handbooks" for their populations. An example is the fifty-plus-page handbook published by Fuzhou People's Press (Yang F. 2006). Linking etiquette with harmony,[38] it reads like a combination of Emily Post and the NLM rules, covering how men and women, young, old, and middle aged, should behave, dress, stand, sit, walk, eat, speak, greet guests, use the telephone, and address others. There are sections on how offspring,

---

37. Pornographic DVDs are widely available.
38. "The utility of etiquette is harmony" (*li zhi yong he wei gui*).

including adult children, should show respect and consideration toward their parents and, citing the *ba huxiang*, the "eight mutuals" of Zhou Enlai and his wife, Deng Yingchao, which provide a model for how spouses should interact. The handbook also includes instructions on proper behavior in the neighborhood, at school, when driving, riding a bicycle, flying, touring, going abroad and using elevators.

The Teaching of Civility in Taiwan and China

An important question for the validity of the comparison between Taiwan and China is the extent to which the civility-related values and concepts advocated in each society are similar. This is especially important in light of the attacks on traditional morality and the emphasis on class struggle and hating class enemies and bad elements during the Maoist period. At that time, despite the various civil values that "Learning from Lei Feng" symbolized, many of the actions the Chinese government periodically encouraged groups such as the Red Guards to emulate were anything but civil. Likewise, the Lei Feng morality expressly did not apply to the Five Black Elements, who were neither part of "the people" nor citizens.[39] In his diary Lei states, "One should be warm as spring to one's comrades and cold as winter to one's enemies" (Ci 1994, 114).

Moreover, an earlier comparative analysis of Chinese language texts by Roberta Martin shows that there were significant departures in the Maoist-period Chinese texts from the kind of traditional morality found in the NLM and in post-1950s Taiwan, most clearly in the de-emphasis on family and filiality in favor of the collective. In China a child helps mother in the home, not out of filial respect but so that she can spend more time with her work team; a child studies hard not for the sake of family or self but in order to make a greater contribution to the nation. Parents appear in stories not in their parental roles but as workers furthering the goals of the state, and even children are depicted not as family members but as Young Pioneers or members of work groups (Martin 1975).

However, as stated in the previous section, one of the goals of the reforms in the late 1970s and early 1980s was to repair the damage done to the Chinese social fabric and its ethical principles under radical Maoism, and, as demonstrated above, the various KMT and CCP government campaigns have targeted very similar behavior. This section will confirm those similarities in what constitutes civility in the two societies by examining four sets of primary school moral education texts, two each from Taiwan and China, two sets that were used in 2011, and two sets used in the 1980s.[40] The text sets compared are:

- *Thought and Moral Character*, 1988, People's Education Publishers [RMP];

---

39. Sidney Rittenberg, personal communication.
40. There are striking and remarkably similar pedagogical changes between the earlier and the later sets; see Schak 2012.

- *Life and Ethics*, 1970, National Translation and Editing Office [TWP];
- *Moral Character and Life* and *Moral Character and Society*,[41] 2002–2009. People's Education Publishers [RM];
- *Comprehensive Activities*, 2011, Taipei: Hanlin. [TW].[42]

The China texts are labeled RMP and RM for the 1988 and 2011 sets. The Taiwan texts are similarly labeled TWP and TW for the 1970 and 2011 sets, respectively. TW stands for Taiwan, RM for Renmin, both Chinese sets being published by the Renmin (People's) Education Publishers. All text sets follow the respective Ministries of Education guidelines and are officially recognized.[43] Each set has two volumes per grade, which are numbered sequentially in text notes; thus, TW 1 refers to the first volume in the 2011 Taiwan grade one text; RMP 6 refers to the second volume in the 1988 China year three set. Although the early Taiwan set was published in 1970 and the early China set in 1988, they are contemporary in that the Taiwan set was, according to persons who used it, little changed until a year or so before Taiwan democratized following Chiang Ching-kuo's death early in 1988.

The civility-related lessons in the texts can be roughly divided into those that relate to proper attitudes toward the public space—such as not littering and protecting public property—and those that relate to proper behavior toward others—such as queuing and yielding seats to the elderly and others deemed needy. In some cases, a behavior relates to both, for example, when damage to public facilities inconveniences others.

Public space

Lessons aimed at raising concern for the public space focus on three sorts of action: not littering, protecting public property and protecting the environment. All sets have lessons enjoining against littering. In a TW lesson students clean up a public park (TW 8, 40–43); in one from TWP a father, walking with his son in a park, sees some paper on the ground and tells his son to pick it up. The boy obeys but complains that the park keepers did not do their jobs. The father replies that the keepers would be unable to keep the park clean on their own and that keeping the park clean is everyone's responsibility (TWP 5, 49–51).

Lessons in the Chinese texts are more graphic and probably more effective with young children. The RMP 1 text has a comic strip lesson featuring Pigsy and Monkey:[44] Pigsy is thirsty, so he buys some watermelon, eating, spitting out the

---

41. The first title is used in grades 1–2, the second in grades 3–6, but they are all of one set.
42. Taiwan did away with a specific unit on moral education in the 1990s, infusing it throughout the curriculum. According to teachers I interviewed, this set contains the moral education lesson materials.
43. The People's Education Press set is one of four officially approved sets in China and is one of two sets used in both rural and urban areas. In addition, there is a set aimed at rural students and another at urban students. The sets use different stories, but they teach the same concepts and notions. Taiwan has only one set.
44. Pigsy and Monkey are characters from Journey to the West (*Xiyou Ji*). Pigsy is characterized as sloppy,

seeds, and tossing away the rind as he walks along the road, inconveniencing others. Monkey sees this and blows all the seeds and rind back onto Pigsy, who then slips on the rind and falls. Chastened, Pigsy picks up his refuse and disposes of it in a bin, regretting his misconduct (RMP 1, 38–39).

A hard-hitting RM lesson includes a discussion of chewing gum left on Tiananmen Square after the long Chinese New Year holiday. It cited a report estimating that a total of six hundred thousand wads had been dropped there, which a reporter calculated to average five wads per square meter. The square had to be cleaned up by human labor. The text asks the students what they learned from the report and what they thought of those who left their gum: "What would you think if you were someone who spits gum onto the ground . . . ? If you were one of the workers who had to remove the gum . . . ? If you were a tourist . . . ? If you were a foreigner . . . ?" The lesson is followed by a report on improvements in public behavior on Tianjin public buses: spitting phlegm and littering have become less common; people now spit into tissues and put their rubbish into bins if provided inside the buses or wait till they get off and put it into street bins (RM 8, 11–13).

Spitting is also taken up in other lessons. Chapters in both TWP and RMP state that spitting spreads germs and should not be done except into a tissue (RMP 1, 37–41; TWP 1, 53–56; 4, 53, 70). An RM lesson states that spitting is uncivil and that being civil is the key to people getting along harmoniously (RM 11, 13).

Lessons on protecting public property emphasize school supplies, equipment and facilities, public parks, and public facilities. Primary school is the students' first experience on their own in the public realm. Their desks, paper, pencils, textbooks, and sports and music equipment must not be damaged or wasted, whether deliberately or carelessly (TWP 2, 15, 53; RMP 1, 42–49; RM 3, 4–5). One reason is that they are public property. Another is that all goods are produced by the labor of workers and farmers (RMP 1, 42–49; TWP 2, 28–29).[45] In addition, a Taiwan text states that damaging them is wasteful and deprives others of their use (TWP 5, 43–45). When visiting public parks one should not walk on the grass or climb trees, pick flowers or other plants, or catch butterflies. They should be left for all to enjoy (TWP 1, 28, 41–42; RMP 2, 26–29; TW 3, 40–41; RM 5, 33). This notion of consideration of unseen others—strangers—is a very important civility message and is aimed at correcting the traditional attitude of not caring about them.

An RMP text discusses damaging other kinds of public facilities and property, stating that some students put slugs into the coin slots of the public telephones to see if they can make a call. This ruins the phone box, depriving others of its use. Some also break streetlights by using them as targets for their slingshots, causing the alleyways to be dark. In addition, some people take the light bulbs and clothes

---

licentious, and gluttonous, while Monkey is clever, mischievous, and not bound by convention.
45. Two other RMP lessons, one on clothing, the other on steamed bread, stress the importance of understanding where goods come from and the labor that goes into producing them.

hooks from public toilets for their own use, causing inconvenience to others.[46] The text states that public facilities are part of public property and are protected in China by law. To damage public facilities is to damage public property, which impairs public order and is illegal. "We should take it upon ourselves to protect public facilities" (RMP 8, 37–39).

There is no lesson on the environment in TWP, perhaps reflecting its 1970 publication date. There is a brief but informative one in RMP, stating that humans have a great impact on the earth and do it much harm. The lesson notes that China's environmental problems include pollution from waste water, erosion, disappearing forests, and atmospheric pollution, especially near cities; these affect the weather and pose dangers for humanity (RMP 12, 32–37).

The later sets both give the environment much stronger emphasis. RM lessons are more detailed and emotive, seemingly trying to shock students into environmental consciousness. A grade two lesson begins by showing Our Great Mother Earth as a crying face: There is water and air pollution, forests cut down, and industrial smokestacks. Mother Earth nurtures us, but she now suffers great harm. Tell us why. Look at the surrounding area and describe what kinds of litter and water, air and noise pollution you find. Beautify your surroundings. Properly dispose of rubbish. Separate paper, metal, plastics, batteries and organic rubbish. Do not dump rubbish into waterways (RM 4, 16–24). The spirit of this lesson is repeated in year six with a lesson entitled "We Have Only One Earth": We cannot leave this earth and we cannot create another one. Investigate the population, resources and environment of the earth. How do you feel about this? Ask yourself, what can I do for the earth? Investigate the effects we have on the environment. What can we do to reduce desertification? We need to use less water and reduce rubbish and pollution (RM 12, 20–29).

The TW lessons are less emotive and more sophisticated, reflecting Taiwan's more than 30-year-old environmental movement. One lesson describes Taiwan's environmental heritage and lists the problems society now faces: landslides caused by house construction in mountain areas, coral bleaching, invasive species, betel palm stands,[47] and destruction of habitat for migratory birds. Another introduces the various workers, such as rangers and researchers, as well as community and other voluntary associations that protect the environment. It suggests that students organize a class project to contribute to these efforts (TW 8, 20–29; 11, 44–49).

TW lessons strongly stress recycling as well as volunteering, both of which are major concerns in Taiwan. Up to the mid-1970s scavenging was still a viable

---

46. As anyone familiar with China, or with Taiwan before the 1990s, would know, public toilets do not supply toilet paper. People either brought their own tissues or could buy them from vendors at the entrances of toilets at places such as a railway station. One reason for not supplying tissues was that users would steal them.
47. These are carved out of hillside forests and are jarring to the eye because the betel trees stand out glaringly from the natural vegetation and look very out of place. Moreover, because the palms have a shallow root system, they have a negative effect on soil conservation, and the plantations have increased mudslide hazards during heavy storms (Lee 2003).

economic activity, so ordinary householders did not need to be concerned about recycling because between the time that they set out their rubbish and the time the rubbish collector came around, scavengers would have harvested all the recyclable goods. However, as Taiwan became more prosperous scavenging ceased to be viable, and rubbish began to accumulate. By the late 1980s, there was a severe rubbish disposal problem, most strikingly manifested by a large "garbage mountain" south of Taibei that spontaneously combusted and emitted smoke for many months before the fire burned itself out. In the 1990s, the government began a recycling program, and the Taibei City Government went so far as to limit the amount of rubbish that its collection service would take from individual households. Householders have to buy garbage bags from the city government, and rubbish collectors will take only one bag per household per collection.[48] Moreover, many shops have stopped supplying or charge for plastic bags.

Civility toward others

Lessons teaching civility toward others are based on the tacit assumption that all, not just those within one's social circle, are figurative brothers and sisters and fellow members of society. Thus, all should be treated fairly and considerately, with a modicum of concern, as one would one would want to be treated by others. Queuing is a good example. In the texts, queuing brings order to a potentially disorderly situation and avoids danger from crowding or pushing (TWP 2, 18; RM 1, 11; 3, 28–31). It also connotes fairness and respect to others, as anecdotes in RMP show. When Comrade Lenin went to get his hair cut, he would first greet everyone and then ask whose turn it was just before his. Always busy Premier Zhou Enlai, preparing to go abroad, went to a photo shop to get his picture taken. Although the photographer and the soldier who was about to be served repeatedly asked him to go first, he insisted that he be treated as anyone else and that his picture be taken in turn. When Chairman Mao went to the theater in Yan'an, he would always sit in back. When others discovered his presence, they would compete to give him their seat, but he would always say that if everyone kept their seats the theater would be orderly: "Don't disrupt order on my account" (RMP 8, 40–43).

In China texts, as the messages above connote, order generally refers to the way people comport themselves in society. An RMP text notes the consequences of disorderly conduct and disregarding rules: motorists driving aggressively, hawkers blocking pedestrian walkways, and people talking in theaters or using loudspeakers late at night. Such behavior causes inconvenience to others (RMP 8, 40–43; see also TW 8, 10–17). In Taiwan texts, order can also refer to neatness. For example, at school students should place the materials they are using at the time on their desks in an orderly fashion; rubbish should be put into bins, not dropped onto the

---

48. This has a down side; there are now very few public rubbish bins in Taibei.

floor; books and equipment should be properly put away when not in use; and coats should be neatly hung up (TW 1, 28–32). In addition, conforming to social order shows respect for others—for example, not interrupting when another person is talking and not "spying on" neighbors or eavesdropping on their conversations through the window (TWP 4, 14–15; 11, 44–46).

Disregarding laws and rules has been a perennial problem in Chinese society when affective relations (*guanxi*) are involved, as the earlier text sets recognize. TWP lessons call for fair and equal treatment for all according to the law and not playing favorites, judging people on their merits rather than on personalistic criteria and choosing the best person for the task (TWP 8, 44–47, 10, 41–43). A story from the Spring and Autumn period (771–476 BCE) tells of Douguyutu, a high official. His kinsman commits a crime but the judge releases him in deference to Douguyutu. Douguyutu, however, takes his kinsman back to court and upbraids the judge for not following the law (TWP 12, 39–41). RMP lessons teach this with more contemporary stories. One tells of a Wang Yu who, to help his friend Ding Jie with an assignment, tears a page out of a library book. The story then asks whether Ding should protect Wang as his friend or expose the matter, allowing him to learn from his mistake (RMP 9, 39–40). Another story is of a group of friends who cover for a friend they know to be a thief because of personal loyalty (*yiqi*). However, the thief is arrested, and the others learn the lesson that covering up for someone is not helpful for the thief, the country, or themselves. It is wrong to let personal loyalty stand in the way of what is right (RMP 9, 41–43).

Two related teachings are equality before the law and fairness in the sense of equal opportunities. TWP lessons teach that citizens have an obligation to pay tax, to serve in the military if male (TWP 11, 42–44),[49] and to follow the rules when playing games (TWP 10, 11–14). An RMP lesson about uprightness features Bao Gong, an eleventh-century official who symbolizes honesty, uprightness, and justice, as the exemplar (RMP 10, 1–7).[50]

Consideration and concern for others is also a strong theme in the texts. One aspect of this is assisting the elderly, disabled, and others needing special treatment. This includes yielding seats on buses to the elderly (TWP11 10–12; RM 11, 13), helping a crippled or a blind person board a bus (TWP 11, 10–12; TW 9, 17; RM 7, 64–69), or helping a schoolmate who has polio (RMP 6, 21–24). In addition, China texts have stories about Lei Feng (RMP 10, 13–15; RM 4, 39), the Double Nine festival, at which the elderly are honored and served (RM 3, 35–37), and several mentions of the Young Pioneers, a primary school–level youth group, one of whose responsibilities is to do good deeds for the elderly.

---

49. All males had a minimum two-year military obligation at this time to commence when they reached age twenty or graduated from university at bachelor level.
50. Unlike some more arcane historical figures, Bao Gong is a very popular folk hero. As an official, he is said to have sentenced his own uncle, impeached an uncle of the emperor's favorite concubine, and had thirty officials demoted.

Another aspect is being considerate of and not disturbing others. Fathers tell their sons not to disturb neighbors by playing quietly or not playing music loudly (TWP 2, 8–10, 12, 7–9). An RMP lesson describes Little Ning, who is a very thoughtful young girl. When the motor of the school bus starts, she becomes quiet and thinks, "Driver Uncle, drive the bus safely, I won't distract you. She arrives home to find the desk lamp on and her father studying. Seated nearby she thinks, Baba, concentrate on your studies. I won't bother you. Later, the TV is off, and Granny is sleeping. She walks quietly through the room thinking, Granny, sleep well. I won't disturb you" (RMP 2, 14–16).

The more recent texts apply this to frequently encountered real-life situations. A TW lesson focuses on noise, asking what students need to do in order to avoid making noise that "makes others uncomfortable." The pictures that follow show boys dragging a chair across the floor, slamming a door, and tapping a pencil on a desk while doing homework; a girl banging objects on the desk as she unpacks her backpack; three students laughing and talking loudly while another is trying to study; mother and child watching TV while father is on the phone; a family at a restaurant talking loudly, obviously annoying diners at other tables; and a fellow listening to a radio and dancing while someone next door is trying to sleep (TW 2, 22–25). An RM lesson about getting along with neighbors describes society as a big extended family—be thoughtful and considerate of your neighbors. Don't disturb them. Avoid quarrels with them. Pictures follow showing people being noisy, someone watering a plant on their balcony with the water dripping down onto the quilt being aired on the balcony below, children knocking things over as they play, and a family extending their balcony so that it blocks out the sunshine next door (RM 7, 80–85).

Consideration also extends into the playground and the school. "The swing is fun. I swing for a bit and then get off. Why? Because I fear that my schoolmates will be anxious. If there is one booklet with a torn cover, I keep it myself. Why? I want my classmates to be happy. It's raining. I put on my raincoat and leave—but then I go back to the school. Why? Some classmates don't have anything to protect them from the rain." A picture shows a girl sharing her raincoat with another as they walk home. (RMP 4, 13–16; see also TWP 3, 14–16).

The texts also emphasize maintaining harmonious relationships with classmates. TWP lessons teach students to listen respectfully and not interrupt others (TWP 3, 10; 5, 7), to correct their own faults and forgive those in others (TWP 4, 43–44; 12, 34–35), and to be cooperative (TWP 1, 60–62). An RMP chapter shows students doing things together, taking turns sharing a pair of binoculars, helping a fellow student who has fallen down, and resolving a disagreement between classmates (RMP 1, 18–21). The more recent texts have students learning to cooperate in group activities. A TW chapter shows students planning events, discussing what to do, assigning and fulfilling tasks, and participating (TW 4, 22–23, 28–29). An RM lesson shows them electing class cadres and learning not only about proper democratic procedures and actions but also setting rules as to how the election will proceed and how the class cadres will govern them (RM 9, 22–33).

Being kind and considerate is reinforced by lessons on kindness to animals and letting them live their natural lives. An RMP lesson tells students to protect beneficial animals such as dragonflies, geckos, and swallows, as they eat mosquitos and other pests. It also tells them to protect rare birds and animals such as "golden silk monkeys" (*jinsi hou*), the Manchurian tiger, and the Yangzi crocodile. These and other rare species are suffering from habitat loss. They are protected in certain areas and in specified seasons by law, and it is forbidden to hunt them or to use products derived from them (RMP 7, 47–57).

TWP lessons also tell students to be kind to animals and not to tease them (TWP 1, 40; 3, 13, 39). There is an ancient story about Taibaxi. On a hunting trip, his master captures a fawn and tells Taibaxi to take it back and cook it. However, as Taibaxi begins to return, he hears a doe following him and crying mournfully. Believing that the doe is the fawn's mother, he releases the fawn. When his master returns and hears what Taibaxi has done, he angrily fires him, but then, on contemplation, he realizes that Taibaxi acted correctly, that he is not only kind to people but also to animals. He then calls Taibaxi back and makes him his teacher (TWP 9, 30–32).

The RM texts generally repeat the above kindness messages stating that one should not only love one's own life but those of animals and plants as well. A girl, pictured, takes care of plants and feeds rabbits, while two other pictures show a boy swinging a cat by its hind legs and someone pulling a branch off a tree; the text asks how the boy would feel if that were done to him and whether plants, being voiceless, means that they cannot feel pain (RM 7, 2–5).

Kindness also, of course, extends to the public, manifested in one form in the earlier text sets by the use of polite language. Students should use "please" to both adults and peers (TWP 2, 11–12) and should generally be pleasant toward others, smile, and speak reasonably and agreeably (TWP 4, 49–51). Reflecting the five polite phrases campaign, an RMP lesson instructs students to speak politely to others, to use hello, thank you, sorry, please and goodbye, and then has students act out how and in what circumstances to use those phrases. The lesson places special emphasis on the use of "sorry" when accidentally bumping into someone or knocking something off another's desk (RMP 2, 10–13).

The text sets all recognize the greater public. TWP has several stories of historical notables who used their own wealth to benefit the public at large and contribute to the community. For example, Guan Ning, in order to stop people from fighting over water, hired men to draw buckets of water from the well so that those who needed it could get it without contention (TWP 10, 44–46; see also 9, 49–51; 12, 42–44). An RMP chapter shows Young Pioneers helping to plant and care for saplings that will grow to provide shade in the summer. They are also pictured washing buses and a traffic control kiosk, raking leaves in the autumn, and sweeping snow in the winter (RMP 6, 28–31). In addition, the RMP texts have several lessons on people who endured sacrifices in order to help their communities or society in general (RMP 5, 35–38; 9, 30–32; 10, 36–38). RM lessons acknowledge those who serve the community and show love for society as well as those who help students such as teachers, dining hall cooks, school nurses, and the traffic policemen who assist students to cross the street safely. "We should be grateful to them for their work" (RM 6, 12–20).

An RM lesson begins by showing a community in which people behave incorrectly or things do not get done: someone dumps dirty water into a stream; no one clears the streets or footpaths after a big snowfall; a stairwell light burns out, but no one comes to change the bulb. The lesson then asks who will take care of these problems and answers that society is everyone's home, its problems are everyone's problems, and all have an obligation to resolve or fix them. The lesson then shows a community coming together to repair a road, and, by working together, they succeed (RM 7, 86–88; see also 10, 2–7). A comparable TW lesson reflects Taiwan's very robust civil society and community organizations, and it strongly encourages students to get to know their communities and participate in local projects (TW 7, 23–27).

An RM unit goes so far as to include the entire world as a single community in which "we are all under the same sky," and we need to cooperate to tackle the problems of environmental degradation and disease (RM 12, 47–66). However, although we are all one community, we should appreciate that people have different customs and habits, and we should respect these (RMP 7, 1–5; TW 9, 6–17).

In both societies, schoolchildren are exposed to all the basic tenets of civility appropriate to their age, and there is no discernible difference in what they are taught in Taiwan and China. Although TWP uses far more ancient moral exemplars than does RMP, the few that the latter uses are also included in the former. From what the lessons say about fairness, justice, consideration, empathy, and treating others equally, it takes little extrapolation to state that they clearly indicate that both polities aim to create societies that encompass the entire population rather than congeries of inwardly focused communities or families. Everyone should regard themselves and all others as fellow citizens and members of society, and they should generally assume that strangers are persons like themselves who will treat others as they would like to be treated.

The texts also clearly teach that the public space should be kept clean and free of litter. Public facilities, extending to public parks and nature, should be respected and not damaged. The environment, too, is a publicly shared resource and should be protected. By implication, the public should see the public space and public facilities as assets belonging to everyone, rather than belonging to no one and being free for the taking.

However, children learn not only from school but also from their observations of society, what they see adults and peers do. Thus, if they are told to queue when boarding buses and see their schoolmates, their parents, and other adults not doing so, they will learn to answer that they should queue when the teacher asks what they should do, but they will not queue as a natural form of behavior unless a teacher is supervising them. Similarly, if told not to litter but see their parents dropping rubbish on the street, that is what they will likely do themselves. They learn to respect authority when authority figures are present, but otherwise they feel free to do as they wish.

The next chapters, in which I examine the state of civility in China and Taiwan, will indirectly shed light on how effective campaigns and education have been.

4
Civility in China

Introduction: Chinese Foreign Tourists

The uncivil actions by some of its international tourists afford a glimpse into the kinds of behavioral and attitudinal problems that limit civility in China. The list of their offenses is long. A letter to the editor in a Thai newspaper accuses them of speeding and driving on the wrong side of the road, going the wrong way on one-way streets, stopping in the middle of intersections to argue about which way to go, booking a hotel for two but having four to five guests, drying their clothes on balcony railings, not flushing the toilet, queue-jumping, littering, spitting, and being loud, even in five-star hotels (Li 2013a). Elsewhere, Chinese tourists are criticized for allowing their children to relieve themselves on sidewalks, in subways, on airplanes, and near a famous London department store despite a toilet being just inside, for squatting on sit-down toilets and leaving the seats soiled; for eating in Hong Kong subways He 2012); also for smoking where prohibited, declining to tip even when told by their guides that tipping is expected, jaywalking, abusing and fighting with airline ground staff and cabin personnel, causing flights to be delayed or to return to their point of origin (AFP 2014; Nelson 2015d), taking pieces of coral as souvenirs in violation of prohibitions in Palau, and manhandling wildlife to take selfies (Su Yining 2013; Jackson 2015). Moreover, some Chinese tourists act arrogantly toward locals, especially in Hong Kong and Taiwan. When asked by Taiwanese not to litter, spit, or make noise, they retort, "Why not? We do this back home," And when told, "This is Taiwan," they reply, "Taiwan is China's" (Griffiths 2014).

In addition, some individual or group incidents have attracted widespread attention: groups taking away available food at hotel buffets and thus forcing the hotels to ration what guests can take, eating instant noodles in their rooms rather than paying for meals at hotel restaurants, the 15-year-old Nanjing boy who carved his name into a relief at Egypt's Luxor Temple, a Chinese group dancing to loud music at Brooklyn's Sunset Park, two couples fighting in a lavender field in Provence, and tourists in the Maldives arranging fake marriage certificates in order to get honeymoon discounts (Ni 2013; *Changjiang Daily* 2013; Reuters 2013; Zuo 2013).

When tour groups from other countries hear that Chinese tourists are about to arrive, they leave and go elsewhere, encouraging some countries to take measures to cope with their behavior. Switzerland is putting on extra "Asian" (read "Chinese") carriages on the Rigi Railways because the Chinese are so loud that they annoy other passengers. These carriages also have signs showing how to use the toilets—sit, don't squat (Linder 2015b); Japan is considering "Chinese only" zones for tourist visitors (Farrell 2016). Thailand's Wat Rong Khun banned Chinese tourists because of improper toilet use but said it would lift the ban if tour guides agreed to clean the toilets after their tour groups left (Fan 2015). Taiwan, a major Chinese tourist destination, has introduced schemes to attract higher-end independent tourists who will not only spend more but will likely be better behaved (Jennings 2015).

Many of China's newly rich tourists are from rural areas, are poorly educated, and have little exposure to cosmopolitan life (Carrillo 2008, 100–101; see also Hessler 2010, 347), but they have money to spend. In fact, one reason for going abroad is to visit high-end stores and purchase expensive luxury goods that are cheaper abroad than at home. However, they can also be very tight-fisted and irresponsible, peeing in the open rather than paying €0.70 to use a public toilet in Germany (Li 2014) or intensely bargaining over inexpensive items (Yung 2014; Jennings 2015). Some are quite brazen: Anna Fenton, who worked for a time with a hotel catering mainly to guests from China in Tsim Sha Tsui, Hong Kong, writes:

> I realized guest attitudes to hotel property is a moveable feast. We had some who literally stripped the room and removed everything that wasn't nailed down. When challenged, they claimed that they had rented and "owned" the room for the night, so everything inside belonged to them. There was a similar problem with breakages—some took the view that if they cracked the TV screen, the hotel should pay to fix it, not them. (2013)

According to popular Beijing magazine publisher and blogger Hung Huang, Chinese are now more receptive to Western ideas, but that is not apparent in their behavior when they interact with foreigners abroad. "They think, 'The hell with etiquette. As long as I have money, foreigners will bow to my cash'" (Levin 2013b).

However, if one were to go by the tourist behavior that makes the news, one would get a distorted picture of the level of civility in China. It is certainly a good deal lower than that in Taiwan, but although the same breaches of civility take place in China, they are not representative of the general behavior there or even that of its outbound tourists. Moreover, given the number of Chinese international tourists, it is small wonder that some behave inappropriately. In 2011 Chinese made 70 million trips abroad.[1] In 2012 the number increased to 83 million (Branigan 2013; Guilford 2013), and in 2015 it reached 120 million (TCG n.d.). And one reason for the high

---

1. Domestic and international tourism took off in China after May 1995 when it adopted the two-day weekend (*shuangxiuzhi*). The number of public holidays also increased, including week-long breaks (Tomba 2014, 99–100; NBSC).

number of complaints from Thailand is the sheer number of Chinese tourists who visit, 7.9 million in 2015 and an expected 10 million by the end of 2016, many of whom are on "zero-dollar" excursions. These are initially low-cost package tours featuring free food and accommodation, but when the tourists arrive in Thailand they are taken to Chinese, rather than locally run businesses, that sell at jacked-up prices and return the profits to China (Farrell 2016).

Nonetheless, their behavior has become a national embarrassment to their government and many of their fellow Chinese, and stories or videos of their behavior posted on the Chinese internet often draw scathing criticism (Guilford 2013; Reuters 2013b), including demands from netizens that airlines blacklist offenders. Government agencies have issued behavioral guides and lists of dos and don'ts for tourists, have cautioned them against bad behavior abroad (Branigan 2013), and have even banned some from further overseas travel (AFP 2014b). However, it is not uncommon to stereotype a society based on a small number of its people, and their bad behavior has caused much angst in China. Vice Premier Wang Yang labeled such conduct "uncivilized," harmful to the country's image abroad, and stated that the authorities should "guide tourists to conscientiously abide by public order and social ethics, respect local religious beliefs and customs, mind their speech and behavior . . . and protect the environment" (Griffiths 2013a). And President Xi Jinping has suggested that tourists eat fewer packs of instant noodles and consume more local seafood (Farrell 2016). The Chinese government has issued a Civilized Tourist Covenant, a list of eight rules and an appendix of thirty-two four-character phrases instructing tourists on how to behave when abroad.

> Chinese citizens, when you go abroad, pay attention to your manners, and protect your dignity.
>
> Be sanitary, protect the environment, dress appropriately, and don't be noisy or rowdy.
>
> Respect the elderly and the young, take pleasure in helping others—ladies first—be mannerly and yield to others.
>
> When conducting business, be on time, queue, and be orderly, and don't step over the yellow line.[2]
>
> Be civil where you stay, don't waste the supplied goods, eat your meals quietly, and please don't waste.
>
> Choose healthy recreation, improve yourself each day, and resolutely reject gambling and pornography.
>
> When on a tour follow the rules; don't ignore them.
>
> Should you encounter difficulties, contact the Consulate.

---

2. *Huang xian*: a line one meter back from a person accessing an ATM or being waited on by a clerk at a service window behind which the next in line should wait so that the person at the front can transact business in privacy.

Leave home enlightened.

May you have a peaceful journey. (*Changjiang Daily* 2013)

Amy Li, a journalist with the *South China Morning Post*, writes that when stories about rude Chinese tourists all made the top ten most read stories in the paper she wanted to analyze why. A tourism researcher in one of the local universities told her that tourists were not intentionally being rude; they were just being themselves. Not all are discourteous, but the less educated are more so than others. Many in China had their education disrupted during the 1960s and 1970s, so they know little about the world outside, and this, combined with having money, makes many think that they should be able to do or get anything they want. Chinese tourists are also unaccustomed to tipping, and even though their guides tell them that they should tip, they often ignore that advice. They're just acting the way they do back home, no respect for law or rules. They're just doing what their leaders do (2013b; see also Ni 2013, Levin 2013b).

What I have seen in rural areas or of persons from the countryside confirms this. In small towns or villages, one sees litter everywhere. Rural and small town people spit, talk loudly, ignore queues, and make little distinction between the right and left sides of the road. Younger children relieve themselves wherever they happen to be when they feel the need, assisted by the split-crotch pants they wear. Urine is ignored, feces are washed away. Such order as exists is kept through patterns of deference based on authority, age, kinship, and religious belief. Han friends who grew up in Xinjiang say that Uyghurs are much cleaner than the Han, which they attribute to Islamic beliefs about cleanliness and pollution.

This chapter will discuss the present state of civility in China. As stated in Chapter 2, examining civility largely consists of looking at what constitutes civil behavior and then appraising the extent to which people observe it. This predominantly entails surveying breaches and thus creates a critical tone. However, the picture is not all negative. The improvement in civility I have witnessed in the wealthier, better-educated, and more cosmopolitan urban areas that I have visited in China is palpable. However, the implementation of civility is still hindered by the values and attitudes that some display in their actions. This chapter will first examine behavior: toward strangers, road behavior, disturbing others, serving and helping others, queuing, behavior on public transport, littering, ignoring laws and rules, and philanthropy. It will also explain the values, assumptions, and conditions that affect behavior in these areas. It will then analyze the inequalities in Chinese society that contribute to incivility—in particular, the callous, uncaring, outrageous actions carried out by rich or powerful persons against ordinary citizens. These are certainly not everyday occurrences, but they create an atmosphere of oppression and resentment that is made worse because China is not a democracy, making it difficult for victims to seek redress.

Treatment of Strangers in Distress

A number of incidents have occurred in the past several years in which someone, usually but not always elderly, has fallen or been struck, is lying on the ground, and is ignored by passersby. Perhaps the best-known incident is that of "Little Yueyue," a two-year-old girl in Foshan who was run over by a truck, then run over again as the driver reversed to see what he had hit before driving off. She then lay on the road for many minutes while eighteen people, filmed on closed-circuit cameras, passed within a meter of her, ignoring her. Some even changed direction to avoid her. An elderly scavenger woman finally noticed her, picked her up, and took her to her mother. Her parents rushed her to a hospital, but she died of her injuries.

A reporter for the *Yangcheng Evening News* located many of the passersby; most flatly denied having seen anything. Those in nearby shops said they were busy with other matters and did not notice. A trishaw driver drove past and kept looking back at the girl, but he did not stop. Before the incident he went to a nearby scavenger post every day, but he had not been seen for the several days since. Another person clearly identified in the surveillance video denied that he was the same person. When the reporter pressed him he retorted, "It's not your kid, so mind your own business" (ifeng 2011).

There have been several other cases of passersby who either did not stop to help someone in distress or looked on as spectators. A man cycling over the much-trafficked Pearl River Bridge in Guangzhou fainted and lay unconscious and unattended on the ground for fifty minutes before being taken to a hospital. Doctors suspected heart disease and said he may have lived had he been brought to the hospital earlier (Sy 2013). An 88-year-old fell at a vegetable market exit. People stopped to look at him, but no one did anything to help. His relatives came an hour later and rushed him to a hospital, but it was too late (Huang 2011). A five-year-old boy in Shandong playing on a sidewalk was struck by an object that fell from a construction site. His mother pleaded with passersby, including urban management officials,[3] to help, but they all ignored her. By the time an ambulance came to take him to a hospital, it was too late; the boy died en route (Demick 2011a).

In Dongguan a Brazilian attempted to prevent a man from stealing a woman's handbag as she entered a car by blocking the would-be thief with his umbrella. However, the thief's two companions rushed over, and the three of them beat the Brazilian to death. Again, bystanders, including urban managers, simply looked on (McGeary 2012). In Hangzhou a suicidal woman jumped into a lake and was drowning when a Uruguayan woman passed by. Noting that others were simply gazing at the spectacle, some taking photos, one filming the event on an iPad, she dove into the lake, pulled the woman to safety, and left. She was later found and

---

3. Urban managers (*chengguan*) are charged with enforcing bylaws pertaining to hawkers, construction sites, urban sanitation and appearance, pollution, and health. Several have told me that they are very necessary, but they also have a reputation for meting out rough treatment to illegal vendors. See, e.g., Kan 2016.

given a reward by a local NGO (Demick 2011a; Xinhua 2011). At an accident scene in Yunnan involving a truck loaded with watermelons, while the driver was still trapped in the wreckage, local villagers came to scavenge the melons. A reporter asked if this was appropriate behavior. A villager replied, "Of course, the melons are still okay and we can eat them. They'll just be thrown away if we don't take them" (Luo 2013). In a similar incident in Shandong, locals scooped up the chicks a truck was carrying when it overturned (Nelson 2015e).

The closed-circuit footage of Little Yueyue was shown on Chinese television, prompting much soul-searching and consternation (Chin 2011; MacKinnon 2011; Wines 2011b) and sparking projects aimed at improving behavior in the public space (Demick 2011a) as well as giving rise to a discussion of possible laws to indemnify Good Samaritans.[4] However, some said that they understood why people ignored persons in distress—because they feared being accused of causing the person's misfortune.

A reason for this fear is a 2006 case in which a young man, Peng Yu, helped an old woman, Xu Shuolin, who had fallen as she had alighted from a bus. Peng took Xu to a hospital and paid her entry fee, but she later sued him, accusing him of having bumped her and caused her fall. The case went to court, and the judge ruled against Peng, stating that he would not have helped Xu had he not been responsible for her fall.[5] He ordered Peng to pay Xu 45,877 yuan (US$7275) [Xinhua 2012b; about US$6,900].[6] This verdict caused an outcry. First, the judge's remarks dismissed out of hand any possibility of altruistic behavior. Second, and more important vis-à-vis subsequent cases of ignoring those in distress such as those in the cases described above, is that it sent the message to anyone who might render aid, especially aid to the elderly, that they may suffer extortion as a result of their good deeds.[7]

Indeed, there are several reports of older persons doing just that. For example, a bus driver stopped to help an old woman lying under a trishaw, but the woman then told the police that the bus had knocked her down. In this case, surveillance footage cleared the driver. The reporting journalist writes that upon learning this he immediately went to an electronics market to buy a dashboard camera. The shopkeeper told him that sales had been robust since news of the incident, "In the past, I sold only several sets a day; now I can sell several dozens" (Liu 2011). An elderly man purposely fell off his bicycle while crossing an intersection and then, when a student

---

4. The first such law was passed in Shenzhen in 2013. See He Huifeng 2013; *Shenzhen Daily* 2013.
5. This statement speaks volumes for how China's elites, who had been running civility promotion campaigns for over 25 years (not to mention the even earlier promotion of the new socialist man and the Lei Feng spirit), really feel about the level of altruism in Chinese society. One could argue that if the Chinese citizenry were really so self-centered and indifferent, the incidents described above would not have caused the same disquiet.
6. This and subsequent conversions reflect current (October 2017) rates.
7. As it turned out, in 2012 new details of the case revealed that not only had Peng accidentally bumped into Xu but that he had "actively solicited the local news media and online forum moderators to promote him as a martyred Good Samaritan," and that he and Xu had "secretly agreed on a modest financial settlement" (Minter 2012). However, that was six years after the event, and the Peng Yu case still symbolizes *zuo hao shi bei e* (suffer a calamity for having done a good deed).

stopped to help him, accused the student of causing his fall. The police came to investigate, and after viewing surveillance footage, gave the old man a talking to and sent him home. Netizen reaction was strident, many labeling the old man public enemy number one and wishing him an early death. One wrote, "Do you remember the Red Guards? Do you know why all old people nowadays like to blackmail? It's because those hoodlums have all become old" (Liu 2015a)!

Survey results confirm the fear of being taken advantage of. Zhu Hong, a Nanjing University sociologist, found in a survey that 84 percent of those who had not seen reports of the Peng Yu case responded they would help an elderly person who had fallen, while only 8 percent of those who had would unhesitatingly do so (2010, 74). According to a poll carried out by Wu Yilin of Renmin University, shortly before the Little Yueyue incident, 65 percent of respondents would not help an elderly person who had fallen because they feared it would bring trouble (Demick 2011a). A *People's Daily* website poll found that only 13 percent of the 2,425 respondents said they would help someone, while 87 percent would not. And the following incident shows how widespread knowledge of the fear of such extortion attempts is. When fellow passengers declined to help a 75-year-old man who had fallen while getting off a bus, he yelled, "I fell down myself. You needn't worry. It's nothing to do with you" (Huang 2011). However, in one case a man accused of causing the mishap of the person he had tried to help committed suicide to demonstrate his innocence (Dzodin 2014).

Public fear is so strong that various jurisdictions have drafted laws to indemnify those who render assistance to persons who appear to be in distress from extortion. Shenzhen's bill, passed in 2013, not only exempts rescuers from legal liability for unintentional injury unless they have been grossly negligent but also calls for punishment of anyone who receives help and then lies or makes false claims. The government will also compensate a rescuer who dies or is injured in an attempt to assist (He 2013; Baike). Shenzhen's law led to calls for a national law (Dzodin 2014), and Good Samaritan protection is part of the Unified Civil Code recently presented to the legislature (Chin 2017).

State media has tried to counter the string of bad Samaritan stories with more positive ones. Demick cites a video showing several people helping a pregnant woman who had fainted, some carrying her, one hailing a motorist to take her to a hospital. The problem was that the incident was faked (2011a). However, there are genuine Good Samaritan stories.

A Wuhan man who fell off his bicycle was assisted by several passersby. First, a young man crouched over him and asked if he had been hit by a car, and when he did not answer the helper called the emergency service number. Two others came by and inspected his bicycle, and, seeing no damage, determined that a car was not involved. Another used the injured man's phone to call his relatives.[8] After about ten

---

8. The helpers pictured in the article were young men, probably late teens to mid-twenties.

minutes an ambulance came and took the injured man to a hospital where doctors found that his injuries were only cuts to his mouth and nose (*Changjiang Daily* 2012).

A Shanghai petrochemical worker gave up smoking and drinking and lost 22 kilograms in order to be able to donate bone marrow to a stranger. He also donates hematopoietic stem cells (Quan 2014b; Canpadee 2014). A Jinan woman suffered severe postpartum bleeding, but the hospital did not have enough of her uncommon blood type. A message on social media site WeChat telling of her plight resulted in over one hundred donors lining up to help save her (Nelson 2015c).

A Yunnan policeman came across a six-year-old boy who was getting up in the middle of the night to walk 4 kilometers to school because the family was too poor to afford an alarm clock. The policeman not only bought an alarm clock for the boy but some school supplies as well (Quan 2013).

A young woman was walking along a sidewalk when it suddenly caved in, causing her to fall into a six-meter hole. A passing taxi driver who saw what happened stopped his cab and jumped into the hole, shook her until she regained consciousness, then comforted her. The two climbed out a bit later when fire fighters arrived and extended a ladder (*Telegraph*, April 24, 2012).

A Sichuan woman, in addition to raising her own three children, took in four others who had been abandoned by their parents. Because her husband's earnings were insufficient, she worked in construction, mining and scavenging so they could support the family of nine (Quan 2014c).

While saving two students from being hit by an out of control bus a teacher herself was hit, suffering massive injuries and losing both legs. Fellow citizens contributed close to 10 million yuan to pay for her treatment (Yan 2012).

Tang Qijun, a sanitation worker, spent several hours going through already compacted rubbish to find a pair of trousers belonging to an 89-year-old man whose wife had inadvertently thrown them out, not knowing that they contained 3,500 yuan. Tang refused a reward when he returned the trousers and the money (Leroy 2014).

Two other incidents demonstrate admirable kind-heartedness toward strangers and also that condescension toward migrant workers is not universal. A female migrant worker in Fuzhou had 6,000 yuan in a bag tied to her waist as she was being hoisted to clean windows at a high-rise. On reaching the eighth floor, the bag came loose and the money scattered over the streets below. She was able to recover only 300 yuan, but when the story of her mischance spread, she received 15,000 yuan in donations from the public (Canpadee 2014). A similar story has both a civil and an uncivil twist: When Mr. Qin, a migrant worker in Shanghai, fell off his scooter, the wind caught the 15,000 yuan he was carrying and blew it away, where it was snatched by passersby. Only two persons returned any money to him, a total of 700 yuan. However, his calamity was reported in the press, resulting in 14,500 yuan in donations and over 7,000 yuan returned by some of those who gathered up the money when it was lost. He could have received more, but he refused further donations, not wanting to take more from donors than he lost, and he donated the extra money to charity. The uncivil twist is that scammers, whose calls were traced to Guangdong Province, sent messages to people asking them to donate to Mr. Qin's wife. Mr. Qin, however, is divorced (Griffiths 2013b).

Many also show kind-heartedness in response to tragedies. Little Yueyue's family received 270,000 yuan to help defray medical expenses (Chin 2011). Blogger Lauren Hilgers reports that after the 2008 Wenchuan earthquake, blood banks "overflowed" with donations, and in one week domestic cash donations reached 4.185 billion yuan with tens of billions donated in total (2008). Watts reports that 150,000 volunteers went to Wenchuan to help (2008). The 2010 Yushu earthquake also attracted assistance, especially from Tibetan monasteries and NGOs,[9] and although a week after the quake the government set up roadblocks to limit volunteers and outside observers (Branigan 2010), it also included a Tibetan Buddhist temple in its commendations for contributions to relief efforts (Reuters 2013a). In July 2012, following torrential rain, a flash flood hit Beijing, killing thirty-seven persons and paralyzing the public transport system. Over 160,000 people spontaneously rendered assistance, transporting stranded persons and providing food, water and even accommodation (Wu H. 2012). A similar display of public spirit followed the 2015 explosion in Tianjin. Four hundred people lined up to donate blood at Tianjin's hospitals; many brought water to patients and others; some volunteered to drive the injured to seek medical care, and clubs and hotels offered free accommodation to those affected (Liu 2015b).

Finally, a case that demonstrates why some hesitate to be charitable to strangers: a post appeared on a popular BBS (bulletin board system) in which a young female university student from Chongqing wrote that she was willing to sell herself in order to raise the money necessary for a liver transplant for her mother, who had reared her alone since her father's death when she was eleven. Netizens quickly responded, 217 donating a total of 114,550 yuan. However, the woman's story came under suspicion when a netizen claiming to know her wrote that she indulged in expensive luxuries and was of dubious character. This created a crisis for the previously sympathetic netizens, who feared that their trust and faith in society had been betrayed. Two of them, one journeying from Shanghai, traveled to Chongqing, where two locals joined them. The four investigated the story and the woman's bank accounts, finding some discrepancies. They reported their detailed findings back to the BBS, including that approximately one-third of the donations paid for the mother's surgery, the remainder going to a local children's charity (Yang 2009, 175–82).

---

9. The quake site is a Tibetan minority area in Qinghai.

Road Behavior

Civility is not often found on Chinese roads from either vehicle operators or pedestrians. Johnny Lin writes:

> Flouting traffic rules, constant honking, refusing to yield and tit-for-tat verbal attacks between motorists whose patience grows ever shorter have combined to turn Beijing with its overcrowded roads into a riotous street circus every working day. Men peddling flatbed tricycles commonly ignore other automobiles and even sets of lights in bustling traffic. This draws loud curses in Beijing dialect from blocked drivers forced to swerve into the inner lane from outside, triggering even louder foul language from motorists in other cars in a chain reaction of indignation. (2011a)

China's traffic accident and traffic death rates peaked in 2002. WHO reports that, based on Chinese government figures, deaths per 100,000 population show a fall from 8.3 in 2004 to 4.4 in 2013 (2015). However, WHO's own statistics state that China's 2014 rate was 18.49, placing it near the middle for middle-income countries (Worldlifeexpectancy 2015).[10]

Because driver etiquette is still at a relatively early stage, traffic is disorderly, right-of-way is generally honored in the breach, and pedestrians are in danger from vehicles traveling in the wrong lane. An anecdote from James Fallows illustrates the lack of rule-based behavior on Chinese roads. A Chinese engineer visiting Florida was about to take a picture of a school bus that had stopped when police intervened. What the police saw was an adult male taking a photo of a bus containing children. What the engineer saw was a stopped school bus with its "do not pass" flashers and stop sign operating and other drivers obeying them. Fallows writes that in China,

> You'd have motorbikes cutting past on the sidewalk, cars veering into the opposite-direction lane to get around the obstacle, a cacophony of horns complaining about any vehicle that did slow down, and in general the creative-chaos that extends from many other parts of Chinese life to its roadways. (2012)

If one leaves a safe distance between oneself and the car ahead, one or more vehicles will move into the space, often without signaling. If one wants to change lanes, perhaps to exit an expressway, a driver in the other lane may speed up to prevent another car from crossing into the lane ahead of him or her. Missing an expressway exit, some drivers will pull over to the shoulder and reverse or even make a U-turn and go back. Motorists, not sure which way to go, may stop in the middle of an intersection while deciding, holding others up. At the slightest hint of a delay, motorists signal their impatience by sounding their horns. Pedestrians are endangered by cars ignoring crosswalks or speeding up to get through an

---

10. The discrepancy between the official and the WHO figures on traffic deaths is due in part to China's practice of counting as road deaths only those that occur when the person dies at the scene. If someone dies of injuries sustained afterward, it is not counted as a road death.

intersection before pedestrians begin to cross when the driver sees the green walk signal come on.

Several factors are germane to incivility on Chinese roads. First, almost anyone encountered on the roads is a nothing-owed, nothing-expected stranger. Returning in a taxi to my hotel from Tsinghua University on one occasion, we were stopped at a level railway crossing. On each side, drivers moved into the opposing lanes to get ahead of cars in front of them. When the boom gates lifted, rather than two lanes of traffic going south and two going north, there were four lanes going each way, and it took some time before the traffic jam cleared, as drivers weaved their way around each other. I remarked to the cab driver that if drivers obeyed traffic rules, they would probably get to their destinations more quickly. "Yes," he replied, "but they *pa chikui*," fear that they will lose out (by letting others get ahead of them). This notion also inhibits courtesy on the roads because people fear that civility extended will not be reciprocated. A related attitude is *zhengxian konghou*, the desire to be first, an admirable trait in an athlete, but one that can foster aggressiveness in drivers.[11] An additional factor is social expectations—that is, how persons expect others to treat them. Satirist blogger Han Han raises the issue of highway drivers failing to dim their lights as other cars approach (Han 2011). Huang Haifeng explains that even if drivers know they should dim their lights and that it is proper to do so, they often do not because each expects the other not to do so. To dim one's lights when the other driver does not is to be taken advantage of, thus, to suffer a loss—*chikui* (2016).

Second, Chinese motorists behave in ways very similar to those in other societies that are going through the initial stages of motor vehicles coming into common use. Very few have grown up in families that operated a private car, and those with access to a car often had a chauffeur, which meant that they did not have to pay attention to how to drive or to road conditions. Moreover, most have at best limited experience living in a city that has heavily trafficked roads, as the proliferation of private cars is a very recent phenomenon. Furthermore, a considerable proportion of China's urban population is made up of rural–urban migrants who have come from villages and small towns where traffic is much lighter, and few perceive any need for road rules. At home, most could go to their destinations in a more or less direct route, even using the wrong side of the road and weaving to avoid hitting other vehicles or pedestrians when necessary. Peter Hessler describes the result of this inexperience: despite the mandatory fifty-eight-hour driver training course and lengthy written test on traffic rules and proper behavior on the road,[12] Chinese drivers do not have good road skills (2010, 50). One reason for this is that driving

---

11. *Chikui* (literally, to "eat a loss") implies that a person has to be tough to avoid being taken advantage of. It also implies that the world is a hostile place. By *zhengxian konghou*, competing to be first, one demonstrates that toughness. Chinese friends lament that parents teach children to compete to be first from a very young age, which perhaps explains such behavior when they get older.
12. One thing the Chinese education system, with its heavy emphasis on memorization, is very good at is training students to pass tests. However, memorized answers do not necessarily indicate understanding of the questions, let alone how to drive on crowded roads.

instruction takes place inside a driving school and not on public roads. Another factor complicating urban traffic is that although China's larger cities now have a considerable level of motor vehicle traffic, in many places cars, trucks, and buses still share the road with bicycles, motor scooters, and electrical or human powered three-wheelers.

Third is the traffic code, its evolution and level of enforcement as Chinese operate more and more private vehicles.[13] An illustration of at least past inadequacies is how the traffic code has dealt with drink-driving. The first drink-driving statute set the alcohol limit at 0.08, but, as is the case with many laws and rules in China, it was laxly enforced. Then, in 2011, after a public outcry over a spate of deadly crashes, some involving rich and politically powerful persons, the limit was lowered to 0.02 (Li et al. 2012)[14] with a vigorous campaign to show that the police were serious following the change. William Wan writes, "In Beijing alone, 7,000 police officers were deployed to set up checkpoints, armed with tear gas and ten-meter tire-puncturing nail strips. And for several weeks, state-owned media plastered stories of such arrests on their front pages" (2011). A year later, Beijing and Shanghai experienced a 70 percent drop in the number of drink-driving citations; cases involving accidents caused by drink-drivers dropped by 18.8 percent and deaths by 37.7 percent (Xinhua 2012b). Moreover, although the law does permit a 0.02 percent blood alcohol level, many will not drink at all if they will be driving.

Fourth, in part because of the aggressiveness of drivers and their sense of superiority over pedestrians,[15] in part because of the design of roads, the situation for pedestrians is that there is no safe place to cross a road unless someone is directing traffic at a crosswalk or intersection. One factor is that vehicles can turn right on a red light. They are supposed to stop first, but often they do not even slow down and some will even speed up to turn before a crossing pedestrian might delay them. Vehicles can also turn left as soon as there are no vehicles coming in the opposite direction, and there are many busy intersections at which there is no left-turn light that is linked to a "Don't Walk" signal for pedestrians. Vehicles turning either way under these conditions can pose a danger for pedestrians trying to cross.

Another is that it is popularly believed that vehicles are supposed to yield to pedestrians, but the law is vague. The 2011 traffic code says essentially that pedestrians should cross only when it is safe to do so and that cars should avoid pedestrians in crosswalks, but there is no provision that gives unambiguous right-of-way to either. While the code states that vehicles "should" (*yinggai*) stop for pedestrians (NPC 2011), "should" is not *must*, and this makes the provisions sound much like other rules in China for which there are no penalties. Drivers are constrained in

---

13. Private automobile ownership increased from 5.5 million in 1990 to 214 million in 2011 (Li et al. 2012). In 2013 alone, sales of passenger and commercial vehicles reached almost 22 million (Dezan Shira and Associates 2014).
14. This would mean that an adult male of average body weight could have one standard drink, or 10 grams of pure alcohol, at the beginning of a dinner, two to three hours before driving.
15. One could see this as a case of the strong exploiting the weak.

practice because if a vehicle hits a pedestrian or a bicyclist, the driver is deemed to be at fault, though that may be small comfort for the injured person. In 2009 pedestrians accounted for 24.6 percent of traffic deaths and bicyclists for 15.6 percent; of the remainder 22 percent were motorcyclists, 24.1 percent passengers, and 12 percent drivers (Zhang et al. 2013).

However, drivers are not always the problem. There is also what Lin calls the "Chinese style of crossing the road," referring to Chinese pedestrians crossing a road when they see a slight break in traffic, or when they feel there are enough of them to force traffic to stop. Citing a study from Shanghai's Jiaotong University, Lin states that China's roads have been designed for cars with little consideration for pedestrians. Many roads are wide, traffic flows, as noted above, are designed with drivers in mind, and the waiting time for a Walk signal can be a minute and a half or more, followed by 15 seconds to cross an eight-lane road (Lin 2013).

All this creates a potentially dangerous situation as some pedestrians and riders behave as if they believe that it gives them an implied right-of-way, which they take, even going against traffic lights. So there is a gap of ambiguity between what the law states and how road users understand and act on it. Moreover, this gap is exacerbated, according to a Beijinger, because all road users believe that they have the right-of-way.

Civil and Uncivil Behavior toward Strangers

Much of the incivility in China can be explained by a view of strangers that has long prevailed in China and, according to surveys of trust, is still very commonly held (Wang and Liu 2002; Zhu 2010, 2011; Rao et al. 2013). This is that strangers are of no social significance, they are viewed with wariness, and they may even be deemed to be hostile. Thus, how strangers are treated is of no consequence; they simply do not matter. People often ignore the presence of strangers or are oblivious to them; they look at them, but they do not see them.

Among the incivilities found in China and recognized in "Six Guidelines and Six Taboos," a document published for tourists going abroad by Xinhua, is not blocking the way of or pushing other pedestrians. Examples of such behavior are listed below:

- One is a sort of game of chicken in which a pedestrian avoids eye contact with those walking toward him (almost invariably a male) and continues to walk directly ahead, even though it is obvious that he is on a collision course. Such persons appear to have the attitude "look out for me because I won't look out for you." This is not exclusive to China; I also experienced it in 1960s to 1980s pre-civility Taiwan.

- A variation on this is two people approaching very close to each other until one of them suddenly veers off course and crosses in front of the other, forcing that person to stop to avoid a collision.
- Another is A and B (both males) sitting next to each other on a train; A opens his legs so that his knee crosses over the "dividing line" between the seats or extends his arm over the arm rest. B then has a choice of "losing space" to A or pushing back with his knees or arms.[16]
- A group chatting stands across a walkway, blocking it and forcing others to step into the road to pass by them.
- Someone sits in a crowded dining hall with his or her chair pushed out far enough to make it difficult for others to pass through the narrow space between tables.

Goffman describes civil inattention as strangers demonstrating their awareness of each other but not intruding on them in an interactive sense (1963). The behavior in the first of the above actions would be more accurately labeled uncivil inattention: the "offending" person is either oblivious to the presence of others or deliberately avoids eye contact in order not to "notice" them and not to have to make an effort to move out of the way or otherwise acknowledge the others' presence. The first three types of behavior might also be mild forms of "wanting to be first," or of *zhan pianyi* (gaining benefits at others' expense), by making the other person move or appropriating the other's space.

While these behaviors are not commonplace occurrences, others with whom I have discussed them have said that they, too, had had such experiences, and they happen frequently enough to be noticeable.[17] Much more common is to avoid even the very brief eye contact necessary to count as civil inattention. This is understandable on crowded city sidewalks, but it also happens when casually strolling through a public park or encountering someone one has often seen but to whom one has not been introduced in a workplace or a residential compound. This lack of eye contact, even in less crowded conditions, is noticed by Chinese who had spent time abroad. A fellow teacher at a Chinese university said that in Honolulu, where she had studied for several years, people thought it very strange and unfriendly if one did not make eye contact and say hello when passing them on the campus, but at the university at which she taught in Beijing, people avoided eye contact. "They look at a person at a distance of 15 meters or so to determine the other's path but then turn their eyes away as they pass each other." A Chinese couple who taught for several years at an American university in a small city made similar comments.

---

16. In *Shantung Compound*, Langdon Gilkey notes that the foreign POWs in a World War II Japanese prison camp would move their bunks a tiny distance in order to enjoy the psychological satisfaction of getting a fraction more space for themselves (1966).
17. Even here in Australia, a neighbor said that her university student son had complained about Chinese students acting this way on campus.

When someone bumps into another person or steps on someone's foot in a crowded bus, the "offender" often says nothing. However, a grade six moral education text lesson makes clear that this is not the proper civil response. According to the lesson, in the past, when this happened on Tianjin buses, tempers would flare, but now a "sorry" is followed by an "it's nothing" (RM 11, 13).

Another ramification of ignoring or eschewing interaction with strangers is that extending small courtesies such as holding a door open for someone close behind or holding an elevator so that someone coming toward it can get in often results in these actions going unacknowledged, perhaps because they occur so rarely or because many are reluctant to engage with strangers.[18] The major observation from this uncivil inattention phenomenon is that strangers in public places are "just there"; there is no obligation toward them. Thus, there is no need to worry about bothering, disturbing, or inconveniencing them.

Disturbing Others

The notion of not disturbing others is very weak in Chinese society. It is not generally taught to young children, who, before beginning primary school, are loosely disciplined and often allowed to behave as they wish. On a high-speed train from Shanghai, in the seat in back of me was a little girl, between four and five years old. She and her mother were nicely dressed. For the first twenty minutes, the girl drummed on the tray table in back of me with her fists, the vibrations from which I could feel surprisingly strongly through the seat back. I asked her to stop, which she did, but she soon started up again. This happened four times while her mother, sitting next to her, said and did nothing. Discussing this incident with Chinese friends, some said that since her mother tolerated such behavior, she would expect that others would as well. However, such children are referred to in China as "bear children" (*xiong haizi*, or brats) and are widely disliked. Others said that this was evidence of the destruction of Chinese ethical behavior wrought by the Cultural Revolution, that the demise of the former gentry class meant the extinction of the carriers of Chinese moral comportment.[19] It is highly likely that the number of children without siblings has exacerbated the spoiled-child syndrome (Cameron et al. 2013).

The notion behind the mother's toleration of her daughter's behavior is that small children *bu dongshi* (don't understand) but that as they grow older and begin school they will come to realize the need to discipline themselves. An important part of this is learning that there is, as mentioned above, a great difference between

---

18. This is based on observations during approximately eight months of residency in a high-rise apartment building near Xiamen University.
19. There is no doubt that the Cultural Revolution did great damage to human relationships and interpersonal trust (see, e.g., Dikötter 2016). However, as I showed in Chapter 2, there is no evidence that China was a society with civility before CCP rule.

the tolerance inside the home by family members and the much stricter expectations by the outside world. Early year primary school teachers are generally kindly but demand adherence to rules of order and thus provide the discipline that the family generally overlooks.[20] So even when a child's behavior obviously annoys others, parents often do nothing to get the child to stop. Thus, many young children are not taught to be considerate of others.

A common source of disturbance is noise—talking loudly in normal conversation and even more loudly when banqueting, drinking, or playing cards, or playing a radio, stereo, or TV at high volume. While some, generally in the more prosperous cities, realize that being noisy is inappropriate in the general public space, many either are ignorant or do not care. One hears people talking loudly on the street, in coffee shops or restaurants, and in university hallways outside faculty offices and classrooms. In one sense, noise has a positive value in Chinese society. The notion of *renao* (hot and noisy) describes a festive occasion such as Chinese New Year when kin gather together to celebrate. More people is a symbol of prosperity, and when many people celebrate together, the result is a high level of noise, often amplified by firecrackers. The more people, the more noise, the happier the elderly are to see the number of their progeny, who are a symbol of a successful life. A common cause of complaint in cities is groups of usually elderly people square-dancing outside in open spaces to music loud enough to disturb those who want a quiet, relaxing evening in their apartments (Buckley 2016; Xinhua 2015a). Festive occasions with friends or business associates are similar. People toast back and forth, sing together in karaoke, and play very noisy drinking games. One reason why having private dining or karaoke rooms rather than dining or singing in the public restaurant hall with those from other parties is so that the guests can act as they wish, seen and heard only by friends or family, and not disturb or be disturbed by others.[21] When the guests at a dinner are not all familiar with each other or when there are status differences, they are more sedate. They still toast, but the toasts are quieter, more formal, and fewer in number.

Chinese tourists in Taiwan sometimes leave their hotel room doors open so they can talk to friends in other rooms, oblivious to other guests. In Xiamen, a family living in a nearby apartment often left their door open during the day and let their preschool-aged daughter play or even cry for long periods in the hallway. Some even argue in public, in defiance of the Chinese saying that one does not air dirty linen in public (*jiachou buke waiyang*). However, arguing in front of strangers is essentially arguing in private because, since one does not know them, they are insignificant.[22] Such people are seemingly unaware that they might be disturbing

---

20. On spoiling parents and disciplining teachers see Tobin, Wu, and Davidson, *Preschool in Three Cultures: Japan, China and the United States* (1989).
21. Many Chinese restaurants have private rooms large enough for one or two tables in which people can dine without disturbing or being disturbed by others and where others will not hear their conversations.
22. Martin Yang, in his analysis of "face," wrote that to lose face one must commit an act in front of persons one knows (1945, 167–79).

others. A Chinese colleague at Xiamen University who had studied in Japan for several years commented on how noisy Chinese were compared to Japanese.

Loud Chinese tourists also attract complaints in Thailand (Li 2013a), Europe (Fan 2015), Japan (Fifield 2015), Hong Kong (Yung 2014), and Taiwan (Jennings 2015). However, being noisy in China is now "officially" frowned upon. A unit in a Chinese moral education text states that society is a big extended family, and that people should be considerate of neighbors, including not disturbing them by making noise (RM 7, 82–85). Ordinary Chinese also disapprove of other peoples' noise—a friend's father objecting to a group of boisterous, Cantonese-speaking tourists in the restaurant in which we were eating, or a woman sitting across the aisle on an airplane, head bowed and fingers in her ears to block out the din from two men sitting beside her and talking at high volume. Moreover, noise does not have to be loud to disturb others. A student complained that some are not careful about shuffling their books, turning pages quietly, or, worse, switching off their cell phones while studying in the library. When asked whether one can request that noise makers be more quiet, people either say that it would do no good as they would feel that the requestor was meddling (*guan xianshi*), that it was within their right to act as they pleased, or that it could even lead to conflict.

I witnessed the following incident on a high-speed train[23] about to leave Shanghai for Nanjing: A man in the seat across the aisle, A, was reading a newspaper. The man sitting behind him, B, was jiggling his feet on the footrest. A asked B, very politely, to stop, but B ignored him and continued. A few moments later, A again asked B to stop, and again, B ignored him. A then muttered, half to himself, about this being *bu wenming* (uncivil) behavior. B got out of his seat and approached A belligerently. A got up, and B threw a punch. A retaliated, and the two of them fought as B backed A toward the end of the carriage, a distance of about 10 meters. Other passengers finally restrained them, and they went back to their seats.

This sort of unpredictable reaction from a simple request to act with civility is not unique. A woman in an apartment elevator asked a man to stop smoking. Instead, he began to beat her (Hernández 2016b). Wang Tao, the leader of the Green Woodpeckers, a volunteer group in Beijing whose aim is to promote civil behavior, says that his group "risks insult and even injury when asking people to pick up their cigarette butts or when they hand folks a tissue to wipe up their spit" (MacLeod 2013). These incidents involve stubbornness but also a loss of face, which, Harrell notes, can lead to violence (1990, 10–11). Interpersonal violence also results from road rage, persons disappointed by medical treatment they or a relative has received,[24] as well as delayed or canceled airline flights or spats with airline crew. Such incidents are frequently published in Chinese media (Yan 2015; Kenny 2015;

---

23. Such trains are more expensive, so passengers are generally better off and better educated.
24. Violence toward medical staff is a very serious problem in China (Beam 2014; Burkitt 2012; LaFraniere 2010; Rauhala 2014; Zhu 2015), and it is serious enough that airline crew now train in martial arts (Lam 2016).

Jiang 2015; Yu 2015; Roberts 2013). Certainly, not everyone would react as B did, but the problem is that one never knows.

Smoking is another behavior that some find offensive; however, it is very prevalent, and many smoke regardless of whether it is permitted in a particular venue or not. China has the world's largest number of smokers, over 300 million, with 53 percent of men and 2.4 percent of women being smokers (WHO 2016), however, over half of China's population is exposed to second-hand smoke (*Economist* 2014a). Cigarettes are passed around freely by groups of men, and gifts of cigarettes, especially foreign or expensive domestic brands, are welcome gifts. Some wanting to climb the social ladder will switch to a more expensive brand as a part of an image makeover (Hessler 2009, 232–33).

However, according to the World Health Organization, smoking kills 3,000 persons a day in China, is a factor in 80 percent of deaths and is predicted to kill 100 million people this century (Haas 2011). In the larger, more cosmopolitan cities smoking is becoming less tolerated, and there is support for smoking restrictions, although this is not the case elsewhere, where it is socially acceptable.

Legislation enacted on May 1, 2011, mandated that all enclosed public areas such as schools, banks, offices, airports, hospitals, stadiums, and railway stations be smoke free (Haupt 2011). This law directed that such venues prominently display "No Smoking" signs, and employers were asked that employees not smoke in their offices. Failure to comply could attract a fine of up to 30,000 yuan (US$4,500; Haas 2011), though no penalties were set for smokers who violated bans. However, what laws decree and how people actually behave do not always coincide. In 2015 Beijing promulgated its own law, banning smoking in restaurants, offices, on public transport, and in the vicinity of schools and hospitals. The penalty for violating the law was raised from 10 to 200 yuan. Serial violators—those caught more than three times—were to have their names posted for a month on a government website. Businesses that failed to comply became liable to a fine of 10,000 yuan (Reuters 2015). The government sent a thousand specially trained inspectors out into the public on the day the law came into force (Linder 2015a), though it is unclear whether that enforcement effort was sustained.

Elsewhere, despite bans, enforcement is lax or sporadic at best. Some hotel rooms have "No Smoking" cards next to ashtrays on desks and bedside tables. "No Smoking" signs are regularly ignored, especially in restaurants; they are supposed to have a nonsmoking area, but owners rarely enforce this as they fear they will lose trade,[25] and attempted enforcement by customers asking smokers to obey a "No Smoking" sign is more likely than not to be ignored or to cause conflict. Moreover, despite blanket bans in public buildings, there is a de facto exception, men's toilets. Whether in school or university buildings, airports, or bus and train stations, there

---

25. I have seen one restaurant that enforced the smoking ban, a vegetarian restaurant in Xiamen, a stone's throw from the Nanputuo Shan Monastery. When one of the diners at my table pulled out a cigarette, a waitress asked him to go outside to the courtyard to smoke it.

are "No Smoking" signs on the walls, but there are cigarette butts in the urinals and the odor of tobacco smoke in the air. Haas cites a restaurateur as saying, "The police won't enforce the policy. Chinese cops smoke more than anyone" (2011). Moreover, the tobacco lobby is very powerful in China as its products contribute 6 percent of government revenue, about the same as the petroleum and property industries, and it is a major employer, especially in Yunnan (*Economist* 2014a).

Serving and Helping Others

Poor performance by service providers during the period of the planned economy and shortly after the reforms has, in many areas, given way to good service. Service in larger businesses and in large organizations such as banks, airports, and post offices has greatly improved and is on the whole very good.[26] Remaining service problems lie mainly with lower-level administrative staff in state-linked units who have "iron rice bowl" jobs. In two universities where I have lectured or carried out research, I have encountered bureaucratic attitudes, staff robotically carrying out their duties with no effort to be helpful and conveying an attitude that asking them to carry out the services they are supposed to provide is onerous. Students also complain about bureaucratic treatment by administrative staff and by some lecturers as well.

In the past, most would have ignored someone asking directions on the street. People regarded knowledge as capital and were reluctant to share it. My experience in the past decade has been the opposite. On several occasions people have even gone out of their way to direct me to where I needed to go, and when I have asked my students whether those helping me were treating me differently because I was a foreigner some replied that they had received similar treatment. My research assistants concurred, saying that Chinese are generally relatively open hearted to strangers who ask for something simple such as directions, the time, or a light for a cigarette, though they would be reluctant, for example, to help someone whose car had broken down, fearing it might be a ruse. The main exception is that some city residents are condescending toward migrant workers. A research assistant from Shaanxi said that people back home looked down on them, singling out those from Henan, whom they consider poor and uneducated, and itinerant Uyghur traders from Xinjiang, whom they regard as untrustworthy. Amy Hanser found that migrant workers are widely disdained in Harbin (2008, 83–84, 103–5).

I have had a number of experiences in which others acted in a most helpful and civil fashion, and I have also received great kindnesses. At the Nanning airport, while going through exit procedures for a flight to Shanghai and about to have my carry-on items checked, I suddenly realized that I had forgotten to put my Swiss

---

26. Hanser notes that service in retail businesses has improved greatly because of the strong competition in the sector (2008, 34–35).

army knife in my checked bag. I pulled the knife out and showed the inspector, apologizing for my oversight. Very obligingly he told me to put it in my carry-on bag, which he then had checked. In Wuxi, distracted by my conversation with the driver, I forgot my luggage, which was in the trunk of the cab that was taking me to my hotel. Because of roadworks I had to walk about 150 meters from the road to the hotel. As I approached the door, I realized my mistake. Panicked, I rushed to the hotel desk, told the concierge what had happened, and gave her the receipt for the cab ride. She told me not to worry and to take a seat in the lobby. After a nervous half-hour wait, she came over and told me that the cab company had contacted the driver, and that he would come to the hotel once he had dropped off his current passenger. When he came all he wanted was the fare from where he had dropped his passenger off to the hotel, and I had to press him to take a modest reward. The behavior of the concierge indicates that bringing my luggage back and not looting it is not unexpected behavior, and when I told my assistants about my experience, they were not surprised.[27]

Queuing and Public Transport Behavior

Consider the following examples of queuing-related behavior:

- Two bus stops near the Xiamen University campus. One is a large terminal area away from other traffic and features three lanes where buses can pick up passengers with designated stops for each bus route. Passengers wait for the bus they want to board in orderly queues on curbed and sheltered sidewalks. The other is on a busy street running along the campus border and near a major campus gate. Passengers wait in a crowd for the bus they want in an area where buses for several different routes stop. There is no room to queue and no exact spot where the bus for any particular route will stop. So when a bus arrives, intending passengers for that bus move toward the entrance, blending into something resembling a queue just before they get to the door. (One sees similar behavior at multiple route bus stops in Beijing).
- A waiting room at the Beijing airport in which many of the passengers are elderly tourists from the countryside. A flight attendant calls for passengers to board, those in rear seats to board first. The rural tourists, all the while talking very loudly, rush to the boarding gate, pushing and shoving each other, ignoring instructions from the flight attendant to queue. Once on the plane, several of them seem to disregard or not understand the seat assignment on their boarding pass and have to be moved.

---

27. However, not all cab drivers are so honest, as then ABC China correspondent Stephen McDonell discovered in Shanghai; see "One Night in Shanghai: How the Police State Rescued My Luggage," *ABC News*, June 30, 2015, http://www.abc.net.au/news/2015-06-30/mcdonell-how-the-police-state-rescued-my-luggage/6582934

In contrast to rural areas, in major cities queuing is the norm at places such as supermarkets, post offices, airline counters, and bus stops. There are, of course, some who jump queues, but they are a small, though brazen, minority. This usually draws no reaction from others in the queue, though occasionally someone will tell the queue-jumper to *paidui* (line up) and this can embolden others to join in the criticism and shame the queue-jumper into going to the end of the line. Queues are sometimes monitored in student dining halls, but the monitors can only exhort queue-jumpers to follow the rules, as they have no other authority. The same is true at busy subway stations in Beijing where monitors try to ensure that boarding passengers line up at the sides of the entrances before they attempt to board in order to allow those alighting to do so from the center of the doorway. Most comply, but some ignore the monitors, wait in front of the doors, and barge in as soon as they open, presumably to increase their chances of getting a seat. In Beijing this is especially common at the Xizhimen and Dongzhimen stations, which act as links between the city proper and the outer suburbs.

However, queuing has become an expectation in many urban areas, and cutting in line can spark outrage as the following incidents show: (1) A woman with a baby in Nanjing jumped the queue in front of another woman to buy some milk tea. The latter woman slapped the queue-jumper twice, got into her car, and as the queue-jumper left, drove after her down the sidewalk. The queue-jumper ran into a beauty shop, and the driver drove her car in front of the door, blocking it. Passersby then surrounded the car until the police arrived (Twigden 2015). (2) A fiftyish worker in Gulangyu asked to be let in line, as she desperately needed to use the public toilet. Another woman, a tourist, refused, but the older woman pushed in line anyway. When she emerged, others in the queue told her to leave quickly as the tourist had phoned someone and said that she wanted to beat the queue-jumper. The older woman left, but the tourist caught up with her and bashed her in the head with a brick (Nelson 2014a).

Another expectation is that passengers on public transport yield seats to the elderly, the disabled, pregnant women, and small children. Buses and subways have nominally reserved seats for them, but the reservation is not enforced and depends on the goodwill of other passengers. However, in reported incidents over the past decade, some elderly and even middle-aged passengers become angry and even demanding when young people do not yield seats.

In one incident a lame man who appeared to be over seventy years old boarded the Qingdao 60X route bus. The bus was full, and the old man struggled to push through the crowd to a reserved seat. A woman, about twenty years old, was sitting in the seat, her head turned to the window. The bus driver announced, "Please voluntarily give the elderly, weak, sick, disabled, or pregnant a seat," and several middle-aged men also told the young woman to give up her seat. She refused and yelled back, "So many seats on the bus, who are you to tell me to give up my seat?" A man wearing a suit reasoned with her, "because you are sitting in the seat reserved for the elderly." The woman then turned her head away and ignored him. Furious, the suited man pulled a 100 yuan bill from his pocket and slapped it across her face, saying, "You give up the seat and the 100 yuan is yours. Will you give it up? Will you give it up?" The woman jumped up angrily and had an intense quarrel with the man, but he pulled her away to the cheers of the surrounding passengers (Fauna 2009). This incident was posted on Weibo,[28] with some comments criticizing the suited man for striking the woman, even if only with a banknote.

This is only one of several recorded incidents of conflicts between the young and the old over yielding seats,[29] but whether the young should be obligated to yield seats has become contested. A survey cited in the *China Daily* states that "most Chinese" believe that yielding a seat should be voluntary rather than compulsory, and the article itself states that "the elderly should not tell others to vacate seats." It cites incidents in which arguments over seats have turned violent, including one in which an elderly man in Henan argued with a younger man who refused to vacate his seat and slapped him several times before collapsing onto the floor and dying. It also states that there are valid reasons not to yield a seat such as if one is ill or very tired (Wu 2014).

A *Global Times* article generally agrees and also states that the expectations and behavior of some elderly people is a problem. Many of them were born around the time of the revolution and did not receive much education. They then experienced the hardships of the Great Leap Forward and the turmoil of the Cultural Revolution, a period "that broke apart the traditional moral concepts of Chinese society. This meant many people from that era were not properly educated by their schools, family or society, and they have no boundaries or taboos" (Zhang 2014). One conflict incident revealed the existence of a "never give up your seat" group on Douban, a social networking website. The group is composed of young people who believe it is unfair that they are asked to give up their seats to the elderly. Judging from the willingness of elderly people to queue for hours to get free goods, this group feels that some older persons are stronger and healthier than young people; some of the elderly regard it as their right to have a seat and show no gratitude when someone yields one to them; and the young support the old in society and deserve a rest to and from work (Mu 2008; Judah 2014).[30]

Littering

Littering illustrates the general attitude toward the public space: since no member of the general public is charged with supervising it, many do not care about it. However, littering is a modern problem. That ancient peoples littered is evidenced

---

28. Sina Weibo is a popular Chinese microblogging site that combines features of Facebook and Twitter.
29. See, e.g., Nelson 2014c; Judah 2014; Chun Wong 2014; *Global Times* 2014.
30. One can only wonder if this is a result of a spoiled-children syndrome created by the Family Planning policy since children are taught in primary school to honor and help the elderly.

by the shell middens, potsherds, and other items that archaeologists study in their quest to understand the past, but population numbers were small then, and their impact on the earth or their surroundings was minimal. Passing a small farm next to the highway one day in Taiwan and seeing the old tires and oil drums on the periphery near the road it struck me that small farmers have always just thrown away items no longer of use to them, the difference being that, in the past, what they discarded was either consumed by farm animals, rats, and the like or was biodegradable and thus did not present a litter problem. That has changed.

China has two littering problems, the amount of litter and the attitude of many of its people toward littering. The amount varies from place to place. A 2015 Shanghai Road Administration Bureau study found that more than 40 tons of litter were cleared from Shanghai's 1,000 kilometers of roads every day (Xinhua 2015; Ke 2013). Maintaining relative cleanliness is assisted by ample rubbish bins on the sidewalks; in the cleaner cities they are no more than 150 meters apart, but in other cities there are far fewer. Recently, some Chinese municipal governments have banned dogs from public areas (Nelson 2015a), not because the officials dislike dogs but because too many owners fail to clean up after their pets.

From my observations, modern, cosmopolitan, and developed cities such as Beijing and Shanghai—coastal cities in general—are relatively clean. Central Wuhan streets are dirty but more from subway and other construction projects than litter. Rubbish bins are rare, but Wuhan has street sweepers. Less prosperous inland cities such as Fuyang are less clean. In the area near the main railway station, between the paved road and a narrow footpath, there is a dirt strip about 4 meters wide that is littered with plastic bags and other rubbish. The outskirts of both Fuyang and Hefei are equally unkempt with mile after mile of two-story buildings, living quarters upstairs and shops put to various industrial uses below. The shop-front areas are only partially paved and are littered with debris or soaked in oil. However, their city proper areas are, in turn, cleaner and better maintained than Taihe, a rural municipality in Fuyang Prefecture some 25 kilometers to the west, or the smaller market areas in between.

Some major cities are relatively clean, thanks to brigades of street cleaners who do their work early in the morning so that at least when most people start their day, the streets and sidewalks are clean, though litter that blows into bushes is often overlooked. Some cities also do supplementary cleaning—for example, Xiamen market areas are cleaned by street-sweeping trucks twice more daily. A significant part of the problem in cities comes from hawkers, who sometimes operate on the sidewalks. For example, on a street corner just across from the West Gate of Xiamen University, late every evening a fellow sets up a small kebab business to take advantage of the high level of pedestrian traffic passing by. Every morning the concrete is stained with oil from cooking the meat, and the surrounding area is strewn with satay sticks, Styrofoam cups, beer bottles, and cigarette debris. The under-road tunnel connecting the two halves of Beijing Foreign Studies University is similar, lined with cooked-food stalls late in the evenings to take advantage of the midnight-snack (*xiaoye*) trade. Using such areas as venues for doing business is illegal, but, according to locals, it is easy to pay off the urban managers, and such businesses are popular and well patronized.

The attitude problem is that many people don't recognize litter as a problem. While visiting his parents, expat Jin Kai observed with disappointment students buying snack foods on their way home from school and then dropping the packaging and wrappers onto the street, despite criticism of such behavior in their moral education texts. He was also surprised at his neighbors' lack of concern about this; they even joked that litter created jobs for the elderly and for migrant workers, who scavenge and recycle refuse such as plastic bottles (see Swift 2013). Jin lamented that moral education wasn't stronger, but he also noted that children's first teachers are their parents, and littering behavior was likely learned from them (Jin 2014). A survey by the Municipal Office of Civil Ethics and the Shanghai College Student Alliance for Environment corroborates this, finding that although 97 percent of respondents regarded littering on elevated highways as bad behavior, 68 percent of car drivers and 95 percent of truck and bus drivers said they discarded rubbish there as a matter of convenience (Ke 2013).

By far the worst litter problem, however, is from tourists and holiday visitors. Scenic areas are often littered. After the 2014 Mid-Autumn Festival, Sanya's Dadonghai Beach was strewn with more than 50 tons of beer bottles, cigarette butts, food wrappers, newspapers, and other rubbish. More than 600 workers toiled for two hours to clean up afterwards (Gilbert 2014; Lau 2012). A Golden Week[31] visit by tourists to Qinghai Lake left comparable scenes. The Qinghai Lake Tourism Group reported that tourists even criticized sanitation workers who asked them not to carelessly discard their rubbish (Pirbhai 2015). On Monday mornings the beach near Xiamen University is in a similar state, covered with fruit peels, sunflower- or melon-seed husks, coconut shells, empty beverage containers, plastic bags, and broken beach toys (see also Cost 2014; Quan 2014a; Crouch 2013).

Some are becoming aware of littering as a problem. Calum MacLeod reports that five tons of rubbish had been left in Tiananmen Square on the day of the 2013 National Day celebrations, but that this was an improvement on the eight tons left in 2012 or the nineteen tons in 2005. Moreover, this prompted expressions of disapproval on Weibo, some coming from official sources such as CCTV and the Beijing city government, some from ordinary citizens and bloggers, several of whom blamed the political system or the lack of law enforcement for the persistence of uncivil attitudes. Others suggested that the Chinese could learn from the more public-spirited Americans (Macleod 2013), an idea that must be especially galling for the authorities, given their campaign to wean the populace off positive attitudes toward the United States or the West in general.

---

31. The one-week holidays for Chinese New Year and National Day.

Related to littering in that both are crimes against the public space and the public assets within it as well as showing inconsideration toward other members of the public, is the theft of public goods. Closed-circuit TV has revealed that some elderly people make several visits to the public toilets at Beijing's Tiantan Park and walk away with large amounts of toilet paper each time[32] (Ye 2017). Zhengzhou buses have hammers to break the glass sheltering the emergency alarm button, but of late 2,000 of them have been stolen per year, people taking them home to crack walnuts. In the past they were attached with a string, which was easily cut, but they now set off an alarm when removed (Ng 2015). Beijing had a more serious problem. According to a 2013 estimate, over 240,000 manhole covers had been stolen and sold for scrap metal in the previous decade. However, electronics company Huawei has developed electronically tagged "smart" manhole covers that can be tracked (Nelson 2015b). While these items may bring a small amount of profit or convenience to the thieves, the potential harm to the public by their theft is serious.

Ignoring Rules and Laws

A grade two primary school moral education text has a story about a baby giraffe in a zoo. Children who visited the zoo loved the giraffe. In fact, they loved it so much that, despite signs telling them not to, they fed it, sometimes giving it fruit still in plastic bags. The giraffe died (RM 4, 16–17). The story itself is largely true. In 1996 a giraffe at the Shanghai zoo died after eating food in plastic bags. The zoo then put up a three-meter high sign reading, "For animals, plastic bags are murder weapons." Yet in 2014 the zoo reported that visitors threw plastic water bottles into the lion's den, where cleaning staff had access for only one hour a day (Nelson 2013). A similar incident happened in a Xiamen's Haiceng wildlife park where a deer died; an autopsy showed that it had four kilograms of plastic packaging materials in its stomach (Nelson 2014b).

On Chinese commercial aircraft, as soon as a plane touches ground or even before, passengers have turned on their cell phones. Before planes come to a complete stop, many will have undone their seat belts and some will have stood up to retrieve their carry-on baggage. If the aircraft hits turbulence midflight and the seat-belt indicator comes on, some will still leave their seats. Fights with airline crew can break out when economy passengers try to take a seat in first class or when told they must fasten their child's seatbelt (Nelson 2015d).

As noted above, "No Smoking" signs are generally ignored. Also noted above, many drivers do not stop for pedestrians in crosswalks or when making right turns, and traffic police on site often disregard it. Pedestrians, bicyclists, and three-wheeled cart drivers sometimes ignore stop signs and lights, and pedestrians cross

---

32. These toilets are supplied with toilet paper because the park is a major tourist attraction. The toilet paper dispensers are next to the washbasins rather than inside the cubicles.

in the middle of blocks, sometimes stepping over barriers in the middle of the road put there to prevent them from doing so.

Some recognize rules but feel that exceptions can be made "just for me/us." The Anzi River Nature Reserve in Sichuan is a panda sanctuary off limits to tourists, but the three rangers at the Reserve, like the monitors at subway stations, have no power to stop them if they insist on coming in. One of the rangers said that when he and his companions tried to stop a group of tourists one of their number replied, "Just this once, let us through, we're just 'going to have fun,'" then pushed their way in—and left the detritus from their picnic when they departed (Shanghaiist 2015). That this "exception for me/us" attitude is relatively common is demonstrated by a lesson in a grade two Chinese textbook: a family wanting to travel through a scenic mountain area that was closed because of potential danger is stopped by a ranger, but the father says to her, "Just make an exception for us" (RM 4, 31; see also Bo Yang 1985, 21).

The Chinese government has laid down numerous rules in support of the Five Stresses, Four Beauties, and Three Fervent Loves campaign and repeated many of these in the more recent Establish New Customs drives, yet adherence to those rules is spotty at best and is better explained by the increase in what might be called the new middle strata than because citizens pay heed to the propaganda or listen to the government. A question could be asked: Why are Chinese not more rule abiding? The answer, I believe, is multistranded.

First, the rules of Confucian piety set such a high standard of selflessness and self-rectification that only the most dedicated and disciplined could live up to them. As Confucianism became the orthodoxy, its virtually sacred tenets became codified and, as such, were beyond challenge or criticism. They also linked virtue, as defined by these rules, with legitimacy to rule. Rulers, of course, claimed to be good Confucians, and one questioned such claims at one's peril. Elite status was also linked to being a good Confucian. This created tension between craving a high moral reputation and earthly desires. Because the rules could not be challenged, criticized, or changed, people created personal facades, publically paying lip service to Confucian moral rectitude but privately doing as they pleased. In his novel *Family* (*Jia*), Ba Jin describes his uncles as being members of a Protect Confucianism Society while surreptitiously spending their evenings drinking and whoring. Moreover, except for criminal law, there has never been a tradition of rule of law in China. Imperial governments eschewed law in favor of *li*, etiquette, and the judgment of highly educated—and ipso facto moral—officials.

Second, traditionally law was infused with morality, one implication of which is that there was much to enforce but few means to enforce it. Serious crimes and acts that might lead to disorder were enforced as strongly as means allowed, but rules less threatening to the government were often dealt with through moral lectures at the village compact level or by religious practitioners at funerals, urging mourners to engage in proper conduct and threatening supernatural punishments for those who failed to do so. Such breaches were rarely handled through criminal punishment. In the Republican China New Life Movement, officials wrote essays and gave speeches in which they inveighed against various moral misdemeanors, though it is likely that they did so more to be seen to be supporting the movement or as a substitute for making efforts and expending resources to enforce its rules of conduct than as a step in their actual implementation.

However, moral-based enjoinments to obey rules that are widely ignored serve merely to undermine the principle of obedience and teach the young, "Just don't get caught." Children are taught in school to obey rules, some of which are necessary for classroom order. However, as mentioned, aside from learning from their teachers and textbooks, they also learn from observing the behavior of their parents and others, who also often talk about obeying rules but break them in various ways. This sends the unspoken message to children that they should learn the rules taught in school so they can give the correct answer if a teacher asks them, but otherwise they can ignore them. Children also learn from their parents, sometimes directly, sometimes indirectly, that the most important thing is to get ahead, and that in China's highly competitive society finishing second can mean losing out. All this teaches them that, aside from the formal rules and morality there are "hidden" or unwritten rules (*qian guize*) that more accurately portray the way people actually behave.

Third, many rules have no penalties attached, for example the recent National People's Congress amendment to the Law on the Rights and Interests of the Elderly, which states that grown children who do not live with their parents must visit them "often," and "frequently visit and pay their respects." But neither "often" nor "frequently" are defined, nor is there a stipulated penalty for noncompliance (Lubman 2013). As Lubman also states, Chinese laws usually lack precision. Cao writes that this lack of precision comes in part from the ambiguity of the Chinese language, but that vagueness can also be a deliberate and desired quality. Laws are sometimes purposely general and imprecise, giving them a state level universality while allowing flexibility reflecting the diverse conditions of local areas. It also allows various jurisdictions to act as they see fit from case to case (Cao 2004, 96). Further reasons for the ambiguity is that laws still appeal to moral considerations, allowing officials to make arbitrary decisions (113).

Fourth, there is a lack of respect for the fairness of the court system. Johnny Lin writes that cases in which the innocent are convicted while the powerful get off create an apathetic society (2011b). An American lawyer with whom I taught and who also worked with a law firm in Beijing recited several incidents he had witnessed or been told about in which people saw laws being broken (purse snatching, pickpocketing, theft, assault) but did nothing because (1) they wanted to avoid matters involving the police, which can have unpredictable outcomes; and/or (2) they feared that the perpetrators may react violently.

Philanthropy

Philanthropic activity is an important indicator of civility, but data from China are mixed. Chinese demonstrate a strong willingness to donate and volunteer during times of disaster; however, they are not regular donors, and donations fluctuate from year to year based on whether there have been misfortunes (Armstrong and Toh 2014). Donations reached 100 billion yuan in 2008, the year of the Wenchuan earthquake and very heavy and unseasonal snowfalls in Hunan, but they dropped to 54.2 billion in 2009 when there were no disasters. Another earthquake took place in 2010 in Yushu, Qinghai Province, and donations increased to 70 billion yuan.

The fluctuations are mainly in individual donations. In normal years the major proportion of funds come from the corporate sector. For example, in 2006 and 2007, individuals contributed less than a quarter of all donations, though this percentage increased in 2008 to 54 percent, a year of disasters, then but dropped back to 30 percent in 2009 (*Global Times* 2011). Companies remain the primary source of donations, giving 47.44 billion yuan in 2012 according to a China Charity and Donation Information Report (*China Daily* 2013).

From the above it is apparent that individuals show great compassion when disasters strike their compatriots, but, for a variety of reasons, they do not donate on a regular basis.[33] In the early 1950s China made charity a government monopoly, partly for ideological reasons[34] and, extrapolating from its policy of paying for blood donations rather than relying on voluntary donors,[35] partly because the government had little faith in the altruism of the public. Charity was dispensed through government bodies such as the Young Communist League and GONGOs (government-organized nongovernmental organizations) such as the Chinese Red Cross and the Soong Ching-ling Foundation. This situation continued into the 1980s when the government recognized that religion would not die out as Communist ideology predicted, and it allowed, even encouraged, religious and other organizations to engage in philanthropy on their own. After a slow start, donations picked up in the 1990s, stimulated by the 1991 eastern China floods (Wang 2008, 231–32).

In 2014 Zhou Sen, a National People's Congress deputy for Henan and the honorary vice president of the China Charity Federation (a state body) identified the lack of a genuine philanthropic culture in China as a challenge. Cui Yongyuan, a CCPPC delegate, celebrity talk show host and manager of the Cui Yongyuan Public Foundation agreed, saying that China lacks a culture of charity.

---

33. An exception may be charity "donations" through the China Welfare Lottery, which has dispensed over 360 billion yuan in public welfare funds since 1987. See CWL 2015.
34. Foreign charities had too close a connection with foreign powers, and the government regarded philanthropy from the wealthy as feudal, deeming charity from elites to be "sugar-coated bullets" aimed at fooling the people.
35. Jun Jing explains the scheme of paying for blood donations on the basis of government belief that a scheme of voluntary donations would not work (Jing 2011, 96).

It is true that China rates relatively low in terms of philanthropic donations. In 2010, a year of multiple natural disasters, donations reached 103.2 billion yuan, but that was only 0.26 percent of GDP. In 2009, donations reached only 0.01 percent of GDP according to the Social Science Research Institute, or 0.16 percent according to the Chinese Charity and Donations Information Center. Li Liguo, then Minister for Civil Affairs, commented that this was not only lower than the 2.0 percent in the USA but also less than Brazil's 0.5 percent and India's 0.3 percent (MCA 2012). According to an OECD report on prosocial behavior, defined as volunteering time, donating money, and helping strangers, China's scores were 14 percent, 4 percent, and 41 percent, respectively (IAST 2011). Among a group of mostly wealthy countries it ranked thirty-ninth, next to last (OECD 2011). In the 2012 World Giving Index, China came 141st out of 146 countries, "a nation which does not give a lot to charity or philanthropy" (Yu 2014). In 2013 it improved slightly to 133rd. By comparison, Taiwan was 52nd and Hong Kong, with its strong grassroots civil society organizations, 17th (WGI 2013). Moreover, in the past, China supported a large number of Buddhist clerics who, in turn, were a major force in charitable organizations.

Another reason why people are reluctant to donate to charity is the scandals over the past few years involving government-linked charities such as the China Red Cross and the Soong Ching Ling Foundation. Scandals involving those two broke in 2011 and are widely blamed for the 18.1 percent drop in donations in 2012 and a further 3.31 percent year on year drop in September 2013 (*China Daily* 2013; see also Ng 2013; Wong 2011; Wang 2011). Corporate donations are also down because of mistrust. According to the 2012 Hurun Report, donations from China's top 100 philanthropists fell by 44 percent to US$890 million. This followed a drop of 53 percent in the previous year (Armstrong and Toh 2014). However, Jia Xijin, director of the Nongovernmental Organization Research Center at Beijing's Tsinghua University, commented that suspicion about the accountability of charities had existed for some time (Wong 2011). These suspicions were not hers alone: in 2009 a Protestant woman told me that her church group had collected money for Wenchuan relief and then discussed how to make the contribution. "We first looked at the China Red Cross," she said, "and then we decided to give the money to the Hong Kong Red Cross."

The scandals prompted calls from the public and the state media for transparency of charity organization income and spending, but they were initially mostly unheeded (China Daily 2011a). The 2013 release of the *China Charity Transparency Report* found that fewer than one-third of China's charities met international standards of transparency, and the average score of its charities was forty-three out of one hundred (Chengcheng Jiang 2013). More recently a Sohu article asked where close to 5 billion yuan (over US$750 million) had gone. The money had been collected since 2005 from enterprises in Shenzhen and was meant for occupational therapy for disabled persons. An employee of the relevant unit said that about two hundred cases were handled each year, but the accounts were not open for independent inspection (Sohu 2014). Efforts are currently underway to increase the level of transparency of the Chinese Red Cross and other charitable organizations (*SCMP* 2016).

A third reason for the low individual donation level is that some government actions are a drag on charity. Much of the "voluntary" donations of time or money is, to some extent, involuntary. Party members and government employees are levied whenever donations are required, such as after a natural disaster or whenever volunteers are needed.[36] Corporations can be pressured to give as well, as they were after the Wenchuan earthquake when corporations that had declined to donate were labeled in an internet campaign as "iron roosters"—that is, tight-fisted—"from which not even one feather can be plucked" (Makinen 2009). At some universities students have a quota of "credit hours" (*gongshi*) of volunteer service to perform before graduation. They receive credit when they volunteer for Communist Youth League organized or approved projects but not for those initiated by students themselves. These hours are recorded in their dossiers, and while failure to volunteer would not prevent someone from graduating, it could affect future job prospects in the state sector.

"Coerced" donating and volunteering have a negative effect on attitudes toward party and government. A man in Beijing said that, as a public servant, he had to donate to the Wenchuan earthquake relief effort, which he did, but because he wanted his donation to express his own motivation, he then joined a queue on the street so that he could give voluntarily.

Finally, although the number of grassroots organizations, including philanthropy focused groups, have greatly increased in the past several years, by far the greater proportion of donations go to charities linked to the government. Most grassroots groups are small and have been unable to attract much funding. In 2010 they received only 1.3 percent of private donations, while government controlled charities got 58.3 percent. Many need government support to carry out their work (Global Voices 2012). One reason for the small amount going to the grass roots charities is that, being small, they are not well known. Another is that corporate donors get tax breaks when donating to government-linked groups but not for donations to nongovernment organizations. This also creates inefficiencies in the system because corporate foundations tend to carry out the work they do themselves rather than contracting it out to smaller and more specialized groups that can perform it more proficiently and cost-effectively (Browne and Mozur 2014).

One reason for the government's favoring charities linked to itself rather than letting grassroots groups carry more of the weight is because it wants to monopolize the credit for assisting society and protect its dominant position. Xu wrote that

---

36. In Xiamen I saw city government personnel picking up rubbish on a major road leading to the university. Upon inquiry I learned that an environmental maintenance inspection by a higher-up authority was to be made the following day.

there was resistance to public acknowledgement of religious organizations for their contributions to Wenchuan earthquake relief efforts at the expense of giving credit to the government, the Party, and the People's Liberation Army (Xu 2009). This is a hindrance to the growth of citizen-initiated charity. Wan writes, "They don't want other entities competing with them for the people's hearts. But if they continue holding back philanthropy, it may not win the people's hearts either" (2010). Browne and Mozur add, "Private philanthropy is just taking off in China, but it faces many practical and political hurdles. The Communist Party jealously guards its monopoly on power and is reluctant to cede too much autonomy to civil society" (2014).

A sub-type of philanthropy is donating blood. Until 1998 blood for transfusions came from two sources, compulsory donations from state employees and paying others to donate. Government units were given a quota of perhaps 5 percent of employees to donate within a given period. Other donors, mainly peasants, were recruited by blood contractors (*xuetou*), also called blood lords (*xueba*), to give blood in exchange for payment (Ye 2007). It was the latter method that led to the 1990s Henan AIDS-tainted blood scandal (Jing 2011), after which the blood collection system was reformed, placing more emphasis on voluntary donations. People were slow to react in the first few years after the reform, but donations then picked up and voluntary donations have since become sufficient to meet the needs of most locales (Ye 2007; Yang and Song 2006).

Students make up the largest category of donors, and they donate for reasons of idealism, a desire to contribute, or to build up their resumes. Workers make up the next largest group. Some of them may also have idealistic motivations for donating, but another important reason they give is that it makes them and their families eligible for free transfusions. This is especially important for reasons of cost but also because most workers are not official residents of the cities in which they work and live and so cannot access local supplies unless they have donated to them. Thus, in Beijing, outsiders donate to the mobile blood collection units more than do Beijing residents because many are students, migrant workers, or soldiers. Those who donate 200 milliliters of blood are eligible to receive up to a liter of blood within five years. Public servants are a small minority of donors; they can access medical care through their work units (Gong, Gao, and Zhang 2002).

Large corporate philanthropists have only recently emerged. When Bill Gates and Warren Buffett arranged a banquet to meet China's billionaires in 2010 and talk to them about giving away their wealth, initially many were reportedly looking forward to meeting the two, but a third of them backed away, fearing that they would be pressured at the dinner to make a pledge (Armstrong and Toh 2014). Another reason for their reluctance to contribute was fear that giving would draw attention to their riches, prompting questions about how they accumulated so much. According to a Credit Suisse–sponsored report, China's wealthy may be hiding up to $1.4 trillion in corruption-tainted money (Wan 2010). Moreover, of the super wealthy as listed in the Hurun Report,[37] only three of its ten most wealthy were among the top ten donors to charity in 2012 (Chengcheng Jiang 2013).

Over the past several years wealthy people have begun to establish personal foundations. In 2011, Cao Deren, who made his fortune making automobile window glass, set up the Heren Charitable Foundation, contributing 3.5 billion yuan, 15 percent of the shares in his Fuyao Glass Industry Group. Cao has donated 5 billion yuan since 1983 (*China Daily* 2011b). More recently, two other large foundations have been established. Alibaba CEO Jack Ma (Ma Yun) announced that he and his business partner were contributing US$3 billion to create a foundation dedicated to improving education, health, and the environment. Ma is also a director in Hong Kong film star Jet Li's One Foundation (Yu 2014). Sohu CEO Zhang Xin and her husband, Pan Shiyi, set up a US$100 million endowment to enable Chinese children from poor families to be able financially to study at elite universities abroad, beginning with a US$15 million donation to Harvard (Brown and Chen 2014; see also Zhang, Sheng, and Li 2017).

The Rich, the Powerful, the Privileged, and the Rest

I posited in Chapter 2 that civility would be negatively affected by rifts in society between various groups based on such criteria as race, ethnicity, social strata, or religion. In a society such as China, in which the notion of civility has only recently been broadly introduced, people are unlikely to feel the need to be civil toward those to whom they feel superior, and those who are treated as second-class citizens are quite likely to resent those who treat them as such. The most common rifts in Chinese society are based on rural versus urban household registration, Han versus minority ethnicities, power differentials between officials and ordinary citizens, and the large and growing levels of income and wealth inequality, all of which greatly overlap.

One privileged group is those who have urban household registration (*hukou*).[38] They have access to all the facilities, such as schools and hospitals, of the city in which they live. However, urban populations have swelled since the 1980s because of the influx of rural–urban migrants (*nongmingong*). As they constitute the major manual labor workforce and do many of the menial tasks such as rubbish collection, cities could not operate without them. However, many urban residents look down on them as dirty, poorly educated, uncouth, rustic and prone to crime. Because of the cost of urban housing they are often confined to "migrant villages" on the urban periphery. In one Beijing compound they are walled off from the rest of the city,

---

37. The Hurun Report is a sort of Fortune 500 for China.
38. Because of China's official population registration system, or *hukou*, only persons who are registered to live in a jurisdiction are official residents and hence eligible to avail themselves of services such as education, medical care, and pensions. In the past there were strong efforts to prevent rural residents from moving to the cities, but migration is now encouraged. However, becoming an official resident of a major city is very difficult.

supposedly to keep criminals from victimizing them. Police say this has reduced crime in the area, but some migrants see it as a way to isolate them. Moreover, not having household registration where they are working, which is very difficult to obtain except for the highly skilled, they are ineligible to receive the urban services that residents get such as education, medical care, or pensions. In many cities, migrants have established their own schools, though in Beijing, at least, the authorities have sometimes closed them; in 2011, for example, it closed thirty migrant schools (*SCMP* 2011; Gao 2010). According to a Renmin University survey, as a result of suffering from discrimination, migrants see themselves as on the bottom social rung and feel alienated, lonely, and powerless to chart the course of their lives (Zhuang 2013; see also French 2009). Alexander and Chan argue that the treatment of migrant workers amounts to a quasi-apartheid pass system (2006).

There is also resentment against some ethnic minorities, especially Tibetans and Uyghurs, on the basis of the large differences in their cultures and appearance from those of the majority Han. Moreover, although the central government has spent large sums on development projects in their homeland areas, there is still resistance against political inclusion into China, which raises Han complaints that Tibetans and Uyghurs are ungrateful. However, there is also condescension toward and high-handed treatment of minorities in areas where there is competition for resources—for example, Mongol herders protesting being run over and killed by Han workers driving mining company trucks across their paddocks (Reuters 2011). Mongols were also recently insulted by a popular blogger and TV show host who said their ancestors, who conquered China in the thirteenth century, were "uncivilized illiterates" who were "unable to speak Chinese fluently" (Lipes 2013).

China's level of income and wealth inequality has surged. Under the commune system, differences in family incomes were due mainly to life-cycle factors such as whether children were old enough to earn or were still young and dependent; Blecher found Gini coefficients in communes he studied were below 0.2 (1976). More recently, official Gini coefficients are in the very high 0.4 range (Chen 2012; Zhongguowang 2013; Bloomberg 2013), with other studies, which include rural data,[39] putting them as high as 0.61 (A. Li 2014) or 0.73 (Mingbao 2014). According to the latter estimates, the wealthiest 1 percent owns one-third of the property in China while the bottom quarter owns only 1 percent. Moreover, the earnings gap, already very large, continues to increase. The Chinese government's stated goal is for the minimum wage to be set at 40 percent of average regional wages, but that has not happened yet. The highest minimum wage is in Shanghai where it stands at 32.2 percent of the region's average wage. That is twice the level of Qinghai or Guizhou (Wong 2013).

Worsening this inequality in the cities is the decline in access to wage goods such as medical care and housing. Formerly provided by the state, these have

---

39. According to the *Economist*, the China's official figures are based heavily on urban incomes (2016). The article also states that rising incomes for migrant workers has incrementally reduced the rural-urban income gap.

been marketized since the reforms,[40] and although the quality of such goods has improved, the costs to consumers have risen far more rapidly than have most families' incomes. This means that families must save a high proportion of their incomes to provide for medical emergencies or housing (Mingbao 2014). However, for those on lower incomes in the larger cities, buying an apartment is out of reach, and obtaining more than basic medical care can mean waiting in line for days to get an appointment with specialist practitioners. The better off can buy appointments from scalpers, who sell them openly, or bribe hospital staff, and the well-connected can use *guanxi* to bypass the queue (Pierson 2010).

Family wealth also influences the kind of justice one receives. Shai Oster writes, "Before handing down a sentence, judges in criminal cases typically take into account how much compensation is paid to victims and their families, creating the impression that the rich can literally get away with murder" (2009). Access to higher education is also unequal. Residents of places that have many universities, such as Beijing and Shanghai, are advantaged by the higher quotas of places that residents of those cities receive. This gives them a greater chance to further their education and get a better job (see also Gao 2014). Those in provinces with large populations but few universities such as Shandong and Henan are especially disadvantaged.

Inequality manifests itself not only in income and wealth but also in power differentials between ordinary people and officials. In Karamay, Xinjiang, twenty-five officials on an inspection tour were being treated to a show performed by students in a cinema hall crammed with seven hundred people when a fire broke out. The children were ordered to stay seated while the officials and cadres exited the building. Three hundred thirty students died in the blaze, but the officials all got out safely (Cheung 1994). In 2011 a nine-seat van packed with sixty-two children and being used as a school bus in Gansu crashed into a coal truck. Twenty-one children and two adults died. The year before, despite new government regulations requiring that buses transporting primary school children have emergency exits, seat belts, and data recorders to log driver behavior, fourteen died when a farm tractor being used to transport students plunged into a river in Hunan. Not long afterward, highway patrolmen stopped an eight-seat van carrying sixty-four kindergarten students. A few days after the Gansu crash, the *21st Century Business Herald* published a chart, one side depicting numbers of student fatalities in school bus accidents, the other showing amounts particular government departments spent on cars for officials in 2010. Officials also have a penchant for building splendid offices and otherwise providing well for themselves (Wines and Johnson 2011).

Despite the glaring levels of inequality, Whyte finds general satisfaction with distributive justice in China. He argues that most have benefited from China's economic growth and are optimistic, believing that they will be better off in five years. Moreover, they do not want the state to limit incomes, though they do want it to

---

40. These were provided to urban residents by their work units; rural households had to provide their own housing, and medical care was rudimentary.

provide equality of opportunity. They also believe that talent, ability, education, and hard work are important in getting ahead, and they do not begrudge those who have become rich honestly and through skill and hard work. However, they do object to wealth that has been obtained through illicit means, *guanxi*, or access to power. Moreover, while Whyte fully accepts that there is unfairness in Chinese society (2010, 43–59), others see it as a factor in the phenomenon known as *choufu*, hatred of or resentment toward the rich (see, e.g., Lümang 2009; Beam 2015; Li 2008).

What makes unfairness all the more serious is that the notion of equality as a principle of Chinese society preached in the Maoist period has not disappeared despite Deng Xiaoping's encouraging economic growth and endorsing some to get rich before others. Li Hongmei, in a *People's Daily Online* column celebrating the number of wealthy persons in China, still felt it necessary to call for an end to "poverty mentality." By this she referred to the long-held belief that there is something inherently bad in being wealthy and called for a change in thinking to the belief that "everybody can escape poverty and get rich through efforts" (2009).

According to Zang, "there have been heated discussions on 'wealth hatred' in the mass media and Internet" since 2000. People he interviewed over a five-year period "rejected categorically any claim that people were rich because of their business acumen, risk-taking behavior, hard work, or sheer luck, instead being convinced that they had resorted to dishonesty or breaking the law in making their fortunes. Moreover, they had little respect for the rich, whom they perceived as selfish, cheap, heartless, showy, contemptuous, sneering, and most of all, that they had amassed wealth at the expense of ordinary people and had no sense of social responsibility or citizenship." He notes that the rich are referred to as "problematic rich" (2008, 59–60), while Li Hongmei reports terms such as "corrupt rich," "stinking rich and other much harsher things." The reason stems from beliefs that the rich used illicit channels to accumulate their wealth (2009; see also Pew 2012).

There are, in fact, many reasons given for resenting the rich. First, they are seen as accumulating their wealth at the expense of the poor. For example, when property is resumed for development, the compensation given to the original owners, who are generally poorer people, is far below the amount reaped by developers or the local government and officials (Wu 2009). Second, although private and corporate foundations are increasingly common, people do not see corporations and wealthy entrepreneurs as fulfilling their philanthropic responsibilities (Li 2009).

Third, the rich evade taxes. A Credit Suisse study, based on research directed by Professor Wang Xiaolu of the China Reform Foundation, estimated that in 2008, there was approximately 9.3 trillion, equal to 30 percent of GDP, in hidden income. About 63 percent was held by the top 10 percent of urban households, who also received 51.90 percent of the income pie (Credit Suisse 2010).

Fourth, there is a strong confluence between the wealthy and the politically powerful (i.e. officials and their relatives). Officials can become rich through direct corruption such as bribes and kickbacks; their children (*guan erdai*) do so through their connections (see, e.g., Koons, Gopalan, and Sidel 2013). Frank writes that 90 percent of China's billionaires are children of high-level officials, as are the same percentage of leaders in finance, construction, foreign trade, and share trading (2009). A Zhejiang Academy of Social Sciences survey found a widely held perception that the rich became so at the expense of the poor and that they did so through *guanxi* rather than through their own efforts. In addition,

- 16 percent of respondents attributed the success of the rich to their own capabilities and diligence while 74 percent attributed it to their networking abilities;
- 96 percent of respondents felt resentful toward the rich;
- 91 percent feel that rich families have "deep political backgrounds";
- 86 percent were leery of the close ties between businessmen and officials and cast doubt on the ability of the former to have succeeded without such links;
- 69 percent had negative opinions of China's *nouveaux riches*, only 3 percent viewing them positively. (cited in Martin 2010)

There are also frequent reports of stock fraud, bribery, and corruption. A survey from Renmin University found that only 5.3 percent of respondents thought that the rich had followed the law (Beech 2011).

Fifth, ordinary people have to worry about contaminated or adulterated products: pork dyed with borax and other ingredients and sold as beef or cat meat sold as rabbit (WCT 2013; Phillips 2013), wine made from chemicals and coloring agent with little or no grape content (Liu 2010), buns past their use by date that are ground up and recycled into new buns (Tan 2011), foods contaminated with heavy metals (Adams 2014), fake rice made from paper or synthetic resin (Linder 2015c), gutter oil[41] (Fisher 2013), bleached mushrooms, pork from pigs fed clenbuterol (Liu and Li 2107) and melamine added to milk.[42] In addition, there are fake or adulterated drugs sold to hospitals by bribing staff (Yan 2011), drug capsules tainted with chromium (Stanton 2013), and counterfeit airplane parts (BBC 2012).

The melamine scandal demonstrates the callousness with which public safety is treated. Fontera, one of the companies selling the milk, confirmed the contamination shortly before the Beijing Olympics, but the central government ordered that no negative news be aired that might take the shine off the event. It was thus five weeks after the confirmation before the problem was publicly announced and the products taken off shop shelves. Meanwhile, children continued to consume it. In total, over 50,000 children became ill, almost 13,000 of whom were hospitalized,

---

41. So-called gutter oil (*digouyou*) is either recycled from restaurant fryers, grease traps, sewer drains, or waste from slaughterhouses or is made from boiling down discarded animal parts, perhaps combined with expired oils. According to the *Economist*, about 10 percent of cheap restaurant meals are prepared using gutter oil.
42. Melamine is a plastic, the nitrogen content of which boosts the protein count when added to milk powder. Consumption can be deadly.

and 6 died. In addition, a popular Chinese candy was found to have traces of melamine, as were products from Cadbury, Nestlé, and Unilever (Mooney 2008; C. Liu 2014). However, the use of melamine as a bogus protein booster did not end there. Authorities found more melamine contaminated milk powder in 2011 and again in 2014, when the Guangdong Public Security Bureau announced that it had seized 25 tons of contaminated yogurt candy. Moreover, that year the United States found over forty melamine-laden food products from China (Liu 2014; see also Mooney 2008).

Unsurprisingly, a Pew report shows a rise in concern over food safety: from 2008 to 2012 the proportion of people concerned over food safety rose from 12 to 41 percent (Pew 2012; see also WCT 2013; Adams 2014). The issue is so serious that some Chinese students created a database of foods to avoid. "Throw It Out the Window" received 25,000 hits in its first two hours before it crashed (Wu and Han 2012)! However, there is a "special supply" (*tegong*) system through which officials receive supplies of safe, organically grown food. The Zhejiang government, for example, operates special "green" farms in Suichang County with all the produce going to various government departments. Special-supplies is fairly widely known and has been satirized in popular song and on Weibo[43] (WCT 2011c; Demick 2011b; Su 2011).

Sixth is the sense of privilege, condescending attitudes, and unregenerate behavior of some officials, wealthy persons, and their offspring. This is not a blanket condemnation, but because incidents of such behavior have received extensive exposure through internet chat rooms and Weibo, they are very well known and can easily confirm the thinking of those inclined to find fault with such people. Below is a sample of such incidents.

Case One: In 2009, Hu Bin, son of a wealthy Hangzhou businessman, killed Tan Zhuo, a recent graduate of Hangzhou University, while driving his car at excessive speed. Tan was in a crosswalk when the incident occurred. It outraged the public, including students at Hangzhou University and netizens, because of Hu's irresponsible behavior and because of the initial police handling of the case. First, the police grossly underreported the speed of Hu's car and denied that it had been illegally modified, which led people to believe that Hu's father had used his connections to get his son off. When challenged, the police changed their report. Second, Hu's father paid Tan's parents US$165,000 in compensation, and Hu was sentenced to three years in prison, which many regarded as lenient. Third, the person who appeared at the trial looked much heavier than Hu had immediately after the incident, leading many to believe that he was a body double (Oster 2009; see also Sant 2012).

---

43. Although the internet may not bring democracy to China anytime soon, it has made information a lot more accessible despite government censorship and attempts to steer internet discussions in preferred directions (see, e.g., Hewitt 2010).

A news commentary article on the incident referred to the killing of a fellow from a poor, rural family that had scraped together the funds to complete a degree at Hangzhou University by a teen from a rich Hangzhou family who was racing another driver at the time. It noted the coalescence of wealth and political power and stated that the behavior of the second-generation rich was creating class opposition (Di Yi Jinrong Wang 2009) in what was ideologically a classless society. The article states that the driver's photo was uploaded to the web, where it spread rapidly, triggering feelings of "millions" to cry out against the unfairness between those of different social strata and hatred of the privileged. Although the incidents of such arrogant behavior are few, because of widespread increases in internet access over the past several years, they quickly become widely known despite government censorship efforts.[44]

Case Two: In October 2010 an intoxicated Li Qiming drove his girlfriend back to her dormitory, but while leaving the Hebei University campus, he hit two young women who were in-line skating, killing one and injuring the other. Li sped away, but he was stopped by security guards at the campus gate and surrounded by about fifty people. He reportedly yelled, "Sue me if you dare. My father is Li Gang [the then deputy director of the local Baoding Public Security Bureau]" (Wang 2010). By the time attempts were made to suppress news about the incident, it had already reached internet blogs and chat rooms where it was not only kept alive but generated comment and satire. "My father is Li Gang" became a popular phrase for shirking any sort of responsibility (Wines 2011a) or for overbearing arrogance. Li was later sentenced to six years' imprisonment for drink driving, hit and run, and careless driving. The court said that the sentence was lenient because Li confessed to his crimes, and his father paid compensation of 460,000 yuan (US$69,000) to the dead girl's family and 91,000 yuan (US$13,800) to the girl with the broken leg (Barboza 2011; Wines 2010).

Case Three: Four days after the Li Qiming incident Yao Jiaxin, a 21-year-old music student at the Xian Conservatory of Music and also from a wealthy and well-connected family, accidentally struck Zhang Miao, a young peasant woman, who was riding a bicycle. Yao stopped a short distance up the road and looked back, He saw that Zhang was not seriously injured but that she was memorizing his license plate number. Fearing that "the peasant woman would be hard to deal with," he went back and stabbed her eight times, killing her.[45] Yao was stopped by police later that evening and denied killing Zhang, but four days later he turned himself in and confessed. He was tried, convicted and executed (BBC 2011a). Yao's act reportedly "fanned deep public resentment" against the second-generation rich, and sympathy

---

44. This incident occurred just before I began teaching in Beijing. Students brought it up in class and expressed their anger about it.
45. Some drivers, if they hit a pedestrian, will back up and hit the person again to ensure that s/he dies because the compensation they have to pay for killing someone is less than the cost of paying medical bills for the rest of the person's life (Sant 2015).

for the victim. A Shanghai lawyer's wife donated 540,000 yuan to Zhang's survivors, one yuan for each Weibo message sent to her husband about the case (Wines 2011a).

Although there is no evidence in this case of attempted censorship or that Yao's parents, both of whom worked for a defense sector state-owned enterprise, had tried to use political leverage to interfere as Li Qiming's father had, Yao's case nonetheless generated a high level of debate and criticism on the internet, possibly because his defense lawyer asked for leniency on the grounds that Yao was a model student, a criminal behavior expert claimed in a TV interview that Yao's actions were involuntary because of his training in repetitive actions while learning to play the piano, and one of Yao's friends saying that she, too, would have stabbed Zhang if she had seen that Zhang was trying to memorize her license plate number (Chen 2011; Li 2011). Netizens were incensed by what they perceived as the privileged rallying around the privileged.

Case Four: In 2011, 15-year-old Li Tianyi, the son of a general, had an unlicensed, customized BMW and had already chalked up thirty-two traffic violations. He and a friend were driving their sports cars when they became annoyed at a couple in another car. When the cars stopped, Li and his friend got out and pulled the couple from their car. According to witnesses, they then beat them for about three minutes while the couple's child looked on. The father's nose and right eye were injured, and he had to have eleven stiches to his head. After the beating, as the boys tried to flee, Li yelled, "Who will dare call the police?" However, they were stopped by bystanders, then arrested (*SCMP* 2011; BBC 2011b). The BBC inferred that there were attempts to cover up the story, citing a *Legal System Evening News* story that did not mention the incident itself but referred to it on a micro blog— "Perhaps a way the paper tells its readers to look it up on the micro blog since we [the paper] have orders not to mention the assault." Li served one year in a government correctional facility (Zhang 2013).

Two years later Li and some friends were in a bar where, after drinking and singing, they left with one of the hostesses. Though intoxicated, the hostess realized that she was alone with several men and tried to leave, but Li and his friends overpowered her and took her to a hotel room where they repeatedly raped her. The men were later arrested and tried. According to the court, Li was the main perpetrator and showed no remorse. He was sentenced to ten years in prison (Tatlow 2013). Before the trial, to distract attention from her son's behavior, Li's mother filed a claim against the bar accusing the manager of pimping and extortion; a court dismissed the claim (Zhang 2013).

Case Five: In this case, no one was hurt, but it shows the reckless abandon of some of the rich. This case involves two of the four "Beijing playboys" (*jingcheng sishao*) a name revived from an early twentieth century group of young men known for their wealth and romantic pursuits.[46] The present group consists of four wealthy

---

46. These four included the sons of former president Yuan Shikai and Manchu warlord Zhang Zuolin, a cousin of Pu Yi, the last emperor, and a Peking opera aficionado.

sons[47] of wealthy fathers, unrelated but all with the surname Wang, who are known for their love of luxury cars and actresses. In 2010, after an argument, Wang Shuo pulled a gun on Wang Ke then sped away in his car, Wang Ke in hot pursuit. The chase resulted in both cars crashing and Wang Shuo reversing into Wang Ke's Audi, setting it alight and causing 199,000 yuan in damage. This occurred in Wangfujing, a very crowded and busy part of central Beijing. Moreover, it was later discovered that both cars had license plates they were not entitled to have, one from the Central Guard Bureau, the security unit charged with keeping the top leaders safe, the other from the PLA general staff headquarters (Chan 2011).[48]

In a later incident, Wang Shuo thought that someone in another car was trying to take a photograph of his Bugatti. The woman in the other car, a reporter, wrote that the Bugatti driver "was so crazy, and punched both me and my husband. We had to call to police." Wang reportedly later phoned the couple and apologized. Despite the apology, netizens remained dissatisfied (D. Wang 2013).

In addition to the above cases, a sufficient number of the wealthy flaunt their wealth, arousing resentment on that basis alone. For example, in 2009, twenty-one bachelor billionaires and twenty-two single women attended a ball in Beijing that carried an entry price of 100,000 yuan (US$14,650) per person. The men were all clients of the Shanghai-based Golden Bachelors, a matchmaking agency for wealthy Chinese men (Reuters 2009). A wedding in Wenzhou had a procession of twenty-six luxury cars: four Lamborghinis, four Ferraris, eight Rolls-Royces, and ten Bentleys (WCT 2011a). And the son of China's richest man showed off a picture online of his dog wearing a gold Apple watch on each front paw (Beam 2015).

The rich drive expensive cars and sport luxury products and name-brand accessories such as handbags and watches (WCT 2011b). One manifestation of resentment toward the rich is that their pricy cars are at risk of being vandalized— for example, through *huache*, scratching the side panel with a key as one walks by, though this is more often done to the cars of the middle class as those of the rich are generally parked in more secure spots. The resentment against them can also result in the rich being kidnapped and even killed (Frank 2015; Zang 2008).

A survey by the Zhejiang Academy of Social Science shows that 96 percent of respondents resent the rich, 23 percent strongly. Over half (57 percent) believe that the wealth gap will grow, 9 percent by a large amount. Shanghai University Professor Qiu Liping believes that "the wealth gap is a much more serious problem nationwide," however, people hate "those who are immorally rich" rather than the rich in general (Wu 2009).

As Xi Jinping's anticorruption drive and the amassed wealth of Bo Xilai show (Anderlini 2013; Page and Bisserbe 2013), graft is endemic through the highest

---
47. For example, one owns a Boeing 737.
48. License plates in China generally indicate the provincial level administrative district in which they are registered, but in addition there are plates that designate police, military police, various military services, and regions and embassies. Having such plates deters police from stopping the drivers.

reaches of government and Party officialdom,[49] and there are myriad reports of corruption involving lower-level officials. Also in 2013, exposés came of two lower officials, Cai Bin, an urban management official in Guangdong nicknamed Uncle House because he had accumulated twenty-two homes, valued at an estimated US$6 million, on a monthly salary of only 10,000 yuan (*China Daily* 2012), and Yang Decai, the Work Safety Administration head in Shaanxi, nicknamed Brother Watch. Yang, inspecting the site of a bus crash in which thirty-six people died, was seen smiling in a newscast and wearing a very expensive wristwatch. A "human flesh search"[50] ensued, identifying him, and a subsequent investigation revealed that he owned eleven luxury watches, including a Montblanc (US$5,000) and an Omega (US$10,000). In addition, he had other property worth 5.04 million yuan "from unexplained sources" (*Telegraph* 2013; Osnos 2012). Yang was sentenced to fourteen years in prison, Cai to eleven and a half years. Resentment toward those in power is strongest toward officials at the local level as they deal most directly with the public and the public is most likely to know about their peccadilloes and experience their highhandedness (Forsythe 2015). Accounts of their deeds often spread very rapidly through China's very active internet community, while information on higher-up scandals from foreign sources is more difficult to access.

Not only are officials seen to be corrupt; there are many causes célèbres of them behaving imperiously toward ordinary people, as the following two examples demonstrate. In 2008, as an 11-year-old girl passed by his table in a restaurant, Lin Jiaxiang, Communist Party secretary of the Shenzhen Marine Affairs Bureau, asked her where the toilets were. He then got up and followed her, and, according to the girl, grabbed her by the neck and shoulders and tried to force her into the men's toilet. She escaped his grasp and ran back to her father, who confronted the clearly drunk Lin when he returned. According to state media, Lin retorted, "Yes, I did it. So what? How much do you want? Just tell me. I'll give you the money." He then tried to push the father away and shouted, "Do you know who I am? I am from the Ministry of Transportation in Beijing. I have the same seniority as the Mayor of your city. So what if I grabbed the neck of a small child? You people count for fart! If you dare challenge me, just wait and see how I will deal with you" (Macartney 2008).

Another well-known case is that of Deng Yujiao, a 21-year-old waitress who stabbed a Party official as he attempted to rape her. The official died of his wounds, and Deng was arrested for voluntary manslaughter. However, a blogger learned of her case, and his reports brought her not only popular support but also a lawyer and enough publicity to prevent the authorities from railroading her. Local officials

---

49. See also Barboza 2012; Bloomberg 2012.
50. *Renrou sousuo*; a photo of Yang was uploaded to the internet where someone who noted the watch and had seen other photos of Yang wearing other luxury watches recognized him and made his identity public. Human flesh searches can be used to expose corrupt officials and official misbehaviour as well as to embarrass those who commit uncivil acts (Levine 2012).

imposed censorship, tried to cut off access to the trial site and intimidated journalists, but in the end Deng was acquitted and judged to have acted in self-defense (Wines 2009). Those involved in these cases and those in the several pages above are tiny in number compared with the Chinese population. However, when it is commonly believed that the rich and powerful are arrogant and that official corruption is widespread, these stories are a powerful reconfirmation of those beliefs (see Jacob 2011).

To summarize, some aspects of civility in China are improving, especially in coastal cities that have benefited from economic development and where people are generally better off economically and educationally. Sustained campaigns, such as getting people to queue before the Beijing Olympics, have also been a factor, but the inequality and the condescension illustrated above are impediments to the development of a more positive form of compatriotism that could make strangers into fellow citizens deserving civil treatment. However, for a variety of reasons that I will discuss in Chapter 6, these improvements are uneven in China as a whole. In the next chapter I examine the level of civility in Taiwan and offer an explanation of the process that created a society for itself in which people's mutual identification with Taiwan made them consociates in each other's eyes.

5
Civility in Taiwan

That Taiwan became a society in which people treat others with civility is demonstrated by the impressions of visitors, in particular those from China. As I showed in a previous paper (Schak 2009b), this change in Taiwan society[1] began to appear in the early 1990s and coincided with democratization and the freedom to establish grassroots organizations. This chapter will examine the state of Taiwan's civility, explore how the Taiwanese and others view it, and then trace the path it took to move from being a territory lacking civility and occupied by myriad inward-looking small communities to a civil society with a strong sense of social unity and identification, what I call a society for itself.

The State of Civility in Taiwan

The negative behavior referred to in Taiwan's previous civility campaigns is relatively infrequent now. During two short trips in 1995, and confirmed by several longer stays between 2004 and 2008 and shorter ones since then, not littering seems to have entered the public consciousness. Public areas such as sidewalks and parks are cleaner. During the 1996 presidential election campaign, the Democratic Progressive Party (DPP) made it a point to clean up the sites after their rallies. Not to be outdone, officials of the New Party declared that they, too, must demonstrate public morality by cleaning up. Spitting has become much less frequent, even for betel chewers; in the past they spat the red juice onto the ground, but they now receive a plastic cup to spit into with each box of betel quids, which most then dump into rubbish bins after use. Service in commercial establishments and government offices is friendly and helpful, and people quite willingly give directions when asked.

Traffic became much more orderly in the mid-1990s following the sustained and successful campaign ordered by then Mayor Chen Shui-bian referred to above. Traffic death rates are still high in Taiwan, though they have significantly declined since the 1990s. According to Taiwan's Road Traffic Safety Commission, in 2009

---

1. I use Taiwan rather than Taiwanese society to denote the society that existed in Taiwan which included Mainlanders as well as Taiwanese and first peoples.

Taiwan had 17.5 road deaths per 100,000 people (2009).[2] Queuing is very common, as is letting people out of elevators before trying to get in, holding doors, and other common courtesies that show consideration for others. People have also adopted a habit of standing on the right side as they ride escalators, allowing those who want to walk up or down more quickly to pass them on the left. Passenger behavior on the Taipei Mass Rapid Transit system (MRT) is a good indicator of the level of civility there. The public has taken to heart a public education campaign explaining, prior to its opening, the rules of subway behavior, from no eating, drinking, gum chewing or smoking to respecting the seats near the exits reserved for the elderly, the physically impaired, children, or women with children or carrying packages (Anru Lee 2007).

Efforts to curtail smoking and limit where people smoked began in 1984 with the establishment of the John Tung Foundation, an organization dedicated to tobacco control, mental health, and nutrition. It pressured the government to enact legislation to restrict smoking in public and indoor areas, to control the promotion of tobacco products, and to ban smoking in hospitals. It also organized a "Quit Smoking Alliance" and compiled a textbook about smoking that contained a photo of lungs blackened by the practice (Jiang Chengxuan 2013). Adult smoking rates fell from 32.5 percent in 1990 to 19.1 percent in 2011 (Yau n.d.). Moreover, there was a noticeable change in smokers' attitudes; rather than simply lighting up wherever and whenever they wanted to, they began to defer to non-smokers and to make efforts not to subject nonsmokers to second-hand smoke.

At least partially thanks to Taiwan's socially engaged Buddhist groups, Taiwanese are generous contributors to philanthropic causes. Foguang Shan (Buddha's Light) began operating mobile clinics, schools, orphanages, and old folks' homes in the 1960s. Taiwan's largest Buddhist group, Ciji,[3] has several million members (i.e., persons who make regular donations) and raises hundreds of millions annually. It operates six hospitals and many schools in Taiwan, runs a large bone marrow bank, and is engaged in charity, disaster relief, and environmental cleanup and recycling. It engages in similar activities outside Taiwan through the forty-seven branches it has abroad; in doing so it assiduously avoids pressuring recipients of its assistance to accept Buddhism (Montlake 2010). Three other socially engaged Buddhist groups, as well as Presbyterians and Catholics, are also very active in philanthropy and social service.

A 2010 MasterCard survey found Taiwanese to be the most generous donors in the greater China area. Two-thirds of those surveyed replied that they were willing to buy products online from companies that donate to charities; just over half planned to donate or participate in a charitable event in the next six months and 11 percent said that they would donate 5 percent of their income (Yang 2010). Although Taiwan's GDP per capita is lower than that of Japan, donations per capita

---

2. Cited in Jsphfrtz 2013, which also states that, Japan's ratio was 3.85/100,000 and South Korea's 11.3.
3. The Buddhist Compassionate Merit Association; in Taiwan spelled Fo-chiao Tzu-chi Kung-te Hui.

after the 1999 earthquake[4] were significantly higher than those by the Japanese after the 1995 Kobe earthquake (Moon 2013). Moreover, Taiwan's business community donated much more per capita than its Chinese counterpart to the relief efforts following the 2008 Sichuan earthquake (Lin 2011), and of the ninety-three countries that contributed to post-Fukushima disaster relief, Taiwan's donation effort was sustained, had a high participation rate, and provided the highest total contribution, over 20 billion Japanese yen (NT$68.4 billion; Moon 2013). Several Taiwanese philanthropists are on the Forbes list. Of the four on the 2013 list, two donated money for buildings at their alma maters, one to build four new public libraries, and one to help two hospitals upgrade their levels of medical expertise (Taipei Times 2014).

The level of volunteerism has increased over the past two decades. Interior Ministry data shows a 123 percent rise from 1996 to 2005, and in 2003, one person in seven was a volunteer (Wang 2006, 190–92). More recent data from the World Giving Index examines giving on the bases of volunteering time, helping strangers, and donating money. Based on a five-year running average, in 2013 Taiwan ranked 47th out of 135 countries: 62nd in terms of helping strangers, 31st for giving money, and 60th for donating time (CAF 2014). In addition to volunteering for philanthropic work, people also serve as guides and at information desks in hospitals, museums, the MRT, and at District Offices (*qu gongsuo*), where citizens transact business with local government.

Taiwan also has many NGOs and foundations with missions to assist disadvantaged groups (*ruoshi tuanti*). For example, the Garden of Hope provides shelters for women in danger of domestic violence and fights human trafficking, the Eden Foundation helps those with disabilities, and the Genesis Foundation assists persons in vegetative states. Catholic and Presbyterian charities assist AIDS victims, foreign workers and foreign brides.

People in Taiwan are generous blood donors. Until 1974, all of Taiwan's blood donations for medical use were from paid donors. However, fearing the risk of spreading disease, a group led by the then Red Cross Taiwan chapter chairman, Tsai Pei-Huo, formed the Blood Donation Association of the Republic of China (TBSF 2008). Its donation rate in 2013 was 78.9 donations per thousand people, twice the median rate for high-income countries (A. Hsiao 2013, 3) and substantially more than sufficient for Taiwan's blood product needs.

There are still areas of incivility in Taiwan, for example the treatment of foreign brides. Over the past few decades, farmers and less educated blue-collar workers have found it difficult to attract Taiwanese women to marry them, a situated exacerbated by Taiwan's skewed sex ratio at birth.[5] They have therefore resorted to seeking

---

4. A devastating quake occurred on September 21, 1999; killing 2,415 and injuring 11,305.
5. Yang Wen-shan, personal communication. Poston and Yang calculate that between 1983 and 2010, half a million more males than females reached marriage age. This is not because of government policy—indeed the government would welcome a higher birth rate. It is what a colleague described as an "invisible one-child policy" (*yinxing de yitai zhengce*) because decisions to limit births are made by the couples themselves.

brides from Southeast Asia, especially Vietnam, or China. However, popular prejudices arose against Chinese women, who were perceived by some as a fifth column,[6] and against Vietnamese women based on their lack of knowledge of Chinese, which was seen to limit their ability to help their children with their studies, and on the possibility of their having been exposed to Agent Orange during the Vietnam War (Tsai 2011, 262; Yen 2005). These prejudices, particularly those against the Vietnamese, have ameliorated over the past decade.

How Taiwanese and Others See Civility in Taiwan

Surveys on civility in Taiwan show that Taiwanese are not completely satisfied with their compatriots' behavior. A 2007 Taiwan Environmental Information Center survey identified four "large environmental tumors" caused by incivility: littering in general, litter from cigarette butts and betel juice stains, the poor standard of cleanliness at scenic spots, and the posting of small advertisements on walls and utility poles (TEIC 2007). A Ministry of Education survey on doing a daily good deed returned slightly more positive results; 47 percent of respondents felt that the people around them were uncivil, while 44 percent disagreed; 44 percent said they helped others, and 56 percent believed that many of their acquaintances did as well; 29 percent had participated in community benefit projects and 66 percent in activities to assist in international disasters (CNA 2010; Ministry of Education 2010). A blog about office staff demonstrates that Taiwanese have extended civility to other grievances. It reports complaints about fellow workers taking pens, pencils, and the like from other workers' desks and not returning them, coughing or sneezing without covering their mouth or nose, and other breaches of personal etiquette (Chaizu daren 2011).

While Taiwanese are still critical of their level of civility, foreigners have a more positive assessment. Professor Thomas Gold writes that several Inter-University Program students took time off from their studies in Beijing to visit Taiwan. They were impressed with Taiwan's clean roads, orderly queuing, people speaking softly and replying "you're welcome" to "thank you." They also

> noted the friendliness and hospitality of people in Taiwan, strangers on the street who offered directions, explained the subway system and even bought tickets for them. One reported, "Taiwan has law, reason, humanity, civility and trees—five things the Mainland lacks, not to mention democratically elected leaders, a valid constitution, and a free press. . . . Taiwanese hold doors for strangers, allow subway/bus passengers to get off before getting on, care about the environment, and respond to traffic accidents with CPR and calls for ambulances rather than asking, '*sile meiyou*' ["Is she or he dead?"]. (Gold 2013)

---

6. This is based on suspicion that their loyalties lie with China. By marrying someone from Taiwan they can become citizens and vote in elections; the fear is that if a vote were taken on unification or independence, they could tip the balance in favor of the former.

Hasselle reports that Taiwan is an easier place to visit than China because it is much cleaner, the restrooms have toilet paper and soap, people don't spit, babies are taken to toilets rather than being allowed to relieve themselves on public streets, and people obey traffic rules, which is especially helpful for pedestrians (2014). Rovnick adds that Taiwanese don't push others while walking (2012).

Chinese tourism to Taiwan has brought mixed results. The majority of Chinese visitors come with tour groups for short visits of four to five days and endure a hectic round of museums, scenic and cultural sites, restaurants, and gift shops. Some tour leaders even confiscate tourists' passports, preventing them from venturing out on their own, though there are also reports of tourists who forgo evening sightseeing to watch news and free-wheeling political talk shows on Taiwan television. While the tourism industry welcomes their contribution to incomes, on the negative side these visitors have increased Taiwanese enmity toward China because of the lack of manners and rudeness of some of their number (A. Jacobs 2011). Moreover, short-visit tourists rarely see much of everyday Taiwan society or meet ordinary residents.

However, in 2011 Taiwan introduced a Free Independent Traveler program that allowed tourists to make their own individual arrangements. These tourists were allowed to stay for longer periods, wander through Taiwan, and mingle with locals. What such tourists found was pleasantly surprising: "The elbowing and pushing so prevalent in mainland China's cities is conspicuous by its absence. In Taiwan, the young yield to the elderly on public transport, while the rich apologize after having accidentally trampled on the have-not's foot" (Kastner 2011).

The well-known Chinese writer and blogger Han Han wrote a stirring account of his first trip to Taiwan. A friend traveling with him broke his glasses and was given a free pair by an optical shop proprietor. Han left his cell phone in a taxi; the cab driver, discovering it after dropping him off, returned it to the hotel from which Han had taken the cab, and refused a reward for doing so. Everyone Han met during his short trip impressed him with their genuineness and kindness. He describes a deep sense of frustration that where he came from people were first taught for a few decades to be savage and contentious then for a few decades to be avaricious and selfish. He regrets that the generation before his destroyed their culture and its traditional virtues, interpersonal trust, beliefs and common ground, and in so doing failed to construct a beautiful new world (Han 2012).

Sociologist Chen Chih-jou of Academia Sinica surveyed groups of Chinese scholars and students (N=1720) visiting Taiwan for stays of one to two months between 2008 and 2010, long enough for them to get out and about and to encounter ordinary locals in natural settings. He writes:

> They all came to Taiwan with some stereotypic views: they had absorbed the yearning in the Chinese history books for Taiwan [to (re)unite with the motherland]; they saw Taiwan as a highly-developed economy with lots of tall buildings, beauty spots such as Mt. Ali and Sun Moon Lake, and propagandized notions of its raucous liberal democracy. After two months in Taiwan, they had abandoned these

stereotypes. They saw Taiwan's economy and infrastructure as "okay." Nor had its democratic governance made a deep impression. On the contrary, most, by utter coincidence, were impressed by what they saw as its orderliness and the temperament of the Taiwanese people, that is, its social norms, its values, its grass-roots organizations, and its social relationships. (2008, 340)

Chen found that almost all (96 percent) regarded the Taiwanese, both ordinary people and those in service industries, as friendly and polite, orderly and conscientious. Visitors observed them separating rubbish, obeying traffic regulations, and not eating or drinking on public transport. Interviewees often used phrases such as "welcoming and polite," "modest and agreeable," "take care of those in need" and "gender equality," and they saw Taiwan as an egalitarian and harmonious society. People treated others warmly and civilly regardless of status differences among them. They were happy to help others, including strangers. Scholars were particularly impressed with culture in Taiwan. In ceremonies and religion, architecture, the arts, traditional characters, and the mannerly way people treated each other, they felt they were seeing traditional Chinese culture again, a culture that they felt had been lost in China. They were also impressed by Taiwan's civil society, the number of volunteers in various sorts of organizations, and people's trust in institutions, its pluralism, and its multiple voices, with everyone allowed to express their opinions (Chen 2008, 2010).

The State of Taiwan Society in the Early KMT Period: The Baseline of Change

I've often heard Taiwanese say that the Japanese colonial regime brought order and civility to Taiwan, that the Japanese were masters who governed strictly according to rules they set down and insisted that all follow the law. The orderly and polite behavior of Japanese lends some credibility to this claim, and it may have been to some extent true in urban areas. However, it is more likely the product of nostalgia, of the difference between the behavior of the Japanese colonizers and the chaotic and highly repressive first decades of KMT rule, than an accurate description of the state of Taiwan society as a whole under the Japanese.

I saw little evidence of civility in Taiwan during my first sojourn there, two and a half years in the early 1960s. It is true that Taiwan society had endured considerable trauma and even desperation from the early 1940s. In the latter years of World War II the Japanese government requisitioned much of the food produced to feed its military, causing hunger among the civilian population. In addition, American warplanes carried out bombing and strafing raids in 1943 and 1944, as evidenced by the pockmarked outer walls of buildings and the numerous small air-raid shelters still visible in 1960 (see also Tseng and Chung 2015). The arrival of the KMT government from China in 1945 brought further disruption. At the time it took control, if seen in the context of China, Taiwan would have been its most developed province in both hard and soft infrastructure and human capital. However, the KMT treated Taiwan as a colony and refused the Taiwanese any role in governance. KMT soldiers, being armed, often simply took what they wanted from the locals (Kerr 1965), and government officials treated them condescendingly. Malgovernance and highhandedness led to the 228 (February 28) Incident during which many were killed.[7] China's post–World War II inflation also spread to Taiwan, destroying the value of its currency. From 1948 to 1950, 2 million people from the Chinese mainland, many soldiers but also public servants and officials, business families, intellectuals and ordinary people fleeing from the communists, arrived in Taiwan, quickly swelling its six million population. The transfer of the Republic of China government in 1949 ushered in a 40-year period of "White Terror," during which those suspected of opposing the government or of being communists were imprisoned, executed, or simply disappeared.

Such tumult certainly had significant effects on Taiwan society. It would be remarkable if the Japanese, in what was really only three decades (they spent much of the first two pacifying the population) had been able to bring civility to a poor, largely illiterate society only for this to be reversed by fifteen years of KMT malgovernance and ethnic strife. Such deep sociocultural change could not have occurred so rapidly. The nostalgia Taiwanese felt for Japanese rule was more likely the result of subsequent KMT mistreatment and misrule.

Another reason for the lack of civility in the early 1960s—recall that Baron's op-ed was published in 1963—was the "plate of loose sand" nature of Taiwan society. In 1950, to pick a round date that reflects the year that the governments on both sides of the Taiwan Straits began to consolidate their rule, Taiwan's population consisted of non-Han indigenous peoples, Hoklo, Hakka, and Mainlanders. The indigenous peoples were further divided into tribal groups, each with its own territory, and having no sense of common identity as "first peoples" at that time. The Hakka and Hoklo (Taiwanese) were each divided by village community or faction, these being the primary foci of identity, and to a lesser degree by dialect.[8] They felt little if any loyalty or emotional attachment to those outside their communities. Mainlanders were divided by the area of China from which they came, which connotes differences in language[9] and cuisine. Mainlanders' work units also reinforced divisions among them. Many military units were local militia from various areas in China, and in Taiwan, their family members lived together in "dependents' villages" (*juancun*). Many government bureaus also had housing allocations for their workers, which

---

7. Estimates at the time put the death toll at between 10,000 to 30,000 (T. Durdin 1947; P. Durdin 1947), however recent scholarship puts the numbers much lower, around 1000 (Wu 2015).
8. Among the Hoklo, the dialect difference is relatively minor and does not seriously affect mutual intelligibility. The difference may be greater among the five Hakka dialects spoken in Taiwan; a Hakka friend told me that he and his wife, both Hakka, spoke Mandarin at home because of dialect difference.
9. Although both the KMT and China governments insist, for the purpose of national unity, that there is only one Chinese language, this is linguistically incorrect. There are eight recognized Chinese languages, each of which has myriad dialects. The languages are not mutually intelligible, and even some dialectical differences are great enough to cause difficulties in understanding.

meant that bureau employees lived together in compounds and worked together at the office. Moreover, at least through the 1960s, most Mainlanders believed government claims that it would reconquer the mainland and that they would be able to return to their homes and kin. They thus made little effort to mix with those from other places or to find new friends.[10] As people associated mainly with those in their own communities, strangers remained strangers and society remained simply a congeries of small introverted populations. People had little sense of common identity with or obligation toward others.

Because of the malgovernance noted above, there were considerable tensions between Mainlanders and Taiwanese. Despite some Taiwanese having welcomed the arrival of the KMT government, Mainlander officials distrusted them, suspecting that, having been under Japanese rule for fifty years, they were disloyal. Elite Mainlanders regarded themselves as culturally superior, but the less educated Mainlander soldiers who went to Taiwan were also condescending toward the Taiwanese. The Taiwanese, understandably, strongly resented the autocratic regime imposed on them by the KMT government and the disdain of the Mainlanders. Moreover, the government, assuming that the Taiwanese had been subject to Nipponization during the colonial period, sought to eradicate any Japanese influence and not only to re-Sinicize them but to exterminate any separate Taiwanese identity.

In 1946 schools began to teach in Mandarin and banned Japanese language use in newspapers and magazines, an act that rendered those educated only in Japanese illiterate. In an assault on Taiwanese dignity, non-Mandarin languages were declared to be dialects (*fangyan* or, colloquially, *tuhua*), the Chinese terms being more pejorative than the English and implying inferiority to the national language. In 1956 primary and secondary school students were forbidden to speak in "dialect" and could be fined or worse for doing so.[11] In 1965 this ban was extended to offices of the Taiwan Provincial Government (Hsiau 1997, 305–7). When television began in 1962, TV channels were restricted in how much Taiwanese language content they could air. These bans were rescinded when martial law was lifted in 1987, but their effect had been such that when more Taiwanese language programming was allowed, networks had difficulty finding people who could read the news in Hoklo or Hakka. School curricula taught Chinese history, geography, culture, and civilization to the almost-complete exclusion of information about Taiwan. This bias was paralleled by the presentation of "facts" about the Republic of China in the annual official yearbooks (*nianjian*) that pretended that the ROC government still ruled the Chinese mainland (Chang 2015). The government also ridiculed Taiwanese folk religious practices as superstition and tried to persuade Taiwanese to limit the size

---

10. The carpenter father of a friend whose parents came from Wenzhou worked with Wenzhou carpenters, and in the 1970s over twenty years after he had come to Taiwan, he still could not speak or understand Mandarin.
11. According to Taiwanese, students were fined only if they used Hoklo or Hakka. Speakers of mainland dialects were not.

and frequency of the feasts families held to celebrate the birthdays of their gods and to renew ties with kin and neighbors. The government said this was to limit consumption in a time of economic stringency, but it was widely interpreted as aimed at suppressing the expression of Taiwanese identity. At the same time, individuals' official identities consisted of name, date of birth, and native place.[12] This was to remind Mainlanders to continue the struggle to recover mainland China so they could return home, but it also emphasized the division between Mainlanders and Taiwanese.

Two other factors contributed to people's focus on community and family. First, in the 1950s, Taiwan was poor, and for most, regardless of which ethnic group they belonged to, their overriding concern was to make a living. It was not until the 1980s that workers felt prosperous enough to decline overtime work because they wanted more leisure time for themselves or to spend with their families.[13] Second, before the death of Chiang Kai-shek, Taiwan had an archetypical subject political culture: the KMT government governed, the masses voicelessly followed, and dissension was prohibited. Moreover, the 228 Incident was met with overwhelming repressive force, decimating the Taiwanese elite (Phillips 2003), and was followed soon afterward by the White Terror period. A call for democracy in 1960 by liberal intellectuals associated with the magazine *Free China* resulted in its publisher, Lei Chen (Lei Zhen), being jailed on sedition charges.[14] The message was clear: ordinary people had no role in how the country was run. They should mind their own business and not concern themselves with national affairs.

Over the next four decades, Taiwan gradually became what I call a society for itself, that is, one in which people's social horizons expanded from their small communities of insiders to Taiwan as a whole and in which they felt a common identity as members with other persons, mostly strangers, of that imagined community. Seeing them as fellow human beings and as sharing a common Taiwanese identity created a basis for affording them civil treatment. In the next section I will explicate the events that brought this development about. These include phenomena associated with modernization and industrialization, cultural and social movements, a community project associated with a Buddhist organization, and political struggles that eventuated in Taiwan's democratization. Through these events, the people in Taiwan created a society in which the citizenry could feel a sense of ownership. They also weakened the KMT colonial government's[15] hegemony over education and the definition of the country such that the majority Taiwanese could reclaim their dignity by having their history, geography, customs, and language respected rather than disparaged.

---

12. The term used was *jiguan*, i.e., the county where one's ancestors were from.
13. This is based on interviews with workers and bosses carried out in 1983–1984 and in the early 1990s.
14. Lei was a Mainlander. That he involved Taiwanese in this effort made the government even more upset.
15. I use this term to refer to the period 1945–1988 when Chiang Kai-shek and later his son, Chiang Ching-kuo, were the authoritarian rulers of Taiwan. See J. Jacobs 2012.

Taiwan's Transformation to a Society for Itself

The broadest set of influences creating this change were various forces of modernization that took people out of their small communities and into the wider world where they met and mixed with others, enabling them to see themselves as part of Taiwan rather than just their home communities. In the late 1950s, after several years of import-substitution industrialization manufacturing simple consumer products that had previously been imported from Japan, then—post-1945—from China, Taiwan embarked on a path of export-led growth. This entailed local entrepreneurs creating thousands of small and medium enterprises, the establishment of export-processing zones in which product components from overseas companies were assembled then re-exported, and foreign investment in labor-intensive industries. These activities created hundreds of thousands of jobs, and from very high unemployment rates in the early 1950s, Taiwan achieved full employment by 1970. Employers were so hungry for workers that they would go to schools several months before the end of the school year to recruit students about to graduate. Some factories recruited married women, providing buses to transport them from their homes to their workplaces and back. Many male school-leavers became apprentices and continued work until they reached age twenty, when they had to complete two to three years of military service. Female school-leavers worked in factories until they married, frequently changing jobs to move to a new town and see a different part of Taiwan.

Paddy-rice agricultural being very labor-intensive, adult men initially remained at home to farm. However, as technology improved, handheld tractors and chemical herbicides and pesticides became available. These decreased the amount of energy and time required to farm and increased the slack periods between planting and harvesting, which allowed men to leave the light farming tasks to their wives while they sought day labor work in the cities and increased their family incomes.

As Taiwan's economy grew, so, too, did participation in education. Before 1968, Taiwan had only six years of compulsory education, but in poorer rural areas many girls did not attend school regularly. As factory work became available, however, students needed higher levels of education if they were to be employable. Private post-primary schools helped fill the shortfall of places in the public system in both vocational and nonvocational education, and they continued to do so after 1968 at the senior middle school level when compulsory education was extended through grade nine. Moreover, many private and public schools ran evening classes, allowing students to work during the day and attend classes in the evenings. This enabled students from poorer households to continue their education while contributing economically to their families. Moreover, while doing so they were able to meet fellow students from outside their home areas, increasing the number of schoolmates (*tongxue*) they had, and thus their social capital.[16]

---

16. The schoolmate tie is very important in Taiwan. It can lead to a lifetime of mutual assistance and friendship.

As Taiwan's economy developed, rural–urban migration increased rapidly. In early 1970s Taibei the population comprised approximately 30 percent each of Mainlanders and Taibei natives and 40 percent migrants from elsewhere in Taiwan. Overall, the percentage of population in cities increased from 20.7 percent in 1950 to 50.2 percent in 1985 and 53.3 percent in 1988 (Speare, Liu, and Tsay 1988, 18; Speare 1992, 213). Thus, several million people uprooted themselves from their villages to work, study, and live with strangers, broadening their social horizons in the process.

Taiwan's industrialization assisted the development of civility in other ways. First, it was a famous case of "growth with equity" as economic gains were relatively equally spread (Fei, Ranis, and Kuo 1979). Income inequality, measured by the Gini coefficient, fell from 0.5 in 1960 to 0.35 by the late 1960s, 0.3 in the late 1970s, rising slightly to 0.32 in 1990 (Wang Feng 2011, 3). As full employment was realized, wages began to rise. From NT$5670 in 1960, the average per capita income grew to NT$14,827 by 1970 and NT$77,004 in 1980 (DGBAS). Higher incomes gradually released people from having to devote themselves single-mindedly to earning more money and allowed them to indulge in discretionary spending. From the mid-1970s, buses of mostly elderly people enjoying themselves on tours or religious pilgrimages to visit Taiwan's scenic spots, famous temples, and other cultural sites were a common sight on Taiwan's highways. For many, particularly women, these tours were a rare opportunity to leave the area around their natal or conjugal villages. Touring increased people's awareness that the area in which they lived was only a small part of a larger Taiwan. From 1980 working people had more leisure time as average hours worked per month fell from 216 to 197 in 1990 and 180 in 2000 (Lau 2012, 20). Moreover, the workweek dropped from five and a half to five days, which swelled domestic tourism opportunities.

Another phenomenon that helped people get to know each other was the growth of the two above-mentioned socially engaged Buddhist organizations, Foguang Shan and Ciji. Foguang Shan was the first to experience rapid growth. Its undertakings ranged well beyond meditation, study, and chanting, extending to more social and cooperative pursuits such as community and charitable activities. Ciji also engaged in such activities, even more so than Foguang Shan, but it was much smaller at the time.

However, a dramatic event occurred in the 1980s that attracted a large number of people to become part of a cause, when Master Cheng-yen, Ciji's founder, announced that she wanted to build a hospital in the Ciji headquarter city of Hualian. Hualian is located on the sparsely populated, remote, and less easily accessible eastern side of Taiwan, and although there were already two hospitals there, both were small and limited in the services they could provide. Moreover, intending patients had to pay an upfront registration fee when seeking treatment, effectively shutting out the poor. At the time, Ciji had only a few thousand members, and it is doubtful that they could have raised enough money to build the kind of hospital that Master Cheng-yen wanted on their own. However, journalists got wind of this human-interest story and gave it media publicity. This generated support from Taiwan's provincial governor, who helped Ciji obtain a building site and clear other bureaucratic hurdles. More important, it attracted the attention of the public, who, moved by a frail nun and her hope to provide for the medical needs of an underserved community, contributed the US$20 million dollars needed to build the hospital. The National Taiwan University Hospital offered its expertise in planning the hospital and helped in its initial staffing. This was the first event in Taiwan in which a substantial section of the public demonstrated an affinity with the greater Taiwanese community (see Schak 2009a).

Turning to other events, the KMT governed relatively unchallenged during the 1950s and 1960s, following its own agenda. As mentioned, Taiwan's economy recovered from the shocks of the 1940s. Its small and medium enterprises began to develop from the late 1950s, and most people put their efforts into making a living. However, from the early 1970s things began to go less smoothly for the government. The first such event was a challenge to the KMT's Sinocentric bias, the emergence of Taiwanese "nativist" literature (*hsiang-t'u wen-hsüeh, xiangtu wenxue*). Previously, literature in KMT-controlled Taiwan had been dominated by Mainlander authors whose perspective was "China," who strongly supported the government goal to reconquer the Chinese mainland, and who opposed any expression of Taiwan as a distinct entity. In the 1950s authors wrote anti-Communist literature or escapist, nostalgic stories about the homelands they missed. In the 1960s they wrote in a modernist style that brought to bear concepts from Western literature such as symbolism, surrealism, existentialism, and Freud (Chen 1991, 59–60), and in which style and language use were more important than substance.

Toward the end of the 1960s, the modernist genre came under criticism for being elitist, impenetrable, "art for art's sake," and in complete disregard of society. This paved the way for the nativist literature of the 1970s, a social-realist genre through which Taiwanese authors wrote about village life and in doing so expressed a Taiwanese identity, occasionally using colloquial Hoklo expressions.[17] It was largely a rural literature, reflecting the origins of many nativist writers. Their characters were Taiwanese from the lower strata of society, and their stories were typically about the characters' struggles. Stories also conveyed nostalgia about a way of life that was being lost to industrialization (Chen 1991, 72–77).

Social-realist expression was dangerous under the KMT government's repressive rule because it expressed the difficult conditions workers and peasants faced, descriptions not welcomed by a government that opposed the airing of negative

---

17. Taiwanese nativist literature had been written in the 1920s by authors who insisted on writing in Chinese to express their status as Chinese and their rejection of Japan. The colonial government gradually increased its prohibition of Chinese language publications in the 1930s, culminating in the rigid enforcement of *kōminka* from 1937. In the 1950s Taiwanese authors, having grown up learning Japanese, were hindered by their inability to express themselves in a Chinese literary medium. Some tried to write in a Taiwanese colloquial language, but this was difficult as there were many words for which there were no recognized characters.

aspects of Taiwan society and their implied criticism of the government or calls for social change. Some authors also protested against the KMT's one-party rule and the near monopoly Mainlanders had in the higher echelons of government. The government also feared that, with its focus on Taiwan, nativist literature promoted a separate Taiwanese identity in opposition to its goal of unifying Taiwan with China (Chen 1991, 54–55, 88–90; see also Hsiau 2005).

Mainlander authors, who were largely supportive of the government, disapproved of what they called the subversive nature of nativist literature and said it harked back to the social criticism of the May Fourth period and the even more critical literature by leftist writers in 1930s China. Their debate with the nativist authors ended when two prominent nativist writers, Yang Qingchu and Wang Tuo, were arrested and jailed in the Formosa Incident (see below), leading to accusations that nativist writers were leftists (Chen 1991, 96–98). However, the genre continued to develop in the direction of "de-Sinicizing" Taiwanese literature (Hsiau 2005, 135–36). Nativist literature later became known as "indigenous literature" (*bentu wenxue*), then as Taiwan literature (*Taiwan wenxue*) (Hsiau 2005, 135–36).

A simultaneous event was the 1971 announcement that US President Nixon would visit Chairman Mao in Beijing, which also triggered a UN vote to replace the ROC in the Security Council with China. The latter instigated President Chiang Kai-shek to withdraw Taiwan from the body altogether. According to Lung Ying-tai (Long Yingtai), these events were a severe shock to university students. All their lives they had heard that they, in the ROC, were China, and then, suddenly, the world was saying that they weren't, that the PRC was China. So they started asking themselves, if we aren't China, what are we? "We students organized ourselves and started learning about Taiwan, its geography and society, and began going to rural villages to see what the conditions there were like and to try to help out. We also started writing and singing our own songs" (2015).[18] While this did not eliminate the focus on China, it did bring attention to Taiwan.

Political change began in 1972, when Chiang Ching-kuo (CCK) became premier, and it accelerated after his father died in 1975. This ushered in a softening of authoritarianism and the rise of an opposition force that gradually became more emboldened. CCK portrayed a much softer, friendlier image than his father, who often appeared aloof. Whereas the elder Chiang regularly appeared in public in his military uniform or a long Chinese gown and was often stern-faced, CCK preferred the sort of zip-up jacket worn by much of the public. He looked much more down-to-earth and was known to stop his motorcade occasionally and wade out into a field to talk to a farmer. He also recognized the importance of bringing Taiwanese

---

18. The popular Mandarin music in Taiwan in the early 1960s was music from the 1940s to the 1950s and earlier, mostly sung by stars in pre-PRC Shanghai or from Hong Kong. This music had disappeared by 1969 or 1970, when I did my initial field research, and popular music was mostly American pop and soft rock. By 1974 Mandarin popular music began to appear again. The music Lung referred to was called "campus music" (*xiaoyuan gequ*).

into the KMT, the government, and the bureaucracy. Nonetheless, he still ruled as an authoritarian, as the handling of the 1979 Formosa Incident (below) shows.

When CCK became KMT Chairman, the party began to increase its membership and make efforts to get party members elected in local elections that, in the past, had essentially been nonpartisan local popularity contests. Also at that time, a group that opposed the government began referring to itself as *dangwai* (outside the [KMT] party) to get around the ban on forming new political parties under Taiwan's martial law. The dangwai group grew over the next several years and ran candidates in elections, some of whom were successful in legislative, county executive, and provincial assembly contests (J. Jacobs 2012, 51–53). At the time, the majority in the Legislative Yuan had been elected in China in 1948, and with the loss of mainland China to the Communists, they became "frozen in office" because they could not face reelection in their home districts.[19] This made it impossible for dangwai politicians to defeat the government, but they could at least debate it in the legislature. With their supporters they engaged in a steady stream of activities to remain in the public eye, including publishing politically oriented magazines that pushed the boundaries of what the authoritarian government would allow. When the government closed one magazine, another, with the same format and layout but a different name and color scheme, would soon appear.

On December 16, 1978, the US announced that it would establish formal diplomatic relations with China at the beginning of the new year. The ROC government, which had been informed before the announcement, used it as an excuse to postpone indefinitely legislative elections scheduled for a week later, on December 23.[20] Over the next year, the opposition responded by holding various public activities to keep their cause in the public eye, including launching a new publication, *Formosa Magazine* (*Meilidao Zazhi*), in July 1979. On Human Rights Day, December 10, it held a demonstration in Gaoxiong. The KMT government had never allowed expressions of protest on this scale. When the protesters tried to advertise the rally on December 9 using sound trucks, two of their number were arrested. At the protest itself, security forces surrounded the area before the protesters' arrival, and as the protest began they advanced toward the crowd and then retreated several times. In the end, clashes broke out, and many demonstrators were arrested, with dangwai leaders being targeted. This became known as the Meilidao Incident.

In March and April 1980 the eight most prominent opposition leaders were tried in military courts. Found guilty, six of the eight received jail sentences of twelve years, one of fourteen years and one of life imprisonment. A further twenty-nine protesters were jailed for three to six years. Between the arrests and the trials,

---

19. The KMT government needed to keep them in office to maintain the myth that it was the legitimate ruler of and represented all of China. It was also convenient, giving the government an indomitable majority of legislators.
20. It is likely that a major reason to postpone the elections was that in elections held in 1977, the dangwai increased its number of seats and showed itself to be a viable opposition.

despite 24-hour surveillance by security forces, the mother and two daughters of one of the leaders, Lin Yi-hsiung, were murdered in their home.

Notwithstanding its powerful position at the beginning of the 1980s, the KMT gradually lost its ability to dictate events over the decade, its loss being a gain in influence of the Taiwanese and the opposition. When the previously postponed elections were finally held in December 1980, the public showed their disapproval of the government's prosecution of opposition leaders by giving the wife of one of them the highest number of votes, electing her to the National Assembly, and electing the wife and younger brother of two other jailed leaders to other offices (J. Jacobs 2012, 58). The opposition also gained a generation of younger leaders as several of the defense attorneys gained prominence through the trials. Further KMT losses resulted from a combination of its own overreach, corruption, CCK's failing health, and the steadily increasing strength of social forces, which simultaneously expanded the cohesiveness of Taiwanese society.

In 1981 Chen Wen-chen (Chen Wencheng), a Taiwanese-American professor visiting his family in Taiwan, was found dead on the National Taiwan University campus. He had undergone twelve hours of interrogation by the Garrison Command, Taiwan's paramount security organization, the day before, but his death was described as resulting from a fall from an upper-story window. In 1984 Henry Liu,[21] a Chinese-American writer and author of an unauthorized biography of CCK, was murdered in front of his home in Daly City, California. This was a far more momentous event because Liu, a US citizen, was shot dead on American soil. The FBI traced the murder to members of the pro-Mainlander/KMT Bamboo Union Gang, Taiwan's largest criminal organization, who were acting under the orders of the director of the Intelligence Bureau of the Ministry of National Defense (Chang 1992, 28–29). The US government was understandably outraged and stepped up its pressure on the Taiwan government to curb its methods of controlling dissidents and to democratize.

By 1983 CCK's health was such that he had to turn over day-to-day official affairs to advisors, in particular his close associate, General Wang Sheng. Soon afterward, Wang made a semiofficial visit to the US, where those he met either hoped or expected that he would be CCK's successor. However, CCK decided that Wang had become too ambitious, so he sent him first to an out-of-the-way military post and then to Paraguay as ROC ambassador (Chang 1992, 38; Roy 2003, 180–81). In 1985, the Tenth Credit Cooperative collapsed, causing losses to thousands of savers. Its failure was due to granting illegal loans to companies it knew were in financial straits, many of which were owned by persons in the government. Both the previous and the incumbent finance ministers, the latter also a close advisor to CCK, had to resign over the incident (J. Jacobs 2012, 61; Pempel 1999, 251).

---

21. Liu's Chinese name is 劉宜良. He wrote under the name 江南.

In the 1980s grassroots movements and environmental protests also challenged the authoritarian government. The first of these occurred in 1980 when, in response to two food scandals the year before and the absence of a relevant government body or laws to protect consumers from harmful products, Weng Zhaoxi, Li Kunyi, and Chai Songling founded the Consumer Foundation.[22] Its aims were to educate consumers, enhance their interests as a group, and protect their rights. It played a crucial role in consumer protection over the next decade until the local press was able to engage in investigative journalism. Despite its noble intentions, it was met with hostility by some members of the Legislative Yuan, who regarded it as a rebellious group that upset the system, and by business groups who objected to any interference in their interests (H. Hsiao, personal communication).

Two years later the government faced a more serious challenge, local community-based antipollution protests. Taiwan was one of the original four Asian tigers, enjoying rapid economic growth from the 1960s. However, the government, needing economic development, and local governments, anxious to have economic activities in their jurisdictions, were indiscriminate about what sorts of factories were established, gaining Taiwan a reputation as a haven for highly polluting industries such as electroplating, dyeing, and petrochemicals. The pollution that resulted was exacerbated because much of Taiwan's industrialization took place in rural areas (Williams 1992, 195), which increased the likelihood that pollution could get into the soil and water and contaminate the food supply. By the 1980s many areas were suffering from severe pollution because of the "inefficiency and ineffectiveness of local governments in dealing with the problem" (Hsiao 1990, 225). Surveys in 1983 and 1986 found that over two-thirds of respondents regarded environmental pollution as serious or very serious (Hsiao 1990, 219).

Because the law made companies almost invulnerable, going to the government or the police was useless, as was going to the companies. Moreover, fines for polluting were negligible, only NT$3,000 (about US$75 at the time). Thus, people began taking direct, though illegal, action against companies and officials. The first such action was in Linyuan Shire, Gaoxiong, in 1982, where, after years of no response to their complaints, residents destroyed polluting factories. Protests increased significantly in 1984 and 1985. Being single-issue campaigns and ceasing when goals were met, they had no direct political effect, but they showed that people no longer feared the government. More important, they had demonstration effects, protests in one locale encouraging protests in others as the government took no action against the protesters (Wang 1988, 182–87). In 1986, a local protest successfully blocked a proposal from the very powerful DuPont Corporation to establish a titanium-dioxide plant in the central Taiwan town of Lukang (Lugang).

Two national level environmental movements and several local ones emerged from these protests, a Conservation Movement that focused on habitat protection

---

22. It was established as a foundation rather than an association because of the government's state-corporatist policy.

and an antinuclear power movement aimed at stopping Taipower, the national electricity supplier, from building a nuclear power plant in an earthquake prone area. These two movements differed from antipollution protests in that their momentum and support came largely from the urban middle class (see Hsiao 1990, 221–23). However, all these protests and movements carried with them a sense of problems shared widely in Taiwan and thus made people recognize that their local problems were identical with those of many others. The soon to emerge women's, first peoples, and Hakka rights movements, although they focused on specific populations, had similar effects as the citizenry recognized that the rights of all should be protected.[23]

The 1980s also saw two notable calls for an increased level of civility and in doing so called for Taiwan to become a society inclusive of all. The first came from former economics minister, Li Kwoh-ting (Li Guoding) who, in 1982, advocated a "sixth relationship" (*liu lun*) in order to promote a spirit of citizenship. The Five Relationships (*wu lun*)—ruler-subject, father-son, husband-wife, older brother–younger brother, and friend-friend—is a core Confucian concept. However, echoing Liang Qichao, Li argued that a modern industrial society needed a sixth relationship, between the group and the self (*qun-ji*). This referred to relations with strangers, nature, groups, and organizations. As practiced, the Five Relationships implied love limited to insiders, those with whom one was related or familiar. The sixth relationship was about the ethical responsibility of the individual to society itself and called for love that was boundless (SEA 2013).

The sixth relationship, according to Li, necessitated thoughtfulness toward others. For example, on Taipei streets drivers often parked illegally in bus-stop zones so that intending passengers, including the elderly, the disabled, and pregnant women, had to run to where the bus was able to stop. This sort of harm to people was very concrete. The problem, he said, was that people rarely considered how their actions might affect others, especially those with whom they had no special relationship. They lacked respect toward strangers and were indifferent about harming them (SEA 2013). Commenting on Li's sixth relationship, Chen Ruoshui writes, "Comparing this sort of very common attitude with traditional Chinese ethics we can't but say that the low level of Chinese public morality and our traditional culture's lack of emphasis on everyday people to people relations are very closely linked" (2005, 30–31).

Li's call had no perceptible effect on civil behavior at the time, but in 1991 he and other prominent persons established the Society to Promote Ethical Conduct between Individuals and Groups in order to promote the sixth relationship and as a foundation to foster interaction between them. Since 2001 it has carried out large annual or biennial surveys to provide concrete information about the level of trust in Taiwan (SEA).

---

23. As Taiwan democratized, the rights of specific groups were recognized in amendments to the constitution (J. Jacobs 2012).

The other 1980s promoter of social reforms, prominently including civil behavior, was Lung Ying-tai. After graduating from university in Taiwan, Lung earned a PhD in English and American literature at Kansas State University. She then returned to Taiwan and began writing essays for the *China Times*, many of which were republished, along with essays by others, in two books, *The Wild Fire Collection* (*Yehuo Ji*) in 1985 and a 1987 sequel, *The Wildfire External Collection* (*Yehuo Ji Waiji*).

In the first essay in *Wildfire*, "Chinese People, Why Don't You Get Angry," Lung castigates her fellow citizens for their inaction in the face of incivility: hawkers setting up just outside people's homes to sell cooked food, the smoke assaulting the residents through their windows and the vendors heedlessly discarding food scraps and creating a noise nuisance; taxis driving wildly and stopping in right turn lanes, blocking other traffic; waterways polluted with rubbish, plastic bottles, sewerage and chemical wastes; and the harm this pollution does to the unborn and to developing children. "Why do you just take this with a shrug of the shoulders and a nod of the head?" she asks. "Why don't you get angry? Because the hawkers and taxi drivers are either gangsters themselves or are in league with them? Because the police, public servants and legislators will do nothing" (Lung 1985, 1–6).

Luo Zhaojin's essay "Of course, Chinese Don't Get Angry" follows, answering Lung's question. Echoing her criticisms, he writes that they don't get angry because of their families:

> My family tells me that outside there are many bad people, that I should take what others say with a grain of salt. They are afraid I'll be taken advantage of. They tell me not to rush to a stranger's aid in order that I don't invite disaster upon myself. They're afraid I'll suffer a loss. So I study hard so I can earn well, so people will say I have a good future, not like those people who go to the aid of persons suffering an injustice. Although some are public-spirited, in the end, if they're not pushed aside, they're regarded as heretics and they don't come to a good end. In daily life, smart people just happily go about their business; they don't listen to others' opinions, carelessly express their own, or help out every stranger in need. They are thus able to return home without incident. Only fools and dumbbells help others out of difficulties, express opinion or criticism, stir up trouble, or invite unwanted difficulties. (Luo 1985, 8)

In other essays Lung identified various features of Taiwan society that contributed to its lack of civility: neither police nor officials clamp down on people who make their livings at the expense of others such as hawkers who block streets and footpaths and persons who pollute or exploit publically owned goods; an education system in which even university students are treated as children and taught to respect teachers but not to think for themselves;[24] faults and holes in the legal

---

24. Chinese child socialization practices do not prepare children for an independent adult life, one reason being that sons are expected to stay with their parents and daughters to move in with their husbands, who also live with their parents.

system; too many people with whom it is impossible to reason; authorities who are unwilling to enforce the law; a passive public unwilling to complain yet insistent that their rights be upheld; and people who have no concept of consideration for others. Although Lung did not say so directly, some of these criticisms can be laid at the feet of the authoritarian government whose officials have little pressure to actually serve the people, despite "serving the people" being a prominent slogan of the KMT. And because Lung was so outspoken and her message so effective, and probably also because she was young and a woman, she was cursed and criticized by many and even received death threats (Ling 2001). Two years after *Wildfire* was published, she left Taiwan to live in Germany, returning to Taiwan in 1999 to head the Taipei City Government's Cultural Affairs Bureau.

However, within a month after it was first published, *Wildfire* was into its twenty-fourth printing, and within six months it had been through over fifty printings, selling over 100,000 copies. Only magazines published by the anti-KMT opposition had higher sales. Through *Wildfire* and *Wildfire External Collection*, Lung became a spokesperson for the middle class and the young intelligentsia (Xiang 2005). Whether Lung's writings at this time had a direct influence on the development of civility in the 1990s, I cannot say. However, political activity increased at an accelerating pace from the latter half of the 1980s, and in 1990 the student Wild Lily Movement (*yebaihe yundong*) was an important force in Taiwan's democratization (J. Jacobs 2012). Moreover, in the late 1980s, a new genre of music became popular among the young. Sung in Hoklo, the lyrics provided a stimulus to Taiwanese consciousness. A leading band in this genre was Hei Mingdan, Black List, reflecting the political conditions of the recent past.

Returning to political events, in 1986, emboldened by large demonstrations that toppled leaders in neighboring South Korea and the Philippines, dangwai leaders decided that they would attempt to formally register themselves as a political party despite it being forbidden under Taiwan's martial law. Within half an hour of publicly announcing their intention, police handed CCK a list of the names of participants so that he could give the order to arrest them. Reckoning that a crackdown would do great harm to the country, he declined, "Arresting people won't solve the problem" (Chang 2013). Although the dangwai leaders who made the announcement had been prepared to be jailed, they were able to register as the Democratic Progressive Party without incident and run candidates in elections held at the end of the year.

The following year CCK lifted martial law and bans on people visiting China.[25] Both these events boosted popular identification with Taiwan, the former because the opposition was largely made up of Hoklo and Hakka Taiwanese and was a

---

25. The KMT has claimed that CCK brought democracy to Taiwan, but Jacobs disagrees, arguing that he liberalized but did not democratize. CCK "clearly did not expect the KMT to lose office to an opposition. He improved Taiwanese participation in political processes, but he maintained the firm monopoly of power among Mainlanders. And freedom of speech remained strictly limited" (J. Jacobs 2012, 69).

demonstration that the majority population in Taiwan was on the ascendency, the latter because of a wholly unintended consequence. With the seemingly more liberal conditions in China, many Mainlanders, especially the soldiers who had come to Taiwan with the government in the late 1940s, were clamoring for a chance to return home to *tanqin*, visit their relatives. Many initially intended to stay. However, when they arrived in China, they were shocked by both the backward conditions they found there and by the reception they received from their kin. Rather than being received with open arms, many saw only an open palm extended toward them and their kin wanting to know how much money the returnees had brought them. Some of the relatives expressed bitterness that, while their kinsperson had gone to Taiwan, they had had to stay at home and suffer, "Why you and not me?"[26] A few months after the former soldiers left, almost all had returned to Taiwan, having decided that it was their home.[27]

Already in failing health, CCK died several months later, in January 1988. On the day following the official one-month mourning period, when life could return to normal, a headline in the *Liberty Times* asked if it was now possible that CCK's other two sons[28] would be able to state openly who their father was. This headline was an emphatic announcement that a new era of freedom of expression had begun in Taiwan. After CCK died, Vice President Lee Teng-hui, a native Taiwanese, became president. Reforms began almost immediately after the mourning period finished. Newspapers became bolder and were no longer restricted to eight broadsheet pages. A civil assembly law passed in 1988 gave citizens the right of assembly with the police having only administrative powers to maintain order during demonstrations (Cao, Huang, and Sun 2014, 32). The Civil Associations Law was revised the following year, permitting the formation of civil society groups.

The citizenry reacted quickly. The months following CCK's death saw large demonstrations: by farmers over the prices for farm produce and opposing the importation of agricultural goods, by indigenous peoples over a culturally insulting symbol, and by Hakka over preserving Hakka language and culture. The passage of the Civil Associations Law opened the floodgates of new associations. Prominent among them were religious groups (Chiu 2001, 273), including some large and prominent Buddhist organizations. They not only contribute to eroding regionalism and distinctions between Taiwanese and Mainlanders but also have strong environmental and social welfare missions such as environmental protection, recycling, and social-disaster relief (Weller 1999b; Schak 2009a). Moreover, along with Christian groups, they differ from Taiwanese folk religion in that their philanthropy focuses on society as a whole while folk worship largely centers on

---

26. The irony of this is that in the 1960s it was those Mainlanders "stranded" in Taiwan who felt they were suffering.
27. This account is based on several broadcast reports I heard while in Taiwan at the time.
28. These were two sons born to a mistress and given her surname, Chang (Zhang). Both were prominent at the time, Chang Hsiao-yen (章孝嚴) in the Foreign Ministry and Chang Hsiao-tzu (章孝慈) in academia. Chang Hsiao-yen later changed his surname to Chiang, after his father.

particular village temples and their associated communities. Many other organizations, some inspired by religious beliefs, some secular, have focused on specific problems such as HIV/AIDS, unwed mothers, victims of domestic violence, and maltreatment of foreign workers. The government responded in 1992 with a constitutional provision calling for universal health insurance, promoting women's rights, eliminating sexual discrimination, and safeguarding the rights of the handicapped, the disabled and indigenous peoples (J. Jacobs 2012, 82–83). Recalling what Lin Yutang wrote about Chinese not being socially minded or able to understand why Western women organize a Society for the Prevention of Cruelty to Animals, it is clear that Taiwan is no longer that sort of society.

While one still could not call for Taiwan independence, public discussion of previously forbidden topics such as White Terror, the 228 Incident and Taiwan consciousness became possible. I was stunned on returning to Taiwan in 1992, after an absence of four years, to see a bookshop with about 6 square meters of shelf space devoted to works on Taiwan history, customs, and religion, topics that were previously banned or tightly restricted. Political sociologist Wang Fu-chang documents the increase, also noting that no new books on Taiwan were published from 1952 to 1968.

Table 5.1
Numbers of books published about Taiwan: 1952–1998

Year	Number of books
1952–1968	0
1969	13
1970–1976	19
1977	10
1978–1984	<16/year
1985	22
1986	23
1987	44
1988	65
1989	90
1990	85
1991	135
1992	210
1993	284
1994	288
1995	457
1996	392
1997	472
1998	402

Source: Wang (2005, 71).

In 1989 there were protests in Jilong demanding government apologies for the deaths in the 228 Incident on the anniversary of that event. The following year saw an unprecedentedly large student demonstration over the appointment of a former general as premier. Demonstrators also demanded the retirement of the "frozen in office" officials and the direct election of president and vice president (Chao and Myers 1998, 191–93). Those officials were retired soon afterward, and 1996 saw direct election of the president and full democratization. An empowered citizenry had forced an authoritarian government to democratize and, the Taiwanese had seized control of their government from outsiders.

Strongly implied in these events was the growth of identification with Taiwan and as Taiwanese. According to Fell, in 1989, 52 percent of Taiwan's population identified as Chinese, 16 percent as Taiwanese, and 26 percent as both (2005, 89–90). In 2014 the National Chengchi University's Election Study Center found striking changes: only 3.5 percent identified as Chinese, 32.5 percent as both, and 60.6 percent as Taiwanese (Liberty Times 2014). In part, these changes are generational. Observers of the social movements of the last several years and the 2014 and 2016 elections have noted that the 20–39 age group identifies strongly as Taiwanese rather than Chinese, whether they are of Taiwanese or Mainlander origin.

Being cautious of small sample sizes and non-sampling errors, available data indicate that these impressions are correct. Rigger has examined generational differences in identity and party preference in Taiwan. Taiwanese born before 1932, having spent their formative years under Japanese rule and having little impression of China, identify as Taiwanese. Taiwanese born between 1932 and 1953 passed through their formative years during the most authoritarian period and identify as Taiwanese; Mainlanders of that age group, having migrated from China to Taiwan, identify as Chinese. The third (1954–1968) and fourth (1968–1986) generations, whether Taiwanese or Mainlander, identify as both Taiwanese and Chinese, a difference between them being that third-generation Taiwanese grew up with disparaging attitudes toward Taiwanese language and culture, while the fourth generation saw Taiwan as their home and had a positive attitude toward them. The fifth generation, born after 1986, grew up in a democratic Taiwan, and whether Mainlander or Taiwanese they identify strongly with Taiwan; only 0.89 percent identify as Chinese (Rigger 2016). Members of the two youngest generations have shown their commitment to Taiwan through demonstrations (the Wild Lily, Black Island, and Sunflower Movements) that have altered Taiwan's political and social landscape during the past three decades.

Aside from the effects of the zeitgeist during the formative years of generations, two other factors have brought about the above identity changes. One is the idea that identification with Taiwan is necessary to be a "real citizen" (McLean-Dreyfus and Varrall 2015). The other is the threats and pressure to (re)unite from China (Tseng and Chen 2015), ramified by Taiwan's perceived increased economic dependency on its cross-straits neighbor resulting from a series of trade pacts the

Ma Ying-jeou government (2008–2016) signed with Beijing (Chen 2014). Beijing insists that Taiwan is an inalienable part of China and pressures other countries to adhere to this. Just before the 2016 election, a photo emerged of the members of a Korean girl group holding the flags of their countries of origin. One of them, a 16-year-old Taiwanese singer, was forced by her singing group's sponsors to make an abject public apology for holding up an ROC flag, the sponsors fearing that her action would offend China, where the group often performs (Buckley and Ramzy 2016). According to the TVBS Poll Center research, seeing the video of her apology motivated half a million voters to make the effort to cast a ballot (TVBS 2016).

Post-KMT colonial governments have played a role in the continuation of the identity shift in Taiwan.[29] First, textbook revisions began in the 1990s to focus on the geography, history, and culture of Taiwan, the first major text, *Renshi Taiwan* (*Get to Know Taiwan*), being adopted in 1997. In the process, information about China was reduced, and from 2006 China was presented simply as a neighboring country.[30] Second, in the mid-1990s, the Interior Ministry, through the Council for Cultural Affairs, began a program aimed at strengthening community identity and culture by promoting community development, "new hometowns" in a society that had gone from one in which most lived in small rural committees or relatively stable urban neighborhoods to one that has become very geographically mobile and highly urbanized. The Council for Cultural Affairs encouraged community members and leaders to research community history, beautify the area, and mark significant sites. Residents could apply for small grants to hold community events or exhibitions of community artifacts and to tell their community's story. Residents, including primary school students, are encouraged to become active in community affairs (Taiwan Info 2002; Hsing 2013).

These top-down efforts to build communities had some success. They succeeded in places such as Danshui's Puting District, where neighborhood leaders created a self-guided tour of historic buildings and public art. However, Danshui was already an established tourist spot with significant historical sites and strong commercial interests. In new urban neighborhoods, many of which encompassed old villages as city boundaries expanded, participation was generally limited to or strongest among the elderly. One survey found that those reporting a close or very close relationship with others in the neighborhood or ward dropped 5.1 percent from 1999 to 2003 (DGBAS 2004). According to Hsin-huang Hsiao, the program has remained top-down, in part because recruiting sufficient volunteers to carry out projects is difficult (2013 personal communication).

---

29. For a good overview of identity in Taiwan see Muyard 2014.
30. In 2014, the KMT Ma government began a "fine-tuning" of history texts, drawing up new guidelines. This was seen by many as a re-Sinification effort. When the revised text came out, students from more than 150 high schools demanded that the guidelines be withdrawn (Tsoi 2015). Two weeks of street demonstrations by students followed, including two attempts to occupy the Education Ministry. The minister refused to withdraw the new texts (Marquand 2015; Cole 2015), however, the incoming Tsai government education minister has since scrapped them.

The changes documented above took people out of their communities into a world where they met, studied, worked, did military service with, and lived next door to people they did not know. Political struggles united Taiwanese with each other and with Mainlanders who were opposed to the KMT's authoritarian governance or who simply had never seen their ancestral homes in China, being born and raised in Taiwan where they "drank Taiwan water and ate Taiwan rice." The rash of social movements showed people that they had much in common with those in other communities. The Ciji hospital project united people in a cause that appealed to their humanity and compassion, and participation in Buddhist and other religious organizations and in voluntary associations brought strangers together. Together these phenomena created a Taiwan consciousness, an underlying feeling that others, whether encountered or unseen, whether acquaintances or strangers, are equally part of a significant imagined community. Together, these effectuated the transition to Taiwan as a society for itself.

6

Discussion

What Social Conditions Are Needed for a Society to Develop Civility?

In the last two chapters I have examined the state of civility in China and Taiwan, two societies with very similar cultural foundations and governance histories but, up to this point, quite different levels of civility. Taiwan friends with whom I have discussed this research recall, as I do, the lack of civility in Taiwan several decades ago and the changes that have taken place, but they assume that the evolution to a society with civility is natural. They feel that, just as China's economic takeoff has succeeded, albeit three to four decades after Taiwan's, its level of civility will also catch up with Taiwan's in due time. However, while the pockets of civil behavior in China noted in Chapter 4 lend some credibility to that view, the scale of the problems that China will have to overcome and the differences in social formations and governance between it and Taiwan will make it much more difficult to achieve the level of civility that Taiwan has achieved.

In this chapter I will first examine those problems: differences in size and population, level and quality of social and economic development, including education levels and egalitarianism, degree of social unity, differences in social organization and governance, and levels of trust. I will then test the facilitating and hindering factors presented in Chapter 2 that I posited would affect the development of civility to see if the evidence presented in Chapters 4 and 5 bears them out. I will conclude with a discussion of the links between civility and values, a society for itself, and the role of democratization in developing civility.

There are several social or material characteristics that explain why it is more difficult for China to develop civility than it has been for Taiwan. First, China is 265 times larger in area and, in 2016, fifty-nine times larger in population. It has a much greater disparity in the levels of development and in the number and remoteness of difficult to reach settlements. Even in one of the earliest areas of Han civilization, Shaanxi Province, in the less fertile hilly areas families are dispersed, sometimes several kilometers apart. Taiwan, by contrast, is compact and largely urbanized; there are few rural settlements that are more than 50 kilometers from a city, and Eluanbi, at Taiwan's southern tip, is less than 400 kilometers from the northern port of Jilong (Keelung). This means that communication and the spread of new ideas are more challenging in China than in Taiwan.

Han Chinese dominate in both societies, constituting 94 percent of the population in China and 98 percent in Taiwan. Moreover, in both, indigenous peoples or minority populations are in general less educated and poorer than the Han. However, in Taiwan they are more assimilated, and there are no serious, open conflicts between them and the Han. In fact, over the last two decades, Taiwan's indigenous peoples have been regarded as a disadvantaged group that deserves protection, respect, and empathy by middle-class society. In China, aside from some of the larger groups living on the periphery such as Tibetans, Kazakhs, Uyghurs, and Mongols, there are smaller groups, especially in Guizhou and Yunnan, who live in difficult to access mountain areas. Moreover, particularly in the peripheral areas, there is some tension and resistance to assimilation. A major effect of government investment in these areas is that it finances projects that provide jobs for which Han are more qualified and thus encourages Han migration. This causes resentment among the minorities, which is in turn resented by Han in other parts of China who see only the amounts invested and regard the minorities as ungrateful. It also contributes to an increase in pejorative ethnic stereotypes and weakens any sense of an encompassing imagined community (see HRW 2017).

Second, in economic and social development, Taiwan had a head start. Its economic development and industrialization began in the 1950s and was much less interrupted than China's, which did not enjoy stable growth until the 1980s.[1] Whereas the latter was governed by campaigns in the 1950s and 1960s and had a centrally planned economy, Taiwan's KMT government eschewed disruptive social actions; even its largest, the Chinese Cultural Renaissance Movement, was largely aimed at culture, the arts, and school textbooks and had little effect on the economy or everyday society. This put Taiwan in a position to benefit from foreign investment and open American markets. By contrast, China endured a US boycott into the 1970s as well as the Great Leap Forward, the Cultural Revolution, and other turbulent campaigns.

Education levels rose in Taiwan during its rapid development phase. The school leaving age was raised to completion of junior middle school in 1968, and many middle schools ran evening sessions, allowing students to work during the day to help support their families and continue their education in the evenings.[2] Moreover, many private senior vocational middle schools opened up, creating opportunities for those unable to gain entry into the public system at that level.[3] By 2007 Taiwan's literacy rate reached 96 percent. Overall, throughout the latter half of the twentieth century, Taiwan also had a much higher exposure to advanced economies and

---

1. The two oil shocks in the 1970s were mere speed bumps compared to collectivization, the Great Leap Forward or the Cultural Revolution.
2. This system, known as *bangong bandu* (half work, half study) was used extensively by lower income families and was especially helpful for young women whose families demanded that they go to work after finishing primary school, often to assist a brother in furthering his education.
3. There were few public senior middle schools in Taiwan, and entry was by a competitive exam. Thus, many had to attend private institutions if they wanted to complete secondary education.

societies, especially Japan and the United States, through the media, cultural products, study overseas, and personal contacts.

As result of its development path, Taiwan achieved full employment by 1970, and by the mid-1980s industrial workers were turning down overtime work in order to spend more time following individual pursuits. It became one of the OECD-designated first generation of newly industrialized countries, China, along with India and the Philippines, being named in the third generation. Taiwan achieved high-income country status by the 1990s. According to the IMF, in 2015, China's GPD per capita in nominal US dollars was $8,280 while Taiwan's was $22,083.[4]

Based on recent CIA *World Factbook* estimates of income distribution, China is substantially more unequal than Taiwan, their respective official Gini coefficients being 0.469 (2014) and 0.338 (2012), and their respective ratios of top tenth to bottom tenth of incomes are 21.8:1 and 6.1:1, the China figures representing urban incomes only (CIA n.d.). That said, there are domestic inequalities in each. In Taiwan, income from property and equity investments is very lightly taxed, and there is no tax at all on income from trusts. Under the Ma Ying-jeou government, the tax burden shifted significantly from the wealthy to middle-class salary earners (Chang 2012). In China, urban incomes are much higher than rural incomes, and there are also discrepancies among regions. China's human development index (HDI) value reached 0.727 in 2014, ranking it ninetieth out of 188 countries (UNDP), but urban incomes are 3.2 times those of rural incomes. The top decile earns 9.2 times as much as the bottom decile in urban areas, 7.3 times more in rural regions. The per capita GDP of China's wealthiest province is 9.9 times that of the poorest. The urban-rural income gap widened from 2.79:1 in 2000 to 3.33:1 in 2007, though it improved slightly in 2008 to 3.19:1 because of increased prices for farm goods. Provincial level HDI also varies widely, with Shanghai enjoying the highest HDI, 0.9111, and Tibet the lowest, 0.616 (Bertelsmann 2014).[5]

Third, there are differences in their respective levels of social unity. Taiwan's ethnic mix initially made social unity difficult to achieve, especially during the KMT colonial period when the government used divide-and-rule tactics, but it is not nearly as complex as that of China. Ancestral place of origin, the basis of the earlier ethnic complexity, has become irrelevant to the younger generations, who have only known life in Taiwan. Thus, much of Taiwan's 1950s–1960s complexity has been eroded as the new, Taiwan-born generations have replaced the old. Moreover, except for the very elderly, all speak Mandarin and, especially in the south, most also speak Hoklo. For the past two decades, a major aspect of Taiwanese social unity is the appreciation of living in a democracy.

---

4. These figures should be seen as indicative. Chinese GPD per capita figures from different agencies for the same year vary by around 10 percent. Moreover, several bodies that make such estimates do not have a separate figure for Taiwan, which could mean that they include it in Chinese figures or, more likely, they simply do not count it.
5. The UN does not list such data for Taiwan, nor is it included in listings for China.

In China, following the past two-plus decades of "patriotic education,"[6] constant reminders of China's economic and technological achievements, its securing of the Olympic Games, two World Expos and WTO membership, and warnings of enemies trying to "contain" China, cause it to split, or overthrow its government, the level of patriotic nationalism is probably higher than that in Taiwan, but China is less united as a society. It is far more ethnically and linguistically complex. Some of its minorities are relatively assimilated and integrated, but those on its periphery or in mountain areas are much less so. Linguistically, despite the central government's promotion of Mandarin since 1955, a recent Ministry of Education report states that 400 million people, 30 percent of the population, cannot communicate in the national language (Reuters 2013c). Moreover, local languages have become more popular in music, films, and television programs (Roberts 2014). Government pressure in 2010 to require Cantonese-speaking Guangzhou to use Mandarin in TV broadcasts met with enough resistance that the government backed off, though it began to reapply pressure in 2014 (Sonmez 2014). Furthermore, despite the power of the central government, localism is still strong; some of the actions of regional governments indicate that local interests are more important to them than national interests.

The nature of the two nationalisms also differs. Taiwan's is essentially civic, mostly based on internal unity as Taiwanese. It was forged through struggles against an authoritarian government that had high levels of participation and even higher levels of sympathy for the cause among the population at large. Those demonstrating for this cause have shown strong desires to advance social justice and to maintain Taiwan's hard-earned democracy, the latter desire strengthened by Chinese pressure, threats, and demands for unification. It is a nationalism founded on the democratic institutions that Taiwan has built up over the past three decades. In China's case, on one hand, social unity is rooted in pride in China's rise, its recovery from its "century of humiliation," what it has achieved in terms of economic growth, and its rising presence in the world. On the other, it is based on cultural nationalism tropes—the "greatness of China," its "5,000 years of history," its "glorious culture," and its people's "shared blood" as "descendants of the Yellow and Yan emperors" (*yan huang zisun*)—which the government has increasingly promoted since the early 1990s. There are also jingoistic elements such as the recovery of what is claimed to be lost territory and opposition to the US and Japan, evil enemies who want to overthrow the government and break up China.

Privilege and condescension toward persons from different ethnic groups, different social strata, or different parts of the country play a role in the social disunity in China. Some Shanghainese feel that they are more sophisticated than people from elsewhere, and many in Beijing, which has been the capital of China for most of the past eight centuries, have a sense of cultural superiority. Privilege is a factor in that

---

6. A patriotic education campaign began in the early 1990s in response to the Tiananmen Incident.

the *hukou* (population registration) assigns people, usually based on their mother's birthplace, to a particular place of residence. The main distinction is between rural and urban, but the assignment is for a specific location (e.g., a Beijing *hukou*, which is prized in China). One's *hukou* determines what sorts of rights, privileges, and benefits one is entitled to. Mooted reforms in the *hukou* system will take years to implement and will still exclude the majority of rural–urban migrants.

Two recent issues demonstrate the desire of the privileged to hang on to their advantages. One has to do with the crowded roads and frequent traffic jams in Beijing and the measures the government is taking to alleviate them: limiting monthly additions to the number of vehicles, reducing the number of cars by restricting the number of Beijing registrations through a lottery system; or rationing the roads by prohibiting vehicles according to the last digit of their license plate number on particular days or, on very busy occasions, allowing only vehicles with even- or odd-numbered plates. This has resulted in displays of Beijing nativism, with Beijing residents blaming traffic congestion on vehicles with non-Beijing license plates and demanding that they be banned from using Beijing's roads. A professor suggested changing this to a simple, user pays system as a way to reduce road use, a 20 yuan road-user fee such as those charged in Singapore and London. Furious netizens reacted to his recommendation by uploading his photo enclosed in a black frame such as those used at funerals to portray the recently deceased (Chublic 2016).

The other issue is access to higher education. Those wanting a place in university take a national meritocratic exam called the *gaokao*. However, locations that have universities receive a higher quota of admissions than places without. Thus, students from Beijing and Shanghai, which both have many universities, have a better chance of gaining a place than those from outside. This discriminates against students from poorer areas or populous provinces, such as Shandong and Henan, that have few universities. Government efforts to make the system fairer have met with loud protests from parents of students living in university-rich locations and who see those universities as belonging to their particular areas rather than to the nation as a whole (Hernández 2016a).

Another factor in disunity, one that is more individual or us versus them, is the competition for scarce goods. China remains perennially overpopulated. It was especially so after the peace and stability during the first half of the Qing dynasty (1644–1911) that allowed the population to exceed carrying capacity. Gold sees this competition expressed in

> the deplorable state of public morality and civic consciousness in China. The cutthroat competition for a seat on a bus, the anarchic manner of operating vehicles, the increase in the crime rate, and the notoriously indifferent-to-surly service in stores are examples of how people relate to one another in impersonal or anonymous situations. (1985, 665)

This competition also helps explain the attitudes presented in Chapter 4—striving to be first, fear of suffering a loss, and benefiting at others' expense—which are products of the zero-sum view of relationships with outsiders that lies behind some of the uncivil person-to-person behavior found in Chinese society. Queuing is stressed in Chinese moral education textbooks, but parents urge their offspring to strive to be first from a young age in order to get more attention from teachers.[7] In George Foster's model of the "Image of Limited Good," an individual cannot be seen to possess or compete for scarce goods because, given the strong desire for equality among villagers, it would make others envious and invite undesirable consequences (Foster 1965). However, there are no such fears in China, where, in fact, it would be abnormal not to be competitive; not being so would guarantee that one would suffer both a material loss and a loss of face as one would lose out to others. Better still is to strive to benefit at others' expense.

This high level of competitiveness, in combination with authoritarian governance, also explains the absence of a sense of justice. I mentioned above the special supply system in China that provides officials with organic foods and allows them to avoid the heavy metals, harmful chemicals, and adulterated substances in the foods that ordinary people consume. When I have asked whether people object to this system on the grounds of justice and fairness, I am told that they do not, that justice and fairness are not part of their society, that people's reaction is, instead, to look for ways to become one of those who enjoy the safer goods.

Steven Mosher illustrates this attitude through an incident in the market town in which he did field research in the early 1980s. There was a multistory restaurant in the town. It was public, but only the cadres had access to the top floor, where they disappeared late every morning for a long and, it was strongly suspected by the ordinary townsfolk, sumptuous lunch at public expense. This behavior breached the notion of egalitarianism, and it embittered the townspeople, not because the privilege the cadres enjoyed was unfair—it was—but because of envy, that it was the cadres and not the envious townsfolk—them, not us/me—who were privileged (Mosher 1983). In China's authoritarian society, there is no way to seek redress for such wrongs. Complaining about injustice is useless and may even be dangerous, so endeavoring to become one of the privileged is a logical pursuit.

The competitiveness in Chinese society and the indifference to fairness or social justice also engenders in some a disregard of others. In the early 1980s some local food producers in Fujian began to produce fake medicines that they then, by giving kickbacks to purchasing agents, sold to hospitals. The state acted only a few years ago, when these companies became a competitive risk to state-owned pharmaceutical factories (Yan 2011, 57). Since that time a number of other food or product scandals have come to light, but what is worrying is the callousness displayed toward their fellow citizens by the perpetrators. Yan cites an interview with workers in a

---

7. Some parents, wanting their child not to miss out, do their part by bribing the teachers to give their child a front row seat (Levin 2012).

factory manufacturing a colloidal food additive from old shoe leather. Their reply to a CCTV journalist, who asked if they were aware that the additive would contaminate foods to which it was added, was indifferent. Knowing about the additives, they avoided them; what happens to strangers was not of their concern (Yan 2011, 58). Yan also cites a township government head who, when asked whether he knew that locals were producing counterfeit goods, replied that, to him, "the highest morality under heaven is to let my poor hometown become rich" (Yan 2011, 60). It is sentiments such as these that lead some scholars to conclude that China is experiencing a moral crisis (Ci 1994; Wang 2002).

Fourth is differences in governance. The CCP and the colonial-era KMT share structural similarities, both being Leninist parties; the CCP was organized by Comintern agent Mikhail Borodin, who also helped reorganize the KMT. However, a crucial difference between the two parties was the KMT's commitment through its official ideology, the "Three Principles of the People" (San Min Zhuyi), to phase in popular democracy following a period of tutelage. The CCP, by contrast, was committed only to democratic centralism. The KMT government made little progress toward introducing democracy during its governance of China, though it did adopt a constitution and hold National Assembly and Legislative Yuan elections between 1947 and 1948, just before losing the civil war and fleeing to Taiwan. However, it began to hold elections in Taiwan not long after taking control there; village, township, city council and Provincial Assembly polls by 1951; and National Assembly and Legislative Yuan supplementary elections from 1969. Although fiscal and political authority remained firmly in the hands of the central government executive branch, elections for members of lower-level assemblies provided a forum where legislators could debate the government and voice criticisms.[8]

As related in Chapter 5, Taiwan's democratization was preceded by a period of gradually increased toleration of an opposition and de facto looser social control. As citizens protested successfully against environmental pollution, they became empowered to pursue other causes. With Taiwan's democratization over the decade following the formal registration of the DPP, "ownership" of government moved from an authoritarian political class to the citizenry. This was particularly significant in that the KMT government had come from outside Taiwan and imposed itself on the locals, mistreating them, suppressing their language, disparaging their customs, and discriminating against them in several areas of public employment. The weakening, then fall, of the authoritarian KMT government, the succession of a Taiwanese, Lee Teng-hui, to the presidency in 1988, and his dismantling of the Mainlander KMT establishment over the next several years, increased people's sense of identity with Taiwan as a society rather than with their kin, village, or personal network.

---

8. US pressure was also a factor because of ROC dependency on US aid and diplomatic support.

In China, by contrast, the arrest of five feminists in 2015 for protesting against sexual harassment of women on public transport, something the government also opposes, attests to citizen participation being unwelcome. The government there owns governing, and the citizenry is not to interfere in any way with its social management unless it is specifically invited to do so, such as by participating in government-sponsored campaigns, or is expressly allowed to do so by the terms of an officially permitted grassroots organization.

These differences are reflected in how China and the KMT have governed. Both governments undertook land reform in the early 1950s, but the impact on local social organization was far less destabilizing in Taiwan than in China. During China's land reform, the government dismantled lineages, which had traditionally been the de facto village governance structures, confiscating their property and destroying their genealogies. It also banned temple worship, and it substituted its own control mechanisms by socializing the means of production and putting its cadres in control. Three decades later, when it decollectivized agriculture, it greatly reduced its level of local control, leaving a power vacuum that adversely affected village governance (Liu 2000; Madsen 1984). From the 1950s to the 1980s the Chinese government sought to substitute socialist morality for traditional morality—that is, to replace loyalty to family and kin with loyalty to the collective, the party, and the state—and to replace relations based on friendship, which it regarded as particularistic, with relations based on comradeship, which it saw as universalistic (Vogel 1965; Gold 1985). But when it discarded class struggle as part of Reform and Opening Up (*gaige kaifang*), though it still paid lip service to these reforms, it essentially abandoned them, not only leaving a moral-ethical vacuum but also switching to a market economy with its attendant atomization and promotion of *sauve qui peut* (Ci 2009, 2014; He 2015a, 2015b).

In Taiwan, by contrast, the government created a rural sector of small landowners who engaged in family farming and left kinship and village structures intact. It confiscated land from landlords, but it compensated them with shares in government corporations, turning their focus toward the urban industrial economy. It made superficial but generally ineffective efforts to reduce participation in folk religion, but it did not interfere in ancestor worship and, in fact, strongly reinforced the importance of family and kinship in its public actions.

Both the KMT and the Chinese governments employed policies of state corporatism. Key organizations were directly linked to the government, and any bodies that were not directly associated with it were controlled by requiring them to affiliate with official bodies in their general area of service. Moreover, both disallowed organizational duplication, thus forbidding rival organizations dealing with the same issue. However, this control loosened in Taiwan in the 1980s and was rescinded with revisions to the Civil Associations Law in 1989. Government control of society loosened in China during the 1980s, but tightened up after Tiananmen and has intensified further since Xi Jinping assumed the presidency.

Fifth is the differential levels of trust in China and Taiwan. As stated in Chapter 2, most villagers traveled little historically and had limited social networks. Thus, trust was limited to one's kin and fellow villagers, and strangers were regarded with suspicion. The advent of the Chinese government in the 1950s brought about a good deal of mobility in urban areas, but this did not change radically in the countryside until the 1980s reforms, when villagers were allowed to go to urban areas and coastal regions to find work. Both increased contacts between strangers, though migrants continued to be suspicious of them. Surveys of migrant workers, for example, show that they mainly trust people back home and fellow workers from their home areas[9] (Zhang 2011; Liu and Liu 2012). In surveys in which general respondents are asked if they trust strangers, no more than 30 percent answer that they do (Wang and Liu 2002), although if respondents are given a third choice, "trust," "don't trust," and "not sure" or "depends," the level of distrust drops from around 70 percent to 35 percent (SCCR 2013). If respondents are asked not whether they trust strangers but whether "most people can be trusted," in most surveys over half answer that they can (see, e.g., Inglehart et al. 2010, 139).

Aside from distrust of others, there is much else to be wary of. Peng Siqing a Peking University, Guanghua School of Management, professor of marketing, lists the following:

- Shoddy products ranging from consumer items and services to large construction projects such as the Chongqing pedestrian bridge, Hangzhou's shoddy dike, and the many "bean curd dregs" buildings that have harmed the nation and brought calamity to the people.
- Promotion of products and services, extending to manufacturers and retailers, that makes people feel that others are interested only in profits and causes them to be distrustful of strangers.
- Acquaintances, friends and kin who utilize the lax regulatory system in China that makes it easy for pyramid retailing businesses to take advantage of others. When friends and kin fall out, it is often over business.
- Officials and law enforcement personnel, who are often in collusion with counterfeiters; "in many places, 'striking against fraud (*dajia*)' becomes 'fraudulent striking (*jia da*).'"
- The legal system has many laws against fraud, counterfeit and the like, but there are also too many loopholes and too much lax enforcement.
- Old values have been replaced by new ones that justify self-seeking behavior, and expressing support for the old values is viewed as cynical. (2003)

High survey trust scores for governments in China can be deceptive. A 2011 Edelman Trust Barometer survey asked citizens in twenty-three countries, "How much do you trust government to do what is right?" Its results put the Chinese

---

9. In my 1990s research on Taiwanese-run factories in the Pearl River Delta Region I found that migrant workers stuck very closely to those from their home areas.

government, with an 88 percent positive score, on top, but this finding was met with strong criticism. Peking University scholar of government, Peng Zhenhuai, averred that the finding did not accurately reflect the general views of most Chinese, stating, "The fact is nowadays most Chinese feel distrustful, anxious and deprived" (Zhang and Ji 2011). Articles in the *Global Times*, China's most nationalistic newspaper, state that corruption, mistreatment of citizens, the lack of efficiency and credibility, and media distortions have eroded trust in government (2011; Wu 2009; Zhang and Ji 2011). An illustration is the salt panic that hit China in the wake of the Fukushima catastrophe in Japan. Citizens, believing that iodine prevents cancer from radiation, demonstrated their distrust in government by rushing out to buy (iodized) salt despite announcements on state TV that doing so was useless (Global Voices 2011).

There is little evidence that much has changed over the past several years, but thanks to Weibo and other internet forums, citizens are more aware and more sophisticated. They have expressed their anger over the Wenzhou train crash and the clumsy attempt to cover it up and the shoddily built school buildings that collapsed in the Wenchuan earthquake, killing tens of thousands of schoolchildren. There are also reports of myriad grassroots protests caused mainly by poor-quality governance, workers not being paid, the SARS cover-up and the Henan blood scandal, extremely heavy air pollution, all sorts of food contamination and food frauds, and the sale of improperly stored vaccines.

Trust as a research focus has not attracted much attention from scholars in Taiwan. I have found no dedicated discussions of it, and where it is included in surveys, it is only one among many topics on which opinion is sought. Questions on trust are frequently included in the annual social change surveys carried out by the Institute of Sociology, Academia Sinica, Taiwan, but they constitute a small proportion of the questions. For example, in the 2003 survey, there were three related questions. See Table 6.1 on p. 146. A civil society research project asked about trust in two surveys with samples from China and the United States as well as Taiwan with the results shown in Table 6.2 on p. 146.

The only long-term, systematic project on trust in Taiwan came from the organization established by Li Kwoh-ting. In 1991 he called on socially prominent individuals to create the Society to Promote Group-Self Ethics (SEA) in order to promote the "sixth human relationship" and increase mutual trust, assistance and benefit. In 2001 the society began to undertake large-scale telephone surveys sampling Taiwan residents twenty and older to assess the level of social trust.[10] Survey results are shown in Table 6.3 (see p. 147).

Table 6.3 shows that trust in "most people" increased steadily from 34.1 percent in 2001 to 64.5 percent in 2013. The survey also found that trust levels were positively correlated with level of education, 46.1 percent of those with a primary school education or less believing most people to be trustworthy, rising to 77.7 percent

---

10. Sample sizes range from 1,067 to 1,092. The society states that it is representative regarding sex, place of residence, age, and education level.

Table 6.1
Do you feel that most people . . . (%)*

	Agree		Disagree		Indifferent	
	Face-to-face	Telephone	Face-to-face	Telephone	Face-to-face	Telephone
Can be trusted?	32.4	36.2	27.2	19.0	40.1	44.8
Will take advantage of you if they get the chance?	15.6	14.5	59.9	55.6	24.3	29.8
Are happy to help others?	49.6	43.0	18.5	19.1	31.8	37.9

* This survey was administered to both a face-to-face and a telephone sample.
Source: Chang and Fu (2004, 243).

Table 6.2
How many can be trusted*

Place	Almost all can be trusted (%)		Most can be trusted (%)	
	2004	2007	2004	2007
Taiwan	8.33	11.30	67.02	69.49
China	7.00	6.92	74.73	78.29
United States	16.07	n/a	64.83	n/a

* Data cited were collected in the thematic research project, "Social Capital: Its Origins and Consequences" (Grant No.: AS-94-TP-CO2). The project was conducted by the Institute of Sociology, Academia Sinica, with pilot funding by the Research Center for Humanities and Social Sciences, Academia Sinica. The principal investigators are Lin Nan, Fu Yang-chih, and Chen Chih-jou. I thank Chen Chih-jou for sharing these data with me. Readers may note that the total "trust" figure is higher for China than for Taiwan; this is true for all such surveys that I have seen.

of those with tertiary education. The survey also found that 58.8 percent felt that "most people are well-intentioned and willing to help others" while 33.8 percent believed that they "cared only for themselves" (SEA 2013).

Using a scale from 1 to 5, strong trust to strong distrust with the midpoint 3 denoting no feeling one way or the other, Table 6.4 shows that trust in the family scored highest, above 4.73 in all surveys. Doctors were the next highest, followed by primary and secondary school teachers, neighbors, and basic-level civil servants. In sixth place was "most people" (i.e., strangers), rising from 2.80 in the 2001 survey

Table 6.3
"In general do you trust or distrust most people?" (%)*

	2001	2002	2004	2006	2008	2013
Trust	34.1	38.1	50.6	60.3	60.5	64.5
Don't trust	47.3	44.8	34.7	27.0	27.9	26.7

* A survey was carried out in 2011 but was scored differently, so the results are not comparable.
Source: SEA (2013).

Table 6.4
Levels of trust*

	2013	2008	2006	2004	2002	2001
Family	4.75	4.78	4.79	4.79	4.73	4.77
Doctors	4.05	4.10	4.09	3.98	3.77	3.78
Primary/secondary teachers	4.03	3.95	4.08	3.95	3.78	3.76
Neighbors	3.82	3.90	–	3.88	3.70	3.62
Basic-level public servants	3.55	–	–	3.49	3.13	–
Most people in society	3.47	3.39	3.44	3.18	2.84	2.80
Enterprise managers	3.12	3.06	3.22	3.00	2.94	2.52
Police	3.07	2.97	2.93	3.08	2.96	2.93
Lawyers	2.90	2.99	2.95	–	–	2.84
The president	2.57	3.01	2.73	3.25	3.01	3.51
Judges	2.50	2.88	3.06	3.23	2.85	3.05
Reporters	2.48	2.36	2.32	2.59	2.59	–
Financial managers	2.48	–	–	–	–	–
Real estate brokers	2.39	–	–	–	–	–
Legislators	2.32	2.24	2.12	2.25	2.21	2.29
Government officials	2.27	2.49	2.45	2.64	2.28	2.63

* Dash (–) indicates that participants were not asked about that category in that survey.
Source: SEA 2013.

to 3.47 in 2013. Trust in institutions and those who run them make up the bottom of the list.

Of particular relevance to civility are the levels of trust of neighbors and of "most people in society." As noted above, trust of strangers has risen with each survey; six in ten believe that strangers are well intentioned (*shanyi*) and that most people are willing to help others (SEA 2013; see also Peng 2013).

Factors That Facilitate or Hinder the Development of Civility

In Chapter 2, I set out a number conditions that I intuitively thought would facilitate or hinder the development of people-to-people civility or civility toward the public space. What follows is a discussion of how I see their explanatory power in the light of the research results above.

I proposed that the following four conditions would have a positive effect on social civility:

- People show concern for others.
- People are generally content with life and are optimistic toward the future.
- Government is not oppressive; it generally meets citizen needs and is seen as striving to be efficient, responsive, honest, fair, and competent.
- There is a culture of obedience to road rules and acting courteously toward other drivers.

That people showing concern for others, treating them civilly, will enhance civil behavior is most likely correct. Before the 1990s in Taiwan people turned their heads and walked past strangers who had fallen down. One reason was that if a Good Samaritan took such a person to a hospital, he or she could be held responsible to pay for the person's care. Another reason was that people simply avoided situations that did not directly involve them. A third, based on the embarrassed grins on people's faces when confronting such a situation, is that they simply did not know what they should do. The rise in popularity of socially engaged Buddhism and its emphasis on philanthropy and compassion and the public effort behind the building of Ciji's first hospital helped raise public consciousness about the needs of others. The revision of the Civil Associations Law (*minjian tuanti fa*) in 1989, abandoning state corporatism, sparked off the formation of all sorts of grassroots organizations, including many dedicated to helping the disadvantaged. From the 1990s, candidates for public office began including "love" for people and society among their qualifications for office. In 2014 I saw several ads in subways informing passengers about NGOs whose purpose was to help those with various kinds of problems. Taiwan is also more than self-sufficient in blood donations.

For a variety of reasons Chinese citizens are less inclined to show concern. First, the party/state monopolized the philanthropy sector from 1954 until the 1980s, condemning grassroots or religious charities as having nefarious intentions and announcing that looking after people was a government/party responsibility. Second, since resuming a role as a contributor to philanthropy the public has been generous in times of national or local emergencies such as the 1991 floods in eastern China, the Wenchuan and Yushu earthquakes, the 2012 Beijing flash flood and the 2015 Tianjin explosion. However, the 2011 China Red Cross and Henan Soong Ching Ling Foundation scandals shook people's faith in government-linked charities, which are still the mainstream philanthropic organizations. Third, government wariness of grassroots organizations and their lack of transparency has hampered the growth of civil society and grassroots philanthropy. Fourth, there has been no phenomenon comparable to the rise of Taiwan's socially engaged Buddhism; some Taiwan Buddhist groups, including Ciji, are allowed to carry out relief work in China but not to recruit or accept members. Nonetheless, popular responses to disasters and to persons in need, and the internet outrages in response to reports of cruelty to animals are an encouraging sign of the potential for Chinese citizens to be charitable and caring.

There is indirect evidence supporting a positive link between contentment and optimism with civility. It is generally agreed on both sides of the Taiwan Straits that the Taiwanese are manifestly more civil than are those in China, and according to the World Happiness Report, they are also a good deal happier. In 2016 Taiwan ranked 35th with a score of 6.379 (out of 10), China ranked 83rd with a score of 5.245. Both scores are up slightly from 2015 (Helliwell, Huang, and Wang 2016).

An efficient, responsive, honest, and fair government will certainly have a positive, though perhaps indirect, effect on its citizens' moods and attitudes, and, indeed, the perception of government corruption forms a part of the World Happiness Index. Having such a government should logically predispose people to being more civil, though I have no direct evidence of this. As the effect of government on civility figures in more than one of the factors I am examining, I will discuss it further below.

The 17 million cases of road rage recorded in China in 2015 (Yu 2015) indicate that encountering discourteous or dangerous driving or pedestrian behavior probably does affect drivers' moods and their behavior toward other road users. How it might affect their behavior after they leave their cars is another question. No road-rage figures are available for Taiwan, but driver behavior there improved greatly from the mid-1990s.

I also proposed four conditions that should have a positive effect on civil behavior in the public space:

- people no longer being willing to sacrifice the natural or built environment for economic growth;
- the provision of public places that people enjoy visiting such as parks, malls, nature reserves, scenic drives, mountain trails and beaches;
- public education campaigns not to litter, waste bins on streets, and enforcement of anti-littering/defacing regulations; and
- something like a "no broken windows" policy to keep public space clean and in good repair.

People no longer being willing to sacrifice the natural or built environment for economic growth, even if only for their own comfort or convenience, is a sign that they are becoming environmentally conscious. As shown in Chapter 5, campaigns against environmental degradation were the first popular movements in

Taiwan, and these have continued, the latest example being demonstrations against a nuclear power plant in a northern Taiwan area known to be geologically unstable. Environmental activism in China is more recent, but it has had some impact. In 2007 tens of thousands of Xiamen residents successfully protested against the installation of a paraxylene (PX) plant. It was instead installed in nearby Zhangzhou, and Xiamen residents must have thanked their good fortune when, in April 2015, there was an explosion at the plant—the second in two years (BBC 2015)! In 2001 Dalian residents forced the closure of a PX plant after a dyke protecting it broke. In 2014, protesters in Maoming demonstrated against a PX plant and were joined by sister demonstrations in Shenzhen and Guangzhou (*Economist* 2014b). Protests have also occurred in China over waste incinerator projects and coal-fired power plants, e.g., in Shanghai, Lubu and Wuchuan, and netizens have decried the foul air in Beijing and other cities, especially since the "airpocalypse"[11] (Wainwright 2014; Gan 2016). It may have been easier for those engaged in Taiwan's 1980s protests, as they were generally residents of small population centers and protesting against small businesses. Those in China have targeted large companies backed by the state or at least by local government.

However, the concern about polluted air, soil, and water in China has not yet extended to a general consciousness against littering. Sidewalks are swept in many cities every morning, but the litter in bushes at the side is ignored, and more litter accumulates in the public space during the day. There are scenic spots in China, but they are trashed during holidays when many tourists visit them. Thus, having nice places to visit is not enough. People also need to be environmentally conscious and publically minded.

The same can be said for environmental tidiness campaigns and "no broken windows" policies. Whereas dilapidation invites vandalism in some Western countries, it is much less common in China or Taiwan because, I was told, the density of population makes it much harder to get away with. Sweeping the streets early every morning can be seen as a "no broken windows" effort, and civilizing messages from the government are ubiquitous, probably so much so that they lose their impact. Placing rubbish bins at moderate distances on the sidewalks should make it easier for people to dispose of trash properly, but they will do so only if they are environmentally aware.

Finally, I proposed four conditions that were likely to hinder the development of civility:

- Society is a police state with domestic informers.
- People feel threatened, especially physically, by crime.
- There are ethnic or religious rifts in society creating out-groups "undeserving" of civil treatment.

---

11. The English nickname for the very severe air pollution in Beijing in 2014.

- Society or government is seen as unjust and unfair; democracy, while not a "necessary" condition, may be important in this regard.

That the first three of these conditions hinder civility is self-evident. Living in a police state in which there are informers who spy on others destroys mutual trust, without which people will not be civil to strangers. They will, instead, turn inward, revealing only a facade to others, trusting only a small number of intimates and avoiding interactions with persons they do not know (Vogel 1965, 46; Kleinman 2006, 80; 2011, 5–7). Taiwan experienced this from 1949 until 1987 during the martial law / White Terror period. Some 140,000 people are said to have disappeared or been executed or jailed. This condition was also common during the Cultural Revolution in China when people were instructed to inform on friends and family and had to at least be seen to comply in order not to fall under suspicion themselves (Dikötter 2016). At present, such a level of government surveillance is generally restricted to persons who do something to arouse security-agency suspicions.

Trust, and hence civil treatment of others, will also diminish if people feel physically threatened by strangers (see Helliwell et al. 2015, 6). However, this seems not to be a serious problem in either Taiwan or China. Ten years ago people in Taiwan, particularly women, would complain that the social order was bad, but when I them asked if they were afraid to walk alone on the street at night, none said that they were, and they seemed surprised at the question. I have also been told that cities in China are safe for women, though the countryside is less so. However, in China, confrontations of any kind, even over something as banal as queue-jumping, smoking, or littering, can result in violence.[12]

Civility will also be limited if there are out-groups or other rifts in society. As shown in Chapter 5, there was condescension toward Taiwanese by Mainlanders in Taiwan for the first several decades of KMT rule, though this has diminished because the KMT no longer has a monopoly on government, and Mainlander identity is no longer salient to the younger generations. However, there are many social cleavages in China. In Beijing during the Cultural Revolution, there were even conflicts between youths from the hutong[13] and those from the residential compounds of higher civilian and military officials (Dikötter 2016).

As noted, during Mao's time, the Chinese government attempted to overcome the particularism in Chinese society by advocating universalistic comradeship, but despite this, most relationships were based on a zero-sum game mentality, with competition between those of different place of origin, residence area, work unit, or the like. Even within the party, members formed networks of "good ol' boys (*laohaoren*), to engage in corruption" (Gold 1985, 664).

---

12. As explained to me, if A accidentally steps on B's foot and apologizes, that will be the end of the matter. If, however, A does not apologize and B calls attention to A's act, A may feel a loss of face and react with curses or even with blows. Asking a person not to smoke or litter can provoke a similar reaction.
13. The hutong were the residential areas of the ordinary people.

As for perceptions of government as fair, there are certainly incidents of even violent protest resulting from actions by government agents regarded as highhanded. Demonstrations over selling off lands in Wukan, for example, produced strident clashes with authorities (Economy 2012; Wong 2016). In Hubei crowds clashed with police after the body of a hotel chef was found outside the gate. Police said he left a suicide note, but the crowds did not believe them and suspected them of being in cahoots with hotel personnel who were said to be dealing drugs (Xie 2009). In Wenzhou people rioted and beat five urban managers to unconsciousness after witnessing them use a hammer to beat to death a man who was taking pictures of them beating a female street vendor. Several months before in Xiamen a man poured sulfuric acid over eighteen urban managers who were attempting to demolish his home (Stevens 2014). However, I have no evidence that government repression has a general effect on people's moods, in particular that someone upset by government actions would treat others uncivilly because of it. Only a small minority of persons, such as human rights activists or the politically committed, are affected in their everyday lives by government actions. Most pay little attention to what governments do unless they are directly affected.

Moreover, in China, despite news of civil liberty restrictions or arrests of human rights lawyers and activists, it seems clear that most Chinese, on balance, have a positive overall impression of their government based on improvements to their material conditions and their pride in China's many accomplishments since the 1980s and its place in the world. Whatever its faults, the present Chinese government has performed far better than any previous Chinese government. People are aware of government failings—for example, the Wenzhou train crash (Brannigan 2011), the recent vaccine scandal (Wang and Burkitt 2016), or the privileges officials arrogate to themselves, and although many will vent their anger on social media, they feel powerless to engage in more forceful efforts to seek justice or fairness. In fact, realizing that they can do nothing to change the system, they shift their interests to becoming part of it.

However, it is possible that the Chinese government, through its repression of demonstrations in 1989, may have affected civility. According to Stein Ringen, those demonstrations were widespread, in perhaps one hundred or more cities, not just in Beijing. Moreover, they were genuinely popular, not only with student supporters but also with workers, officials, soldiers, and journalists. Because of the economic reforms and the generally more liberal atmosphere in the 1980s, "Young people thought they had a future in an increasingly open society." Aside from those killed in the crackdown, "what was killed . . . was hope itself . . . The effects have been lasting and can be seen in the nihilistic materialism, moral corruption, cynicism, disaffection and confusion of identity that are now prevalent in Chinese culture and social life" (2016, 4). Such feelings and outlooks are not conducive toward civil behavior but instead feed directly into the moral crisis that many say now plagues China.

Since democratization in Taiwan, people have been willing and able to protest in their quest to influence government action, e.g., the Wild Lily Movement mentioned above). More recently, in 2014, in what has been called the Sunflower Movement, young people occupied the Legislative Yuan for twenty-three days to protest against a proposed trade agreement between Taiwan and China. The government refused to reveal details of the pact and attempted to ram it through the legislature without due consideration of each clause. The protesters argued that the agreement would allow China to dominate Taiwan economically and would destroy many jobs. In fact, satisfaction with the government greatly decreased after 2012 because of perceptions that it was too China-friendly, President Ma Ying-jeou's popularity plummeting to 9.2 percent at one point (C. Wang 2013), but popular ire was taken out on the government itself, not on random members of the public.

Values and Civility

Inglehart and Welzel argue that sustainable democracy becomes possible when a sufficient proportion of the citizenry hold what they call self-expression values (2005). They do not specify what the proportion of persons holding self-expression values might be (Inglehart, personal communication),[14] but judging from the data in the book's tables, it appears to be around one-third. They contrast postindustrial, self-expression values with what they label survival values, which are found in industrial societies. In such societies, manufacturing is the driver of the economy, and people are primarily concerned with increasing their level of material well-being. Industrial society values include rationalism, as opposed to supernatural belief; secularization, as opposed to ecclesiastical authority; bureaucratization; collective discipline; group conformity; and state authority.

Self-expression values become increasingly prevalent when a country reaches a postindustrial stage of development in which high-level services provided by well-educated workers come to constitute a significant proportion of economic activities. The expansion of high-level service industries creates societies in which there are increases in both the complexity of the division of labor and material security. These bring an increase in people pursuing individual interests and desiring to fulfill them. Although they may still want to raise their level of material well-being, they reach a point at which the marginal utility of an additional increment of income no longer outweighs that of spending the increment of time needed to earn it doing something that makes them happy, something that they want to do for the pleasure of it, for self-fulfillment. Moreover, based on the findings of the World Values Surveys,[15] wanting to fulfill themselves, they respect the rights of others to do likewise, which

---

14. In an email exchange in late September 2012, Professor Inglehart wrote that he had not set a specific percentage.
15. Professor Inglehart played a leading role in extending the World Values Surveys to a greater number of societies.

creates the tolerance of those with different ideas that makes sustainable democracy possible. Religion, rather than declining as it does in industrial societies, changes in the direction of individual spirituality.

Heightened material well-being also increases empathy and toleration of interpersonal differences, thus strengthening acceptance of gender, racial, religious, and sexual orientation equality. A postindustrial economy also brings about a rise in the welfare state, which decreases dependence on the family and facilitates increased individualism and diversity in people's interests. Risk perceptions tend to be of long-term perils that threaten humanity as a whole, such as global warming, rather than the sorts of threats to the individual that those with survival values feel (Inglehart and Welzel 2005, 1–45).

Although Inglehart and Welzel focus on democracy rather than civility, the characteristics they identify that make democracy possible and sustainable—tolerance, concern for, and consideration of others, including unseen others—are precisely the same characteristics that are the foundation of civility. They write,

> The shift from survival values to self-expression values is linked with a rising sense of existential security and human autonomy, which produces a humanistic culture of tolerance and trust, where people place a relatively high value on individual freedom and self-expression and have activist political orientations. (2005, 56)

These changes, together with the awareness of others that they create, also encourage a mindset that makes civility a logical way to behave: treat others as one would like to be treated by them. And recognizing others—strangers—as consociates creates a sense of a public that includes everyone and a public space that belongs to all. One can thus argue that a critical mass of people holding self-expression values creates the fertile soil needed to germinate and nurture civility in a society.

Inglehart and Welzel write that, based on World Value Survey results in China, were its levels of growth to be maintained (which they were), they expected that it would democratize fairly soon (2005, 42). This has proved overly optimistic. According to a 2011 Gallup poll, 71 percent of Chinese respondents regard themselves as "struggling," 17 percent as "suffering," and only 12 percent as "thriving" (Chin 2012). Moreover, Inglehart and Welzel state, "The timing and pace of measurable change in a society is not necessarily correlated with change in values, especially if there are legal or structural barriers to such changes" (2005, 39). Although some in China display the kinds of behavior associated with self-fulfillment values, that barrier exists in the Chinese Communist Party's desire for a monopoly of power and control over everything.

Society for Itself

As stated above, a society for itself is one in which being a member is, in some contexts, an important part of people's identities, in which they feel linked to others on the basis of also being members, and in which they recognize an affective bond with their compatriots. It stands in contrast to the mode of social organization that existed historically in Chinese society or in Taiwan before the 1990s. There, persons of significance were limited to insiders, those within the boundary of Fei's concentric-circles model. Others simply existed; at best, they were inconsequential; at worst, they were a potential source of danger. Moreover, by definition, all such groups of insiders were in competition with each other, creating a zero-sum mentality in that anything one did for a member of another kinship group was a potential loss for one's own. There was no reason to extend civil treatment to those outside one's own social circle and every reason not to.

Such societies lack a polity and a public. A polity requires that the citizens who have reached the age of majority are able to participate in public affairs. Some would go so far as to say that such participation is everyone's civic duty because it gives every individual a stake in how society is managed. Polity is linked to public, and according to Alexander,

> In the minds of most democratic theorists, it seems, the notion of the public points to the existence of an actual group, to actual deliberations, and to an actual place. According to the concrete notion of the public, members of a closely-knit polity meet with one another in the same physical environment, vigorously debating the events that affect their lives. (2006, 71)

In present-day societies, rather than discussions in the same physical environment, such as the agora or the coffee house, the meeting of the public mostly takes place virtually and symbolically, through op-eds, letters to the editor, commentaries in various publications, blogs, satire, talk-back radio, internet bulletin boards, social media, documentaries, demonstrations, communication with those in executive and legislative bodies who represent citizens, voting, participation in civil society, public-opinion surveys, and focus groups, including those commissioned by private entities such as political parties.

In 1950 neither a public nor a polity existed for most people in Taiwan because, although it was a modern state, as a society it consisted of myriad small communities in which people interacted primarily with those from within their own areas. Communities of Taiwanese were mostly geographically based in villages and neighborhoods. Communities of Mainlanders were rooted in what part of China they came from, what dialect they spoke, and, for some, in what government department, bureau, office, or military unit the breadwinner worked in. Han Taiwanese were conscious that they were Taiwanese, Hoklo, or Hakka, but except for a small number, mainly intellectuals, subjectively they were much more members of their communities than Taiwanese. They could act on their Taiwanese identity through language or folk practices, but asserting it politically was perilous. For Mainlanders, Taiwan was nothing more than a place of temporary refuge from the Communists, the more temporary the better, and the government did all it could to encourage that feeling through its ubiquitous propaganda about recovering the mainland, through creating dependent's villages to house the families of military personnel, and through making "native place" a part of one's official identity. Because it fit into the government's mainland recovery mission, Mainlanders were free to express their subcultural identity.

As explained in Chapter 5, over the next four decades, these microcommunities blended into a Taiwanese society that encompassed the clear majority of persons living there. Rural–urban migration and compulsory military service pulled people out of their communities and exposed them to the wider society. The 1970s nativist literature movement raised the issue of Taiwanese identity and hence Taiwan consciousness, and the formation of a political opposition meant that voters had a choice. In the 1980s self-help protests demonstrated that issues facing one community were shared by those in other villages and communities. The growth of socially engaged Buddhism and the construction of the first Ciji hospital stimulated participation in society as a whole. And the retreat of authoritarianism generated further pressure on the regime and triggered the formal process of democratization with the first fully democratic election of all legislators held in 1991.

Taiwan thus became a society for itself. It has a polity and a public. Its citizens are able to participate in political life and civil society. At a minimum, they can vote in free elections, and their vote determines who will represent them and who will preside. It has a public because, if they so desire, citizens can participate or vent their opinions without fear of reprisal. The Taiwan public, like that in many Western countries, is a symbolic public; it has people who deliberate on politics through talk-back TV and radio, letters to the editor, public opinion surveys, and focus groups, and it also has a robust civil society. Opinion polling also shows that a strong bond of social unity exists in Taiwan based on the democratic way of life its people have struggled to achieve and their desire to maintain it (McLean-Dreyfus and Varrall 2015; Sullivan 2014).

China, rather than constituting a society for itself, is still largely made up of groups of insiders who generally lack concern for the greater public. As mentioned, one does see genuine manifestations of concern during times of emergency, but philanthropic donations are most noticeable at times of disaster. In everyday life drivers compete to be first. People are more likely to queue, but rushing for seats on subways is still common, while yielding them to others is much less so. Feelings of unity are mainly aroused by government media fanning the flames of circle-the-wagons nationalism to ward off alleged threats of foreign enemies who allegedly want to break up China.

China has no physical venues and no symbolic venues at which a public can meet other than internet bulletin boards, which are increasingly heavily censored.[16] While these web forums do afford a place for critical and satirical comments,

---

16. Young savvy Chinese tell me that the censors are not nearly as effective as the government would like them to be and that for those who know how to look for it, there is plenty of information available.

they are too restrictive for sober discussions. A very tight lid is kept on the Party's "private household," making it almost impossible to see what is hidden inside. As Richard McGregor states, the party headquarters building is not even marked as such (2010). As for a symbolic public, the media are controlled; on public TV or radio there are no talk shows, and op-ed columns and other opinion outlets must have party approval. On the odd occasion that something contrary slips through, there are repercussions. Moreover, government tries to control web communication through the so-called fifty-centers, persons supposedly paid half a yuan for each post they write to try to steer discussions away from criticism and toward what is more favorable ground for the government. There are public opinion surveys, but most are officially commissioned and the results remain in-house; those done for genuine scholarly purposes have to get political approval, which limits the questions that can be asked. Although there are "wildcat" demonstrations by people such as workers disgruntled because they have not been paid, demonstrations are illegal unless at least covertly sanctioned by the authorities, such as those targeting Japan from time to time. It is difficult to form a civil society group. To the extent they are approved, they are closely watched and regulated. It is challenging to see how a case could be made that a public exists in China, given that actual groups, deliberations, and places are subject to stringent limitations.

Democracy and Civility

As a final question, in earlier research on civility in Taiwan I found that Taiwanese began to behave civilly at the same time that Taiwan was undergoing democratization, giving rise to the questions of what kind of relationship there might be between the two and whether a link might be causal. Over the period that I have been visiting China (1983 to the present) it has not democratized, but civil behavior has improved. Thus, democracy cannot be a necessary condition. Moreover, the unlikelihood that civility is widespread in India or South Africa indicates that democracy alone is not sufficient. Furthermore, while there are some who are directly and personally affected by particular policies or actions of officials, this study finds no evidence that democracy or the quality of governance affect how people in general treat random others.

In Taiwan's case, democratization may have facilitated the advent of civil behavior, but prior events and phenomena appear more directly related. First, the struggle to force an authoritarian government to democratize and remove the stigma it had imposed on the Taiwanese identity of the great majority of the population created a common bond among the citizenry, turning strangers into compatriots. That struggle also involved events that linked members of small communities with Taiwan society as a whole. Second, the spread of socially engaged Buddhism, with its emphasis on universalism, service, and compassion affected many in Taiwan, including those who formed civil society organizations that served disadvantaged groups and ordinary citizens who supported them by donating and volunteering. The message of compassion was sufficiently forceful that persons seeking office had to lay claim to it during their campaigns. It is circumstantial, though highly plausible, that these, combined with the civility education that students received in primary school but felt were meaningless at the time, and the attacks on incivility by critics such as Lung Ying-tai, became salient to people as the new, democratic society emerged.

Thus, rather than a causal relationship, the link between civility and liberal democracy is, as I argued above, that both are dependent on the same set of values. Those values shape people's worldviews, making them tolerant and considerate of their fellow citizens. I have also pointed out that successful government efforts to improve aspects of civility in Taiwan were made by then Taibei mayor Chen Shui-bian, who did so because, as the first Taibei mayor elected rather than appointed in close to thirty years, he felt he had to have accomplishments in his first term if he were to have a chance to be reelected for a second. A democratic system of government, one in which people periodically choose who will and who will not govern them, can thus be an incentive to improve conditions that foster civility.

However, while I cannot say that democracy is necessarily, intuitively I find it difficult to believe that civility would develop at a society-wide level in an authoritarian regime. While some such regimes can boast solid accomplishments, China being a prime example, the regime's insecurity betrays leadership doubts about the extent to which citizens accept their legitimacy, and that leads to their taking repressive measures, whether this means disappearances, arrests of critics on spurious or loosely defined charges such as "picking quarrels to provoke trouble," or merely restricting access to information. Moreover, the overriding concern by authoritarian regimes is to stay in power, China again being a prime example (Dai 2009).

It is also questionable whether civility is a priority of authoritarian regimes. An important motivation for the NLM was to change the behavior of the masses so that foreigners would no longer regard Chinese as uncivilized and the desire to discipline them in order to make China strong. That of the Five Stresses and Four Beauties was to repair the damage to the social fabric wrought by the Cultural Revolution and the chaotic, everyone-for-themselves previous thirty years of class struggle. However, both also aimed to strengthen dedication to the regime itself, as have subsequent Chinese civilizing campaigns. In none of these was civil behavior itself the primary goal. In fact, one might question the extent to which authoritarian regimes are willing to commit resources to developing civility as well as whether it is in their power to do so, remembering that civility is the product of a change in values and worldview. There are areas where governments can further this process, such as enforcing no-smoking laws or more strictly enforcing road rules, but measures to eliminate such actions as spitting or littering are far more difficult. Convincing everyone to be considerate toward strangers is harder still.

Glossary

This glossary contains Chinese names and terms used in the text. Names of individuals follow the Chinese practice of surname first, then given name.

bai jiazi	擺架子
baise kongbu	白色恐怖
bangong bandu	半工半讀
barong bachi	八榮八恥
bentu wenxue	本土文學
biaozhun guoyu	標準國語
bu dongshi	不懂事
bu wenming	不文明
changshi	常識
chengguan	城管
chikui	吃虧
China Youth Self-Awareness Promotion Movement	中國青年自覺運動
choufu	仇富
chuangkou fuwu	窗口服務
Ciji	慈繼
Ciji ren	慈繼人
cixu geju	差序格局
da guanqiang	打官腔
dajia	打架
dangwai	黨外
danwei	單位
daode lunsang	道德淪喪
digouyou	地溝油
dingzi jingshen	釘子精神

dixian lunli	底線倫理
dong	動
duanwu	端午
duibuqi	對不起
enka (Japanese)	演歌
ererba shijian	二二八事件
Erya	爾雅
fangyan	方言
fenfu	憤富
feng shui	風水
Foguang Shan	佛光山
Fojiao Tzu Chi Gongde Hui	佛教慈濟功德會
gaige kaifang	改革開放
gaokao	高考
gaoshanzu	高山族
geta (Japanese)	下駄
gong	公
gongde	公德
gongdexin	公德心
gongshi	功時
guan erdai	官二代
guan fang lou guan ma shou guanzhong tangwu jishi chou	官房漏官馬瘦觀眾堂屋雞屍臭
guanxi	關係
guan xianshi	管閒事
guiju	規矩
guojia	國家
guoma	國罵
Hakka	客家
Heimingdan	黑名單
hexie	和諧
Hoklo	鶴佬
hua	華
huache	劃車
huang xian	黃線
huaren	華人
hukou	戶口

huo Lei Feng	活雷鋒
huo pusa	活菩薩
hutong	胡同
jia	家
jiachou buke waiyang	家醜不可外揚
jia da	假打
jiagong jisi	假公濟私
jiang wenming	講文明
jieyun	捷運
jiguan	籍貫
jingcheng sishao	京城四少
jinsi hou	金絲猴
ji suo bu yu wu shi yu ren	己所不欲勿施於人
juancun	眷村
junzi	君子
kanke wenhua	看客文化
keting ji gongchang	客廳即工廠
kōminka (Japanese)	皇民化
Kuomintang (Guomindang)	國民黨
laohaoren	老好人
leng ying tuo ka	冷硬拖卡
li (ceremonial behavior)	禮
li (dynamism)	力
liangxin	良心
limao	禮貌
li ta	利他
liu lun	六倫
li yi lian chi	禮義廉恥
li zhi yong he wei gui	禮之用和為貴
Meilidao Zazhi	美麗島雜誌
mei suzhi	沒素質
minjian tuanti fa	民間團體法
muji (mother hen)	母雞
muji (wooden clogs)	木屐
nianjian	年鑑
ni hao	你好
nongmingong	農民工

pa chikui	怕吃虧
paidui	排隊
pingjing	瓶頸
pingpuzu	平埔族
qian guize	潛規則
qi bu	七不
qing	請
quanmian fazhan	全面發展
qu gongsuo	區公所
qun	群
qun-ji	群-己
ren	仁
renao	熱鬧
ren chi ren de shijie	人吃人的世界
rendao	人道
renkou suzhi	人口素質
renqingwei	人情味
renrou sousuo	人肉搜索
Renshi Taiwan	認識台灣
ruoshi qunti	弱勢群體
ruoshi tuanti	弱勢團體
san de	三德
San Min Zhuyi	三民主義
san reai	三熱愛
shanyi	善意
shehui	社會
shehuizhuyi wenming	社會主義文明
shengfen	生分
shengming ting	生命廳
shengxue jiaoyu	升學教育
shi xingji wenming hu	十星級文明戶
shuangxiuzhi	雙休制
shu xinfeng	樹新風
si	私
side	私德
sile meiyou	死了沒有
sishu	私塾

si you	四有
suanming	算命
suyang	素養
suzhi	素質
suzhi jiaoyu	素質教育
Taiwan wenxue	台灣文學
tamade	他媽的
tamagōtchi (Japanese)	たまごっち
tanqin	探親
tegong	特供
tian	天
tianxia	天下
tie gongji yi mao bu ba	鐵公雞一毛不拔
tongxiang	同鄉
tongxue	同學
tongyi fapiao	統一發票
tuhua	土話
Unity Foundation	統一事業基金會
wang qian (forward) zou	往前走
wang qian (money) zou	往錢走
weibo	微博
wei renmin fuwu	為人民服務
weiyuan	委員
wenming	文明
wenmingban	文明辦
wenming liyi shouce	文明禮儀手冊
wu ai	五愛
wu bu	五不
wu ge limao de ci	五個禮貌的詞
wu hao	五好
wu hao jiating	五好家庭
wu hao wenming jiating	五好文明家庭
wujiang simei	五講四美
wu lun	五倫
wu qin	五勤
wu si	無私
wu si ye	無私也

xiangtu wenxue (hsiang-t'u wen-hsüeh)	鄉土文學
xiangyue	鄉約
xiaoji	小雞
xiao pin bu xiao chang	笑貧不笑娼
xiao ren	小人
xiaoye	宵夜
xiaoyuan gequ	校園歌曲
xiexie	謝謝
Xinshenghuo yundong	新生活運動
xiong haizi	熊孩子
xiushen	修身
Xi You Ji	西遊記
xuanchuan	宣傳
xueba	血霸
xuetou	血頭
yan huang zisun	炎黃子孫
yebaihe yundong	野百合運動
Yehuo Ji	野火集
Yehuo Ji Waiji	野火集外集
ying	迎
yinggai	應該
yingshi jiaoyu	應試教育
yi pan san sha	一盤散沙
yiqi	義氣
yong bu shengxiu de luosiding	永不生鏽的螺絲釘
zaijian	再見
zeren	責任
zhan pianyi	佔便宜
zhengxian konghou	爭先恐後
zhiliang	質量
Zhonghua wenhua fuxing yundong	中華文化復興運動
Zhongyang Ribao	中央日報
Zhongyang wenming weiyuanhui	中央文明委員會
zijiren	自己人
zongzi	粽子
zuo haoshi bei e	做好事被厄

References

Adams, Mike. 2014. "BREAKTHROUGH: Chinese Government Admits One-Fifth of Farms Lands Heavily Contaminated with Toxic Heavy Metals Like Cadmium, Arsenic and Lead." May 1. http://www.naturalnews.com/044950_China_heavy_metals_soils_contamination.html.

AFP (Agence France-Presse). 2011. "General's Son in Road Rage." Cited in *South China Morning Post*. September 10. Accessed September 10, 2011. http://www.scmp.com/portal/site/SCMP/menuitem.2af62ecb329d3d7733492d9253a0a0a0/?vgnextoid=2aa56e377ce42310VgnVCM100000360a0a0aRCRD&ss=china&s=news.

AFP (Agence France-Presse). 2014. "'They Behaved Like Barbarians': State Media Blasts Chinese Tourists Who Scalded Thai Stewardess." *South China Morning Post*. December 16. http://www.scmp.com/news/china/article/1663135/they-behaved-barbarians-chinese-state-media-blasts-tourists-who-scalded.

Alexander, Jeffrey C. 2006. *The Civil Sphere*. Oxford: Oxford University Press.

Alexander, Peter, and Anita Chan. 2004. "Does China Have an Apartheid Pass System?" *Journal of Ethnic and Migration Studies* 30 (4): 609–29.

Alitto, Guy. 1979 *The Last Confucian: Liang Shu-ming and the Chinese Dilemma of Modernity*. Berkeley and Los Angeles: University of California Press.

Almond, Gabriel A., and Sidney Verba. 1963. *The Civic Culture: Political Attitudes and Democracy in Five Nations*. Thousand Oaks, CA: Sage.

Anagnost, Ann. 1997. *National Past-Times: Narrative, Representation, and Power in Modern China*. Durham: Duke University Press.

Anderlini, Jamil. 2013. "Bo World Exposes Lavish World of the Chinese Elite." *Wall Street Journal*. August 23. http://www.ft.com/cms/s/0/f2e2e974-0c12-11e3-8840-00144feabdc0.html.

Anderson, Benedict. 2006. *Imagined Communities: Reflections on the Origin and Spread of Nationalism*. Rev. ed. London: Verso.

Armstrong, Rachel, and Andrew Toh. 2014. "Bill Gates Wants China to Encourage Wealthy Chinese to Be More Giving." Reuters. April 6. http://www.reuters.com/article/us-singapore-gates-idUSBREA3509120140406.

Baike. 2014a. "五好家庭" [Five-good households]. Accessed November 28, 2014. http://www.baike.com/wiki/"五好家庭".

Baike. 2014b. "'五讲四美三热爱'教育" [Five stresses, four beauties, three fervent loves education]. Accessed January 22, 2014. http://www.baike.com/wiki/"五讲四美三热爱"教育.

Baike. 2016. "深圳經濟特區文明行爲促進條例" [Civility behavior promotion regulations of the Shenzhen Special Economic Zone. Accessed August 31, 2016. http://baike.baidu.com/view/10010709.htm.
Barboza, David. 2012. "Billions in Hidden Riches for Family of Chinese Leader." October 26. http://www.nytimes.com/2012/10/26/business/global/family-of-wen-jiabao-holds-a-hidden-fortune-in-china.html.
BBC. 2011a. "China Executes Student for Murder of Hit-and-Run Victim." June 7. http://www.bbc.com/news/world-asia-pacific-13678179.
BBC. 2011b. "China Singer Apologises for Son's Road-Rage Attack." September 9. http://www.bbc.co.uk/news/world-asia-pacific-14855276.
BBC. 2012. "China Fake Parts 'Used in US Military Equipment.'" May 22. http://www.bbc.com/news/world-us-canada-18155293.
BBC. 2015. "China Paraxylene Chemical Plant Hit by Explosion." April 7. http://www.bbc.com/news/world-asia-china-32196103.
Beam, Christopher. 2014. "Under the Knife: Why Chinese Patients Are Turning Against Their Doctors." *New Yorker*. August 25. http://www.newyorker.com/magazine/2014/08/25/under-the-knife.
Beam, Christopher. 2015. "Children of the Yuan Percent: Everyone Hates China's Rich Kids." *Bloomberg*, October 1. http://www.bloomberg.com/news/features/2015-10-01/children-of-the-yuan-percent-everyone-hates-china-s-rich-kids.
Becker, Marvin. 1988. *Civility and Society in Western Europe, 1300–1600*. Bloomington, IL: Indiana University Press.
Beech, Hannah. 2011. "To Be Young, Rich, Chinese—and Hated." *Time*. May 17. http://world.time.com/2011/05/17/to-be-young-rich-chinese-—-and-hated.
Bertelsmann. 2014. "Bertelsmann Transformation Report." Accessed March 20, 2016. http://www.bertelsmann-transformation-index.de/en/bti/country-reports/laendergutachten/asia-and-oceania/china/?0.
Bi Quanzhong. 1989. "急迫任務是提高人的素質——政協委員談商品經濟衝擊下的教育" [The urgent task is to raise the *suzhi* of the people—Members of the National Committee of the CPPCC on education under the impact of the commodity economy]. *People's Daily*. January 4, 2.
Birdabroad. 2011. "Taiwan: China, but Not China." October 17. https://birdabroad.wordpress.com/2011/10/17/taiwan-china-but-not-china.
Blecher, Marc. 1976. "Income Distribution in Small Rural Chinese Communes." *China Quarterly* 68: 797–816.
Bloomberg. 2012. "Xi Jinping Millionaire Reveals Fortunes of Elite." June 29. http://www.bloomberg.com/news/2012-06-29/xi-jinping-millionaire-relations-reveal-fortunes-of-elite.html.
Bloomberg. 2013. "China's Income Gap Narrows to Level That Still Risks Unrest." January 18. http://www.bloomberg.com/news/2013-01-18/china-income-gap-narrows-while-staying-at-levels-risking-unrest.html.
Bo Yang. 1985. 醜陋的中國人 [The ugly Chinese]. Taibei: Linbai Publishing Company.
Brady, Anne-Marie. 2003. *Making the Foreign Service Serve China: Managing Foreigners in the People's Republic*. Lanham, MD: Rowman and Littlefield.

Branigan, Tania. 2010. "Aid-Giving Monks Told to Leave China Earthquake Zone." *Guardian*. April 22. http://www.guardian.co.uk/world/2010/apr/22/china-earthquake-monks-must-leave.

Branigan, Tania. 2011. "Chinese Anger over Alleged Cover-Up of High-Speed Rail Crash." *Guardian*. July 25. http://www.theguardian.com/world/2011/jul/25/chinese-rail-crash-cover-up-claims.

Branigan, Tania. 2013. "Chinese Tourists Warned over Bad Behaviour Overseas." *Guardian*. May 17. http://www.guardian.co.uk/world/2013/may/17/chinese-tourists-warned-behaving-badly-wang-yang.

Browne, Andrew, and Chen Te-ping. 2014. "Chinese Property Power Couple Launches $100 Million Education Fund, Starting with Harvard." *Wall Street Journal*. July 16. http://blogs.wsj.com/chinarealtime/2014/07/16/chinese-property-power-couple-launches-100-million-education-fund-starting-with-harvard.

Browne, Andrew, and Paul Mozur. 2014. "Alibaba's Jack Ma Sets Up Philanthropic Trust." *Wall Street Journal*. April 24. http://online.wsj.com/news/articles/SB10001424052702304788404579521391392085498.

Buckley, Chris. 2016. "'Dancing Granny' Is Shot, but Don't Expect the Music to Stop." *New York Times*. March 12. http://www.nytimes.com/2016/03/12/world/asia/china-dancing-square-grannies-shot.html.

Buckley, Chris, and Austin Ramzy. 2016. "Singer's Apology for Waving Taiwan Flag Stirs Backlash of Its Own." *New York Times*. January 16. http://www.nytimes.com/2016/01/17/world/asia/taiwan-china-singer-chou-tzu-yu.html.

Burkitt, Laurie. 2012. "China Fears Rise in Doctor Attacks." *Wall Street Journal*. December 22. http://online.wsj.com/news/articles/SB10000872396390444592704578066364234583312.

CAF (Charities Aid Foundation). 2014. "World Giving Index: A Global View of Giving Trends." Accessed September 11, 2015. https://www.cafonline.org/docs/default-source/about-us-publications/caf_wgi2014_report_1555awebfinal.pdf.

Caldwell, Mark. 1999. *A Short History of Rudeness: Manners, Morals, and Misbehavior in Modern America*. New York: Picador.

Calhoun, Cheshire. 2000. "The Virtue of Civility." *Philosophy and Public Affairs* 29 (3): 251–75.

Cameron, L., N. Erkai, L. Gangadharan, and X. Meng. 2013. "Little Emperors: Behavioral Impacts of China's One-Child Policy." *Science* 339: 953–57.

Canpadee, Sam. 2014. "Migrant Worker Loses 6,000 Yuan, Receives 15,000 More in Donations from Strangers." Shanghaiist. http://shanghaiist.com/2014/01/11/migrant-worker-loses-6000-yaun-receives-15000-donation.php.

Cao, Deborah. 2004. *Chinese Law: A Language Perspective*. Aldershot: Ashgate.

Cao, Liqun, Lanying Huang, and Ivan Y. Sun. 2014. *Policing in Taiwan: From Authoritarianism to Democracy*. London and New York: Routledge.

Carrillo, Beatriz. 2008. "From Coal Black to Hospital White." In *The New Rich in China: Future Rulers, Present Lives*, edited by David S. G. Goodman, 99–111. London and New York: Routledge.

Carter, Stephen L. 1998. *Civility: Manners, Morals and the Etiquette of Democracy*. New York: Harper Perennial.

CBS. 2009. "Joe Wilson: Don't Expect 'You Lie!' Repeat." Accessed November 1, 2014. http://www.cbsnews.com/news/joe-wilson-dont-expect-you-lie-repeat.

Chaizu daren (拆組達人). 2011. "上班族公德心大調查" [Survey of the civility of office workers]. *International Engineering Group* (blog). November 28. http://blog.iegoffice.com/civic-minded.

Chan, Minnie. 2011. "Game Over for the Beijing Playboys." *South China Morning Post*. September 25. http://www.scmp.com/article/980039/game-over-beijing-playboys.

Chang, Bi-yu. 2015. *Place, Identity and National Imagination in Postwar Taiwan*. London and New York: Routledge.

Chang, Hao. 1971. *Liang Ch'i-ch'ao and Intellectual Transition in China, 1890–1907*. Cambridge, MA: Harvard University Press.

Chang Hsiang-yi. 2012. "Taiwan's Unfair Tax System." *Commonwealth Magazine* 506. Accessed October 4, 2012. http://english.cw.com.tw/print.do?action=print&id=13805.

Chang, Mau-kuei. 2003. "On the Origins and Transformation of Taiwanese National Identity." In *Religion and the Formation of Taiwanese Identities*, edited by Paul R. Katz and Murray Rubenstein, 23–58. New York: Palgrave Macmillan.

Chang, Parris H. 1992. "The Changing Nature of Taiwan's Politics." In *Taiwan: Beyond the Economic Miracle*, edited by Denis Fred Simon and Michael Y. M. Kau, 25–42. Armonk, NY: M. E. Sharpe.

Chang Tieh Chi. 2013. "Chiang Ching-kuo and the Democratization of Taiwan." *China Change*. June 3. http://chinachange.org/2013/06/03/chiang-chang-kuo-and-the-democratization-of-taiwan-2.

Chang Ying-hua, and Fu Yang-chih, eds. (章英華、傅仰止主編). 2004. "台灣地區社會變遷基本調查計劃：第四期第四次調查計劃報告" [Taiwan area basic social change research project: Report of the fourth quarter of the fourth period, 2004]. Nangang: Sociology Institute, Academia Sinica.

Changjiang Daily. 2012. "武漢一中年男倒地留學中帥哥出手相救" [A Wuhan man fell and was bleeding; several admirable chaps came to his aid]. September 18. http://news.cnhubei.com/xw/sh/201209/t2230780.shtml.

Changjiang Daily. 2013. "國家旅遊局發佈文明旅客公約：不再文明物上塗刻" [Civilized tourist covenant announced by the National Tourist Bureau: Do not carve or write on cultural relics]. May 18. http://news.cjn.cn/gnxw/201305/t2275156_1.htm.

Chao, Linda, and Ramon H. Myers. 1998. *The First Chinese Democracy: Political Life in the Republic of China on Taiwan*. Baltimore and London: Johns Hopkins University Press.

Chen, Ai-li. 1991. "The Search for Cultural Identity: Taiwan 'Hsiang-t'u' Literature in the Seventies." PhD thesis, Ohio State University.

Chen Chih-Jou (陳志柔). 2008. "二十年來兩岸文化教育交流現象：游盈隆編，近二十年兩岸關係的發展與變遷" [The cultural and educational exchange across the Straits over the past twenty years], 327–47. Taibei: Straits Exchange Foundation.

Chen Chih-Jou (陳志柔). 2010. "大陸文教交流人士對台灣觀感問卷分析初稿" [Preliminary questionnaire analysis on observations of Taiwan by Mainland cultural exchange visitors]. Commissioned Research from the China Development Foundation Management Association (中華發展基金管理會委託研究).

Chen, Emily. 2014. "Taiwan Operating in a Confined International Space." Diplomat. August 3. http://thediplomat.com/2014/08/taiwan-operating-in-a-confined-international-space.

Chen Jia. 2012. "Wealth Gap Survey to be Published." *China Daily*. February 7. http://usa.chinadaily.com.cn/business/2012-02/07/content_14549582.htm.

Chen Ruoshui (陳弱水). 1996. "A Preliminary Exploration into the Principle of Public Morality: The Dual Orientation of History and Theory." Paper presented at the Seminar on Public Morality and Society, Sociology Institute, Academia Sinica, Taibei, Taiwan, April 19–20.

Chen Ruoshui (陳弱水). 2005. "公德觀念的初步探討：歷史遠流於理論建構" [A preliminary exploration into the notion of public morality: The historical origins and theoretical construction]. In 公共意識於中國文化 [Public consciousness and Chinese culture], compiled by Ruoshui Chen, 3–41. Taibei: Lianjing.

Chen, Shuze. 2011. "Chinese People Say 'Yao' to Death Penalty." USC Annenberg China Media. April 4. http://ascportfolios.org/chinaandmedia/2011/04/04/chinese-people-say-%22yao%22-to-death-penalty.

Chen, Theodore Hsi-en. 1969. "The New Socialist Man." *Comparative Education Review* 13 (1): 88–95.

Cheung, Po-Ling. 1994. "Officials 'Fled Fire,' Leaving Children to Die." *South China Morning Post*. December 20. http://www.scmp.com/article/100498/officials-fled-fire-leaving-children-die.

Chin, Josh. 2011. "'Little Yueyue' Dies Amid Soul-Searching." *Wall Street Journal*. October 21. http://blogs.wsj.com/chinarealtime/2011/10/21/little-yueyue-dies-amid-soul-searching/.

Chin, Josh. 2012. "Gallup: Chinese People See Themselves as Struggling." *Wall Street Journal*. April 21. http://blogs.wsj.com/chinarealtime/2011/04/21/gallup-chinese-people-see-themselves-struggling.

Chin, Josh. 2017. "China Tries again to Stitch together a Unified Civil Code of Law." *Wall Street Journal*. March 9. https://www.wsj.com/articles/china-tries-again-to-stitch-together-a-unified-civil-code-of-law-1489076208.

China Daily. 2011a. "Charities Must Make Public Their Spending." August 25. http://english.peopledaily.com.cn/90882/7580142.html.

China Daily. 2011b. "China Sets Up 1st Charity Fund Financed by Stocks." May 6. http://europe.chinadaily.com.cn/business/2011-05/06/content_12460743.htm.

China Daily. 2012a. "'Good Samaritan' Admits He Pushed Woman." January 7. http://www.china.org.cn/china/2012-01/17/content_24426931.htm.

China Daily. 2012b. "'Uncle House' under Investigation." October 23. http://www.china.org.cn/china/2012-10/23/content_26875046.htm.

China Daily. 2013. "China Sees Drop in Donations." September 22. http://europe.chinadaily.com.cn/business/2013-09/22/content_16983743.htm.

China Daily. 2015. "1000 Volunteers Set to Drive Citywide Anti-Litter Campaign." http://www.china.org.cn/environment/2015-05/23/content_35642031.htm.

Ching, Leo T. S. 2001. *Becoming "Japanese": Colonial Taiwan and the Politics of Identity Formation*. Berkeley and Los Angeles: University of California Press.

Chiu Hei-yuan. 2001. "Lifting Martial Law, Freedom of Religion, and the Development of Religion." In *The Change in the Authoritarian System: Post Martial Law Taiwan*, edited by Academia Sinica Taiwan Studies Promotion Committee, 249–76. Taibei: Institute of Taiwan History, Academia Sinica.

Chublic. 2016. "Road Rage." Accessed June 12, 2016. https://chublicopinion.com/2016/06/11/road-rage/.
Ci, Jiwei. 1994. *Dialectic of the Chinese Revolution: From Utopianism to Hedonism*. Stanford: Stanford University Press.
Ci, Jiwei. 2009. "The Moral Crisis in Post-Mao China: Prolegomenon to a Philosophical Analysis." *Diogenes* 221: 19–25.
Ci, Jiwei. 2014. *Moral China in the Age of Reform*. Cambridge: Cambridge University Press.
CIA. n.d. *World Factbook*. "Country Comparison, GPD per capita." Accessed March 18, 2016. https://www.cia.gov/library/publications/the-world-factbook/rankorder/2004rank.html.
Civil. 2008. "那時的文明口號　五講四美三熱愛" [The civil slogan of that era: Five Stresses, Four Beauties, Three Fervent Loves]. Accessed August 17, 2009. http://gzhnfz.peoplexz.com/5831/20081001163232.htm.
CMI. 2010. "品德與社會" [Moral character and society]. *Curriculum Materials Institute* [課程教材研究所] 9 (1): 58.
CMP (China Media Project). 2011. "Yu Jianrong on Closing Migrant Schools." August 11. http://cmp.hku.hk/2011/08/23/15144.
CNA (Central News Agency). 2000. "ROC President Expresses Views on Relations with China." October 16. http://web.archive.org/web/20060904132848/http://fas.org/news/taiwan/2000/taiwan-001017-chn1.htm.
CNA (Central News Agency). 2010. "台灣民眾有公德心？近五成民眾否定" [Are Taiwanese really civil? Almost half say no]. *Taiwan Libao* [台灣立報]. June 21. http://www.lihpao.com/?action-viewnews-itemid-9520.
CNTV. 2011. "Henan's Soong Ching Ling Foundation accused of misusing funds." China 24. September 6. http://english.cntv.cn/program/china24/20110906/103502.shtml.
Cole, J. Michael. 2015. "Taiwanese Students Occupy Education Ministry over Textbook Controversy." *Diplomat*. July 24. http://thediplomat.com/2015/07/taiwanese-students-occupy-education-ministry-over-textbook-controversy.
Cost, Benjamin. 2014. "Vacationers Celebrate Dragon Boat Festival by Turning Shenzhen Beach into Landfill." Shanghaiist. June 6. http://shanghaiist.com/2014/06/06/look_shenzheners_celebrate_dragon_b.php.
Credit Suisse. 2010. "Analysing China's Grey Income." *Institutional Investor*. August 6. Accessed July 26, 2014. https://research-doc.credit-suisse.com/docView?language=ENG&source=ulg&format=PDF&document_id=857531571&serialid=WabTv3n9BdHCgZ3T53I97qLKOv%2BqNcskKT70z4WvVpI%3D.
Crouch, Erik. 2013. "Tourists Celebrate May Day by Leaving 180 Tons of Trash on Gulangyu Island." Shanghaiist. June 6. http://shanghaiist.com/2013/05/04/tourists_celebrate_may_day_by_leavi.ph.
Culp, Robert. 2006. "Rethinking Governmentality: Training, Cultivation, and Cultural Citizenship in Nationalist China." *Journal of Asian Studies* 65 (3): 529–54.
CWL (China Welfare Lottery). 2015. "1987年–2014年中國福利彩票發行量及籌集公益" [Amount of public welfare funds collected and distributed from the China welfare lottery, 1987–2014]. May 1. Accessed July 12, 2016. http://www.cwl.gov.cn/gyj/gyjcjqk/383051.shtml.
Davetian, Benet. 2009. *Civility: A Cultural History*. Toronto: University of Toronto Press.

de Bary, William Theodore. 2008. *Sources of East Asian Tradition: The Modern Period*, vol. 2. New York: Columbia University Press.

Demick, Barbara. 2011a. "Chinese Told They've Got to Try a Little Kindness." *Sydney Morning Herald*. January 11. http://www.smh.com.au/world/chinese-told-theyve-got-to-try-a-little-kindness-20111111-1nbly.html.

Demick, Barbara. 2011b. "In China, What You Eat Tells Who You Are." *Los Angeles Times*. September 16. http://articles.latimes.com/2011/sep/16/world/la-fg-china-elite-farm-20110917.

Deng Liqun. 1982. "Ideological and Political Work in the Countryside." *Guangming Ribao*. November 7.

Dezan Shira, and Associates. 2014. "China Vehicle Sales Reach 22 Million Units in 2013." *China Briefing*. January 20. http://www.china-briefing.com/news/2014/01/20/china-vehicle-sales-reach-22-million-units-in-2013.html.

DGBAS (Directorate-General of Budget, Accounting, and Statistics [主計處]). 2004. "社會發展趨勢調查報——社會參與" [Survey of social development trends (social participation), Taiwan area, Republic of China, 2003], 行政院主計處編印，中華民國九十三年七月 [DGBAS, Executive Yuan July 2004].

DGBAS. n.d. "國民所得統計常用資料" [Commonly used statistics on citizens' earnings]. Accessed June 7, 2015. http://www.dgbas.gov.tw/ct.asp?xItem=37407&CtNode=3566&mp=1.

Dickson, Bruce J. 1997. *Democratization in China and Taiwan: The Adaptability of Leninist Parties*. New York: Oxford University Press.

Dikötter, Frank. 2016. *The Cultural Revolution: A People's History, 1962–1976*. New York: Bloomsbury Press.

Di Renhua (狄仁華; Don Baron). 1963. "人情味與公德心" [The human touch and public morality]. *Central Daily News* (中央日報). May 18, 6.

Dirlik, Arif. 1975. "The Ideological Foundations of the New Life Movement: A Study in Counterrevolution." *Journal of Asian Studies* 34 (4): 945–80.

Dirlik, Arif. 1982. "Spiritual Solutions to Material Problems: The 'Socialist Ethics and Courtesy Month' in China." *South Atlantic Quarterly* 81 (4): 359–75.

Dirlik, Arif. 2005. *Marxism in the Chinese Revolution*. Lanham: Rowman and Littlefield.

Diyi jinrong wang (第一金融網). 2009. "中國富二代引發階層對立情緒" [Second-generation rich Chinese trigger a mood of class opposition]. Afinance.cn (reprinted from *Lianhe Zaobao*). September 22. http://www.afinance.cn/new/xwpl/200909/230629.html.

Durdin, Peggy. 1947. "Terror in Taiwan." *Nation*. May 24. http://www.taiwandc.org/hst-1947.htm.

Durdin, Tillman. 1947. "Formosa Killings Are Put at 10,000." *New York Times*. March 29. http://www.taiwandc.org/hst-1947.htm.

Dzodin, Harvey. 2014. "Nationwide Good Samaritan Law Needed." *China Daily*. January 17. http://www.chinadaily.com.cn/opinion/2014-01/17/content_17242681.htm.

Eastman, Lloyd. 1974. *The Abortive Revolution: China under Nationalist Rule, 1927–1937*. Cambridge, MA: Harvard University Press.

Economist. 2014a. "Government Coughers: The Tobacco Industry." March 1. http://www.economist.com/news/china/21597958-smoking-course-kill-100m-chinese-people-century-will-latest-anti-smoking.

Economist. 2014b. "Volatile Atmosphere." *Economist,* April 4. http://www.economist.com/blogs/analects/2014/04/environmental-protest-china.

Economist. 2016. "Up on the Far." *Economist.* May 14, 57–58.

Economy, Elizabeth. 2012. "Land Grab Epidemic: China's Wonderful World of Wukans." *Asia Unbound.* February 7. http://blogs.cfr.org/asia/2012/02/07/a-land-grab-epidemic-chinas-wonderful-world-of-wukans.

Elias, Norbert. 2000. *The Civilizing Process: Sociogenetic and Psychogenetic Investigations,* rev. ed. Translated by E. Jephcott. Oxford: Blackwell.

Erbaugh, Mary S. 2008. "Saying 'Hello' to Strangers." *Journal of Asian Studies* 67 (2): 621–52.

Fallows, James. 2012. "Annals of the Security State: China vs. American Department." *Atlantic.* June 5. http://www.theatlantic.com/national/archive/2012/05/annals-of-the-security-state-china-vs-america-department/256778.

Fan, Yiying. 2015. "'Too Loud, Too Rude': Switzerland Introduces Separate Trains for Chinese Tourists." *What's on Weibo.* August 27. http://www.whatsonweibo.com/too-loud-too-rude-switzerland-introduces-separate-trains-for-chinese-tourists.

Fang Wei (方煒). 1998. 小河壩村志 [Xiao Heba village gazetteer]. Tianjin: Tianjin Institute of Social Science.

Farrell, James Austin. 2016. "What's Really Behind Thailand's Hostility to Chinese Tourists?" *South China Morning Post.* December 30. http://www.scmp.com/week-asia/society/article/2058256/whats-really-behind-thailands-hostility-chinese-tourists.

Fauna. 2009. "Girl Refuses to Give Seat to Disabled, Slapped by 100 RMB." *China Smack.* April 3. http://www.chinasmack.com/2009/stories/girl-refuses-to-give-seat-to-disabled-slapped-by-100-rmb.html.

Fauna. 2014. "Deadly Explosion at Chinese Wheel Factory in Jiangsu Kunshan." *China Smack.* August 2. http://www.chinasmack.com/2014/pictures/deadly-explosion-at-chinese-wheel-factory-in-jiangsu-kunshan.html.

Fei, John C. H., Gustav Ranis, and Shirley W. Y. Kuo. 1979. *Growth with Equity: The Taiwan Case.* Washington, DC: World Bank.

Fei Xiaotong (費孝通). 1948. 鄉土中國 [Rural China]. Shanghai: Guancha she.

Fell, Dafydd. 2005. *Party Politics in Taiwan: Party Change and the Democratic Evolution of Taiwan, 1991–2004.* New York: Routledge.

Fenton, Anna Healy. 2013. "One-Third of Chinese Travellers Admit Stealing Hotel Furniture." *South China Morning Post.* October 17. http://www.scmp.com/comment/blogs/article/1333515/one-third-chinese-travellers-admit-stealing-hotel-furniture.

Fifield, Anna. 2015. "In Japan, Chinese Tourists Are a Welcome Boost—If a Loud, Messy One." *Washington Post.* February 20. https://www.washingtonpost.com/world/asia_pacific/in-japan-chinese-tourists-are-a-welcome-boost--if-a-loud-messy-one/2015/02/19/ef650636-b0b4-11e4-bf39-5560f3918d4b_story.html.

Finanne, Antonia. 2008. *Changing Clothes in China: Fashion, Modernity, Nation.* New York: Columbia University Press.

Fisher, Max. 2013. "You May Never Eat Street Food in China Again after Watching This Video." *Washington Post.* October 28. https://www.washingtonpost.com/news/worldviews/wp/2013/10/28/you-may-never-eat-street-food-in-china-again-after-watching-this-video.

Forsythe, Michael. 2015. "Q. and A.: Tony Saich on What Chinese Want from Their Leaders." *Sinosphere: Dispatches from China.* September 11. http://sinosphere.blogs.nytimes.

com/2015/09/11/anthony-saich-china-communist-party/?emc=edit_tnt_20150912&nl id=16767078&tntemail0=y&_r=0.

Foster, George M. 1965. "Peasant Society and the Image of Limited Good." *American Anthropologist* 67, no. 2: 293–315.

Fowler, Geoffrey A. 2008. "Where Have You Gone, Lei Feng?" *Wall Street Journal*. April 28. http://online.wsj.com/article/SB120767852552198631.html.

Frank, Robert. 2009. "In China They REALLY Hate the Rich." *Wall Street Journal*. December 11. http://blogs.wsj.com/wealth/2009/12/11/in-china-they-really-hate-the-rich.

French, Howard W. 2009. "Tucked Away in Shanghai, Hidden Lives." *New York Times*. August 29. http://www.nytimes.com/2009/08/29/world/asia/29iht-letter.html.

Friedman, Sara L. 2004. "Embodying Civility: Civilizing Processes and Symbolic Citizenship in China." *Journal of Asian Studies* 63 (3): 687–718.

Gan, Nectar. 2016. "Chinese Protest against Incinerator Plant Turns Violent." *South China Morning Post*. July 3. http://www.scmp.com/news/china/policies-politics/article/1984955/chinese-protest-against-incinerator-plant-turns-violent.

Gao, Helen. 2010. "Migrant 'Villages' within a City Ignite Debate." *New York Times*. October 4. http://www.nytimes.com/2010/10/04/world/asia/04beijing.html.

Gao, Helen. 2014. "China's Education Gap." *New York Times*. September 7. http://www.nytimes.com/2014/09/05/opinion/sunday/chinas-education-gap.html.

Gilbert, Karoline. 2014. "China Litter Laws." Prezi. November 26. https://prezi.com/3fu8hxqnyeta/china-litter-laws.

Gilkey, Langdon. 1966. *Shandong Compound: The Story of Men and Women under Pressure*. New York: Harper and Row.

Global Times. 2011. "Trust Has Become an All Too Rare Commodity." March 22. http://china.globaltimes.cn/society/2011-04/636422.html.

Global Times. 2012. "China: NGOs Struggle under the 'Big Government.'" June 23. http://globalvoicesonline.org/2012/06/23/china-ngos-struggle-under-the-big-government.

Global Times. 2014. "'Old People Grow Bad' an Absurd Saying." September 13. http://www.globaltimes.cn/content/881203.shtml.

Global Voices. 2011. "China: Salt Radiation Rumors Fuel Widespread Panic Buying." March 16. http://globalvoicesonline.org/2011/03/16/china-salt-radiation-rumors-fuel-widespread-panic-buying.

Goffman, Erving. 1963. *Behavior in Public Places: Notes on the Social Organization of Gatherings*. New York: Free Press.

Gold, Thomas B. 1982. "China's Youth: Problems and Programs." *Issus and Studies* XXVIII (8): 39–62.

Gold, Thomas B. 1985. "After Comradeship: Personal Relations in China since the Cultural Revolution." *China Quarterly* 104: 657–75.

Gold, Thomas B. 2013. "Complex Characters: Relearning Taiwan." In *Mobile Horizons: Dynamics Across the Taiwan Strait*, edited by Wen-hsin Yeh, 235–58. Berkeley: Institute of East Asian Studies, China Research Monograph.

Gong Wei, Gao Dongying, and Zhang Guizhi. 2002. "北京市街頭無償獻血情況統計分析" [A statistical analysis of mobile unit unpaid blood donations in Beijing]. *Zhongguo Lunxue Zazhi* 15, no. 4 (August): 268–69.

Griffiths, James. 2013a. "Vice Premier Condemns Poor 'Quality and Breeding' of Chinese Tourists." Shanghaiist. May 17. http://shanghaiist.com/2013/05/17/wang_yang_tells_reporters_chinese_tourists_are_uncivilised_and_harming_countrys_image.php.
Griffiths, James. 2013b. "Migrant Who Lost 15,000 Yuan in Shanghai Receives over 22,000 in Donations." Shanghaiist. February 7. http://shanghaiist.com/2013/02/07/migrant_who_lost_15000_yuan_in_shan.php.
Griffiths, James. 2014. "Taiwanese Man Beaten by Mainland Tour Group for Asking Them to Behave." Shanghaiist. September 14. http://shanghaiist.com/2013/09/14/taiwanese_man_beaten_by_mainland_tour_group_for_asking_them_to_behave.php.
Guilford, Gwynn. 2013. "China Is Starting to Get Embarrassed about Its Tourists' Obnoxious Behavior Abroad." Quartz. May 27. http://qz.com/88334/china-is-starting-to-get-embarrassed-about-its-tourists-obnoxious-behavior-abroad.
Haas, Benjamin. 2011. "China Smoking Ban May Have Little Effect." *Los Angeles Times*. April 30. http://articles.latimes.com/2011/apr/30/world/la-fg-china-smoke-20110430.
Habermas, Jürgen. 1989. *The Structural Transformation of the Public Sphere*. Translated by Thomas Burger and Frederick Lawrence. Cambridge, MA: MIT Press.
Hall, John A. 1998. "Genealogies of Civility." In *Democratic Civility: The History and Cross-Cultural Possibility of a Modern Political Ideal*, edited by Robert W. Hefner, 53–77. New Brunswick and London: Transaction.
Hall, John A. 2013. *The Importance of Being Civil: The Struggle for Political Decency*. Princeton, NJ: Princeton University Press.
Han Han. 2011. "韓寒最新博客大談革命：最終收貨者一定心狠手辣" [Han Han's latest blog diatribe on revolution: The ultimate beneficiary will definitely be vicious and merciless]. Wenxuecity.com. December 22. http://www.wenxuecity.com/news/2011/12/22/1576946.html.
Han Han. 2012. "太平洋的風：韓寒台灣初體驗" [Pacific winds: Han Han's first impressions of Taiwan]. *United Daily News*. May 11. http://udn.com/NEWS/MAINLAND/MAI1/7085652.shtml.
Hanser, Amy. 2008. *Service Encounters: Class, Gender, and the Market for Social Distinction in Urban China*. Stanford: Stanford University Press.
Harrell, Stevan. 1982. *Ploughshare Village: Culture and Context in Taiwan*. Seattle: University of Washington Press.
Harrell, Stevan. 1990. Introduction to *Violence in China: Essays in Culture and Counterculture*, edited by Jonathan N. Lipman and Stevan Harrell, 1–26. Albany: State University of New York Press.
Harrell, Stevan. 1995. "Introduction: Civilizing Projects and the Reaction to Them." In *Cultural Encounters on China's Ethnic Frontiers*, edited by Stevan Harrell, 3–36. Seattle and London: University of Washington Press.
Hasselle, Caroline. 2014. "Taipei vs Beijing: A Traveler's Perspective." Shanghaiist. January 10. http://shanghaiist.com/2014/01/10/taipei-vs-beijing-a-travelers-perspective.php.
Haupt, Angela. 2011. "Health Buzz: Smoking Ban Takes Effect in China." *U.S. News & World Report*. May 2. http://health.usnews.com/health-news/family-health/cancer/articles/2011/05/02/health-buzz-smoking-ban-takes-effect-in-china.
He Huaihong. 2015a. *Social Ethics in a Changing China: Moral Decay or Ethical Awakening?* Washington, DC: Brookings Institution Press.

He Huaihong. 2015b. "中國人的道德究竟去了哪裏？" [Where did Chinese morality go?]. ifeng. Accessed September 19, 2015. http://news.ifeng.com/exclusive/lecture/special/hehuaihong.

He, Huifeng. 2012. "Tempers Flare Over Snacking Tourist on MTR." *South China Morning Post*. January 20. http://www.scmp.com/article/990603/tempers-flare-over-snacking-tourist-mtr.

He Huifeng. 2013. "Shenzhen Introduces Good Samaritan Law." *South China Morning Post*. August 1. http://www.scmp.com/news/china/article/1293475/shenzhen-introduces-good-samaritan-law.

Helliwell, John F., Haifang Huang, and Shun Wang. 2016. *The Distribution of World Happiness*. Accessed March 29, 2016. http://worldhappiness.report/wp-content/uploads/sites/2/2016/03/HR-V1Ch2_web.pdf.

Hernández, Javier C. 2016a. "China Tries to Redistribute Education to the Poor, Igniting Class Conflict." *New York Times*. June 12. http://www.nytimes.com/2016/06/12/world/asia/china-higher-education-for-the-poor-protests.html.

Hernández, Javier C. 2016b. "She Asked Him to Stop Smoking. To China's Shock, He Beat Her Instead." *New York Times*. October 21. http://www.nytimes.com/2016/10/22/world/asia/china-smoke-elevator-attack.html.

Hessler, Peter. 2010. *Country Driving: A Journey Through China from Farm to Factory*. New York: Harper.

Hewitt, Duncan. 2010. "The March of the Netizens." BBC. November 2. http://www.bbc.co.uk/news/world-asia-pacific-11576592.

Hilgers, Lauren. 2008. "Giving in China." *Balkinization* (blog). August 11. http://balkin.blogspot.tw/2008/08/giving-in-china_11.html.

HRW (Human Rights Watch). 2017. "Chinese Netizens Attack Minority Uyghur Muslims." Dispatches. February 26. https://www.hrw.org/news/2017/02/26/chinese-netizens-attack-minority-uyghur-muslims.

Hsiao, Alison. 2013. "Taiwan Leading in Blood Donation Safety." *Taipei Times*. June 15. http://www.taipeitimes.com/News/taiwan/archives/2013/06/15/2003564851.

Hsiao, Hsin-huang Michael. 1990. "The Rise of Environmental Consciousness in Taiwan." *Impact Assessment* 8 (1–2): 217–31.

Hsiao, Kung-chuan. 1960. *Rural China: Imperial Control in the Nineteenth Century*. Seattle: University of Washington Press.

Hsiau, A-chin. 1997. "Language Ideology in Taiwan: The KMT's Language Policy, the Tai-yu Language Movement, and Ethnic Politics." *Journal of Multilingual and Multicultural Development* 18 (4): 302–15.

Hsiau, A-chin. 2005. "The Indigenization of Taiwanese Literature: Historical Narrative, Strategic Essentialism, and State Violence." In *Cultural, Ethnic and Political Nationalism in Contemporary Taiwan*, edited by John Makeham and A-chin Hsiau, 25–155. New York and Houndmills, UK: Palgrave Macmillan.

Hsing, Yu (邢瑜). 2013. "政策變遷對社區意涵的影響：台灣一九九四年至二〇〇二年的社區總體營造政策" [The influence of policy change on the connotation of community: Overall community construction policy from 1994 to 2002 in Taiwan]. *Chinese Public Administration Review* 19 (4): 1–23.

Huang, Haifeng. 2016. "Personal Character or Social Expectation: A Formal Analysis of 'Suzhi' in China." *Journal of Contemporary China* 25 (102): 908–22.

Huang Jingjing. 2011. "Fallen Old Man Dies as Bystanders Look On." *Global Times*. September 5. http://www.globaltimes.cn/content/673997.shtml.
Hughes, Christopher R. 2006. *Chinese Nationalism in the Global Era*. London and New York: Routledge.
Huntington, Samuel P. 1991. *The Third Wave: Democratization in the Late Twentieth Century*. Norman: University of Oklahoma Press.
Hu Qingyun. 2013. "Lei Feng's Last Words?" *Global Times*. March 11. http://www.globaltimes.cn/content/767356.shtml.
IAST. "India Lags behind Neighbours in Civic Engagement: Gallup Poll." 2011. *Pakistan Defence*. January 19. http://defence.pk/threads/india-lags-behind-neighbours-in-civic-engagement-gallup-poll.92777.
ifeng. 2011. "Xinwen: 'foshan luren' lüyi nan juli yimicheng wei kandao: kandao wo si gei nin kan [News: Foshan Pedestrians a Man in a Green Shirt a Meter Away Didn't Notice: If I Saw Something, I'll Die." October 18. Accessed October 19, 2011. http://news.ifeng.com/society/special/nianyanvtong/content-4/detail_2011 _10/18/9929905_0.shtml.
IMF (International Monetary Fund). 2015. "2015 World Economic Outlook Database." World Economic and Financial Surveys. Accessed March 20, 2016. http://www.imf.org/external/pubs/ft/weo/2015/02/weodata/weorept.aspx.
Inglehart, Ronald, and Christian Welzel. 2005. *Modernization, Cultural Change, and Democratisation: The Human Developmental Sequence*. Cambridge: Cambridge University Press.
Inglehart, Ronald, Miguel Basáñez, Gabrilela Catterberg, Jaime Díez-Medrano, Alejandro Moreno, Pippa Norris, Renata Siemienska, and Ignacio Zuasnabar, eds. 2010. *Changing Human Beliefs and Values, 1981–2007: A Sourcebook Based on the World Values Surveys and European Values Studies*. Mexico: Siglo XXI Editores, S. A. de C. V.
Interior Ministry (Taiwan). 2014. "各縣市人口數按性別及五歲年齡組分" [Sex ratio by cohort for each municipality and county]. Accessed May 2, 2015. http://statis.moi.gov.tw/micst/stmain.jsp?sys=100.
Iwai, Eiichi. 1937. *Ranisha ni Kansuru Chōsa* [Investigations into the Blue Shirt Society]. Tokyo: Gaimushō Chōsabu.
Jacka, Tamara. 2009. "Cultivating Citizens: *Suzhi* (Quality) Discourse in the PRC." *Positions* 17 (3): 523–35.
Jackson, Dominic. 2015. "Palau Islands Overwhelmed by Chinese Tourists, Say Locals." *Shanghaiist*. March 15. http://shanghaiist.com/2015/03/15/palau_islands_overwhelmed_by_chines.php.
Jacob, Rahul. 2011. "Beijing Worries as Sense of Injustice Deepens." *Financial Times*. June 15. https://www.ft.com/content/596a378c-976d-11e0-af13-00144feab49a.
Jacobs, Andrew. 2011. "As Chinese Visit Taiwan, the Cultural Influence Is Subdued." *New York Times*. August 10. http://www.nytimes.com/2011/08/11/world/asia/11taiwan.html.
Jacobs, Andrew. 2012. "Monday in Observance of 'Learn from Lei Feng Day.'" *New York Times*. March 5. http://www.nytimes.com/2012/03/06/world/asia/lei-feng-day-draws-chinese-cynicism.html.
Jacobs, J. Bruce. 2012. *Democratizing Taiwan*. Leiden: E. J. Brill.
Jennings, Ralph. 2015. "As Spats Mount, Taiwan Courts 'Cream' of Chinese Tourists." VOA News. June 19. http://www.voanews.com/content/as-spats-mount-taiwan-courts-cream-of-chinese-tourists/2828747.html.

Jiang, Chengcheng. 2013. "Chinese Deterred from Donating to Their Country's Dubious Charity Sector." *Time*. September 25. http://world.time.com/2013/09/25/chinese-deterred-from-donating-to-their-countrys-dubious-charity-sector/.

Jiang Chengxuan (江承軒). 2013. "台灣菸害治理機制的形成" [The advent of the management of the harm from tobacco]. Master's thesis, Sociology Institute, National Tsinghua University.

Jiang, Stephen. 2015. "China to Its Reckless Drivers: Rein in Your Road Rage." CNN. May 26. http://edition.cnn.com/2015/05/24/asia/china-road-rage.

Jin Kai. 2014 "'Littering Creates Jobs': The Need for Moral Education in China." *Diplomat*. January 22. http://thediplomat.com/2014/01/littering-creates-jobs-the-need-for-moral-education-in-china.

Jing, Jun. 2011. "From Commodity of Death to Gift of Life." In *Deep China: The Moral Life of the Person: What Anthropology and Psychiatry Tell Us about China Today* by Arthur Kleinman, Yunxiang Yan, Jing Jun, Sing Lee, Everett Zhang, Tianshu Pan, Wu Fei, and Guo Jinhua, 78–105. Berkeley, Los Angeles, and London: University of California Press.

Jones, Susan Mann. 1987. *Local Merchants and the Chinese Bureaucracy, 1750–1950*. Stanford: Stanford University Press.

Jou, Emerson M. F. (周明峰). 1996. "人情味與公德心" [The human touch and public morality. Memorial page for Don Baron]. Accessed December 18, 2013. http://don-baron.jimdo.com.

Jsphfrtz. 2013. "Traffic Deaths in Taiwan: Know the Truth." Accessed September 9, 2015. http://jsphfrtz.com/traffic-deaths-in-taiwan-know-the-truth.

Judah, Sam. 2014. "The Row over a Bus Seat in China." BBC. September 10. http://www.bbc.com/news/blogs-trending-29130357.

Kan, Karoline. 2016. "Chengguan, Widely Despised Officers in China, Find Refuge and a Kind Ear." *New York Times*. September 29. http://www.nytimes.com/2016/09/30/world/asia/china-nanjing-chengguan.html.

Kastner, Jens. 2011. "Taiwan Shocks China's Independent Tourists." *Asia Times*. July 6. http://www.atimes.com/atimes/China/MG06Ad01.html.

Keane, John. 1998. *Civil Society: Old Images, New Visions*. Stanford: Stanford University Press.

Ke Jiayun. 2013. "Highway Littering a Problem in Shanghai." *Shanghai Daily*. April 23. http://en.people.cn/90882/8219297.html.

Kelling, George L., and James Q. Wilson. 1982 "Broken Windows: The Police and Neighborhood Safety." *Atlantic* (March), 29–38. http://www.theatlantic.com/magazine/archive/1982/03/broken-windows/304465.

Kenny, Jamie. 2015. "Chinese Travellers Turn to Air Rage to Make a Point." *National World*. March 16. http://www.thenational.ae/world/east-asia/chinese-travellers-turn-to-air-rage-to-make-a-point.

Kerr, George. 1965. *Formosa Betrayed*. Boston: Houghton Mifflin.

Kesler, Charles R. 1992. "Civility and Citizenship in the American Founding." In *Civility and Citizenship in Liberal Democratic Societies*, edited by Edward Banfield, 57–74. New York: Paragon House.

Kim, Sungmoon. 2014. *Confucian Democracy in East Asia: Theory and Practice*. New York: Cambridge University Press.

Kipnis, Andrew. 2001. "The Disturbing Educational Discipline of "Peasants." *China Journal* 46: 1–24.

Kipnis, Andrew. 2006. "Suzhi: A Keyword Approach." *China Quarterly* 186: 295–313.

Kleinman, Arthur. 2006. *What Really Matters: Living a Moral Life amidst Uncertainty and Danger*. Oxford: Oxford University Press.

Kleinman, Arthur. 2011. "Introduction: Remaking the Moral Person in New China." In *Deep China: The Moral Life of the Person: What Anthropology and Psychiatry Tell Us about China Today*, edited by Arthur Kleinman, Yunxiang Yan, Jing Jun, Sing Lee, Everett Zhang, Tianshu Pan, Wu Fei, and Goa Jinhua, 1–35. Berkeley: University of California Press.

Knapp, Ronald G. 2007. "The Shaping of Taiwan's Landscape." In *Taiwan: A New History*, edited by Murray A. Rubenstein, 3–26. Armonk, NY: M. E. Sharpe.

Koons, Cynthia, Nisha Gopalan, and Robin Sidel. 2013. "Banks' 'Princeling' Hires Were Widespread in China." *Wall Street Journal*. September 2. http://www.wsj.com/articles/SB10001424127887324202304579050550432355702.

Kwong, Julia. 1997. *The Political Economy of Corruption in China*. Armonk, NY: M. E. Sharpe.

LaFraniere, Sharon. 2010. "Chinese Hospitals Are Battlegrounds of Discontent." *New York Times*. August 12. http://www.nytimes.com/2010/08/12/world/asia/12hospital.html.

LaFraniere, Sharon. 2011. "In China, Concern over Radiation Spreads." *New York Times*. March 18. http://www.nytimes.com/2011/03/18/world/asia/18china.htm.

Lam, Tiffany. 2011. "Kung Fu Compulsion for Hong Kong Airlines Cabin Crew." CNN. April 18. http://travel.cnn.com/explorations/life/hong-kong-airlines-makes-cabin-crew-learn-kung-fu-398473.

Lau, Lawrence J. 2012. "The Long-Term Economic Growth of Taiwan." Institute of Global Economics and Finance, Chinese University of Hong Kong, Working Paper No. 13.

Lau, Mimi. 2012. "Tourists to Mainland Hotspots Leave Massive Litter Problem." *South China Morning Post*. October 3. http://www.scmp.com/news/china/article/1052589/tourists-mainland-hotspots-leave-massive-litter-problem.

Lee, Abby. 2003. "Betel-Nut Faming Area Reaps What It Sows." *Taiwan Today*. May 9. http://www.taiwantoday.tw/ct.asp?xItem=20227&CtNode=122.

Lee, Anru. 2007. "Subways as a Space of Cultural Intimacy: The Mass Rapid Transit Systems in Taipei, Taiwan." *China Journal* 58 (July): 31–55.

Leroy, Aliaume. 2014. "Saintly Sanitation Worker Finds 3,500RMB in Dump, Returns It to Owner." Shanghaiist. June 6. http://shanghaiist.com/2014/06/06/good_sanitation_worker_finds_lost_m.php.

Levenson, Joseph. 1959. *Liang Ch'i-ch'ao and the Mind of Modern China*. Berkeley: University of California Press.

Levin, Dan. 2012. "A Chinese Education, for a Price." *New York Times*. November 21. http://www.nytimes.com/2012/11/22/world/asia/in-china-schools-a-culture-of-bribery-spreads.html.

Levin, Dan. 2013a. "Chinese Tourists Spend, and Offend, Freely." *New York Times*. September 16. http://www.nytimes.com/2013/09/17/business/chinese-tourists-spend-and-offend-freely.html.

Levin, Dan. 2013b. "In China, Cinematic Flops Suggest Fading of an Icon." *New York Times*. March 12. http://www.nytimes.com/2013/03/12/world/asia/in-china-unpopular-films-suggest-fading-of-icon.html?ref=global-home.

Levine, Jessica. 2012. "What a 'Human Flesh Search' Is, and How It's Changing China." Tea Leaf Nation. October 4. http://www.tealeafnation.com/2012/10/what-a-human-flesh-search-is-and-how-its-changing-china.

Li, Amy. 2013a. "Chiang Mai Locals Shocked by 'Rude' Chinese Tourists." *South China Morning Post*. February 28. http://www.scmp.com/news/china/article/1162131/chiang-mai-locals-shocked-rude-chinese-tourists.

Li, Amy. 2013b. "Why Are Chinese Tourists So Rude? SCMP Offers an Insight." *South China Morning Post*. June 1. http://www.scmp.com/news/china/article/1251239/why-are-chinese-tourists-so-rude.

Li, Amy. 2014. "Rude Awakening: Chinese Tourists Have the Money, but Not the Manners." *South China Morning Post*. December 31. http://www.scmp.com/news/china/article/1671504/rude-awakening-chinese-tourists-have-means-not-manners.

Li, Gan. 2014. "Income Inequality and an Economy in Transition." Presentation slides to Texas A&M University and Southwestern University of Finance and Economic. July 28.

Li Guicheng (李貴成). 2008. "社會公平的仇富問題探析" [An analysis of hating the rich from the perspective of social fairness]. *Lilun Tansuo* 5 (173): 99–105.

Li Hongmei. 2009. "Don't Hate the Rich, Be One of Them." *People's Daily Online*. April 2. http://english.people.com.cn/90002/96417/6628619.html.

Li Meilian. 2011. "Legal Expert Says Murder Case Not Ideal Symbol of Campaign to Abolish Death Penalty." http://special.globaltimes.cn/2011/04/646927.html.

Li, Ying, Donghua Xie, Guangmeng Nie, and Junhua Zhang. 2012. "The Drink Driving Situation in China." *Traffic Injury Prevention* 13 (2): 101–8.

Liang, Shuming (梁漱溟). 1949. 中國文化要義 [The essentials of Chinese culture]. 上海書店民國叢書影印本 [Shanghai Bookstore ROC series photocopy].

Liberty Times Net. 2014. "政大調查 台灣人認同、台獨支持率均攀新高" [Chengchi University survey rates for Taiwan identity and Taiwan independence both reach new highs]. *Ziyou Shibao*. July 11. http://news.ltn.com.tw/news/politics/breakingnews/1052425.

Lin Cho-shui. 2011. "Charity Work Differs in Taiwan and China." *Taipei Times*. February 2. http://www.taipeitimes.com/News/editorials/archives/2011/02/02/2003495007.

Lin Guoxian (林國顯). n.d. "Chinese Culture Renaissance Movement." *Encyclopedia of Taiwan*. Accessed January 19, 2014. http://taiwanpedia.culture.tw/web/content?ID=3968.

Lin Jingyue. 2013. "Eradicating 'Chinese Style Road Crossing.'" *Economic Observer*. May 31. http://www.eeo.com.cn/ens/2013/0531/244665.shtml.

Lin, Johnny. 2011a. "Rules of the Jungle: How to Survive on Beijing's Roads." WCT. June 5. Accessed June 8, 2011. http://www.wantchinatimes.com/news-subclass-cnt.aspx?id=20110605000001&cid=1503.

Lin, Johnny. 2011b. "Weak Laws in China Are Creating an Apathetic Society." WCT. September 8. Accessed September 11, 2011. http://www.wantchinatimes.com/news-subclass-cnt.aspx?id=20110908000002&cid=1103.

Lin, Qinghong (Delia). 2009. "Civilising Citizens in Post-Mao China: Understanding the Rhetoric of Suzhi." PhD diss., School of Humanities, Griffith University.

Lin Shuzhi (林樹枝). 1992. "統中會案始末" [The Unity Foundation case from start to finish]. Accessed December 18, 2013. http://www.ios.sinica.edu.tw/cll/friends/soc22.html.

Lin Yutang. 1939. *My Country and My People*. New York: John Day.

Linder, Alex. 2015a. "Beijing Smoking Ban Claims First Victim as Popular Hot Pot Restaurant Served Warning." Shanghaiist. June 2. http://shanghaiist.com/2015/06/02/beijing_smoking_ban_1st_victim.php.

Linder, Alex. 2015b. "Swiss Railway Launches Special Trains for Chinese Tourists Following Complaints of Rude Behavior." Shanghaiist. August 29. http://shanghaiist.com/2015/08/29/special_swiss_trains_for_chinese.php.

Linder, Alex. 2015c. "Fake Rice Made with Paper Found in Guangdong." Shanghaiist. September 6. http://shanghaiist.com/2015/09/06/fake_paper_rice.php.

Ling, Connie. 2001. "Former Taiwan Social Critic Works to Promote Taipei's Urban Culture." *Wall Street Journal*. March 12. http://www.wsj.com/articles/SB984147226750729821.

Lipes, Joshua. 2013. "Chinese Talk Show Host Apologizes to Mongolian Viewers." Radio Free Asia. April 24. http://www.rfa.org/english/news/china/apology-04242013183630.html.

Liu Aiyu and Liu Mingli (劉愛玉、劉明利). 2012. "城市融合，組織新任御農民工的社會信任——以對紡織服裝業農民工的調查為例" [Urban assimilation, organizational trust and migrant worker social trust: An example from textile and clothing migrant workers]. *Journal of the Jiangsu Institute of Administration* 2: 78–84.

Liu, Charles. 2014. "Melamine-Laced Yogurt Candy Seized in Guangdong." *Nanfang*. August 1. http://www.thenanfang.com/blog/melamine-laced-yogurt-candy-seized-in-guangdong.

Liu, Jiaying and Li Sijia. 2017. "Minor Officials Become Scapegoats in Food-Safety Scares." Caixin. February 22. http://www.caixinglobal.com/2017-02-22/101057957.html.

Liu Linlin. 2010. "Fake Wine Stuns Nation, Six Wrongdoers Detained." *Global Times*, December 27. http://www.globaltimes.cn/content/604367.shtml.

Liu, Lucy. 2015a. "Sichuan Senior Takes Dive Off His Bike, Tries to Frame Good Samaritan Student, Gets Caught on Camera." Shanghaiist. July 25. http://shanghaiist.com/2015/07/25/senior_tries_to_frame_good_samaritan.php.

Liu, Lucy. 2015b. "Volunteers Rush to Give Out Water, Offer Free Car Rides and Donate Blood in Wake of Explosion." Shanghaiist. August 15. http://shanghaiist.com/2015/08/15/volunteers_rush_to_tianjin.php.

Liu Shinan. 2011. "Controversial Verdict Has Damaged Society." *China Daily*. September 7. http://www.chinadaily.com.cn/opinion/2011-09/07/content_13636204.htm.

Liu, Wennan. 2013. "Redefining the Moral and Legal Roles of the State in Everyday Life: The New Life Movement in China in the Mid-1930s." *Cross-Currents: East Asian History and Culture Review* 7: 30–59.

Liu, Xin. 2000. *In One's Own Shadow: An Ethnographic Account of the Condition of Post-reform Rural China*. Berkeley: University of California Press.

Lubman, Stanley. 2013. "Social Change Leaves China Struggling to Define Role of Law." *Wall Street Journal*. February 27. http://blogs.wsj.com/chinarealtime/2013/02/27/social-change-leaves-china-struggling-to-define-role-of-law.

Lümang. 2009. "'炫富'與'憤富'" ["Flaunting wealth" and "hating the rich"]. *Lumang* (blog). October 20. Accessed December 15, 2015. http://blog.sina.com.cn/s/blog_40bc98c40100gvjx.html.

Lung Ying-tai. 1985a. "中國人，你們為什麼不生氣？" [Chinese people, why don't you get angry?]. In *Wildfire*, compiled by Ying-tai Lung, 1–6. Taibei: Yuanshen.

Lung Ying-tai. 1985b. 野火集 [*Wildfire*]. Taipei: Yuanshen.

Lung Ying-tai. 1987. 野火集外集 [*Wildfire Collection* appendum]. Taibei: Yuanshen.

References

Lung Ying-tai. 2015. Interview with author. September 30.
Luo, Chris. 2013. "Villagers Pillage Food from Scene of Multiple-Vehicle Collision." *South China Morning Post.* March 13. http://www.scmp.com/news/china/article/1201697/villagers-pillage-food-scene-multiple-vehicle-collision.
Luo Zhaojin (羅肇錦). 1985. "中國人當然不生氣" [Of course Chinese don't get angry]. In *Wildfire*, compiled by Yingtai Lung, 7–11. Taibei: Yuanshen.
Lu Xun. 1990. *Diary of a Madman and Other Stories.* Translated by William Lyell. Honolulu: University of Hawai'i Press.
Macartney, Jane. 2008. "Abusive Chinese Official Sacked after Internet Hunt." *Australian.* Reprinted from the *Times.* Accessed July 19, 2014. http://www.theaustralian.com.au/archive/news/abusive-chinese-official-sacked-after-internet-hunt/story-e6frg6t6-1111117953848?nk=63af51a66017bcc326a92a82618f501f.
MacKinnon, Mark. 2011. "Chinese Toddler Struck by Van, Ignored by Passersby." *Toronto Globe and Mail.* October 17. http://www.theglobeandmail.com/news/world/chinese-toddler-struck-by-van-ignored-by-passersby/article558392.
MacLeod, Calum. 2013. "Trashy Habits Leave China Pondering Patriotism, Civics." *USA Today.* October 2. http://www.usatoday.com/story/news/world/2013/10/02/china-trash-tiananmen-square/2908251.
Madsen, Richard. 1984. *Morality and Power in a Chinese Village.* Berkeley: University of California Press.
Madsen, Richard. 1990. "The Politics of Revenge in Contemporary China during the Cultural Revolution." In *Violence in China: Essays in Culture and Counterculture*, edited by Jonathan N. Lipman and Stevan Harrell, 175–202. Albany: State University of New York Press.
Makinen, Julie. 2009. "In China, Philanthropy as a New Measuring Stick." *New York Times.* September 24. http://www.nytimes.com/2009/09/24/business/global/24donate.html.
Margalit, Avishai. 1996. *The Decent Society.* Translated by Naomi Goldblum. Cambridge, MA: Harvard University Press.
Margalit, Avishai. 1997. "Decent Equality and Freedom: A Postscript." *Social Research* 64 (1): 147–60.
Marquand, Robert. 2015. "In Taiwan, Protests over History Textbooks Are about the Future." *Christian Science Monitor.* August 4. http://www.csmonitor.com/World/Asia-Pacific/2015/0804/In-Taiwan-protests-over-history-textbooks-are-about-the-future.
Martin, Jorge. 2010. "Whither China?" *Marxist Update* (blog). March 3. http://marxistupdate.blogspot.com.au/2010/03/whither-china.html.
Martin, Roberta. 1975. "The Socialization of Children in China and on Taiwan: An Analysis of Elementary School Textbooks." *China Quarterly* 62: 242–62.
MCA (Ministry of Civil Affairs). 2012. Xinhua News Agency. Press conference, March 6. http://www.mca.gov.cn/article/zwgk/mzyw/201203/20120300280349.shtml.
McGeary, Kevin. 2012. "Brazilian Man Beaten in Dongguan, Passers-by Watch." *Nanfang.* May 7. http://www.thenanfang.com/blog/brazilian-beaten-in-dongguan-passersby-watch.
McGregor, Joan. 2004. "Civility, Civic Virtue, and Citizenship." In *Civility and Its Discontents: Essays on Civic Virtue, Toleration, and Cultural Fragmentation*, edited by Christine T. Sistare, 25–42. Lawrence: University of Kansas Press.
McGregor, Richard. 2010. *The Party: The Secret World of China's Communist Rulers.* London: Allen Lane.

McLean-Dreyfus, Marie-Alice, and Merriden Varrall. 2015. "Through Protests, Taiwan Forges Its Own Identity." Accessed August 24, 2015. https://www.lowyinstitute.org/the-interpreter/through-protests-taiwan-forges-its-own-identity.

Meng, Xin, and R. G. Gregory. 2002. "The Impact of Interrupted Education on Subsequent Educational Attainment: A Cost of the Chinese Cultural Revolution." *Economic Development and Cultural Change* 50 (4): 935–59.

Mingbao. 2014. "1%人掌全國1/3財富" [One percent of the population holds one-third of the nation's wealth]. July 27. http://news.mingpao.com/20140727/caa1.htm.

Ministry of Education. 2010. "教育部「99終身學習行動年331」日行一善——小市民大善行活動記者會" [Ministry of Education "99 Lifetime Study Activity Year 331" Do a Good Deed Everyday—Citizens' Great Good Activity Press Conference]. Accessed August 2, 2014. http://epaper.edu.tw/print.aspx?print_type=news&print_sn=3268&print_num=0.

Minter, Adam. 2012. "China's Infamous 'Good Samaritan' Case Gets a New Ending." Bloomberg. January 18. http://www.bloomberg.com/news/2012-01-17/china-s-infamous-good-samaritan-case-gets-a-new-ending-adam-minter.html.

Montlake, Simon. 2010. "Taiwan Charity Has Global Reach." *Wall Street Journal*. March 11. http://online.wsj.com/news/articles/SB10001424052748704353404575114661869717700.

Moon, Rona. 2013. "Two Years on, Japan Remembers Disaster Aid from the US, Taiwan and Bhutan." *Rocket News*. March 12. http://en.rocketnews24.com/2013/03/12/two-years-on-japan-remembers-disaster-aid-from-the-u-s-taiwan-and-bhutan.

Mooney, Paul. 2008. "The Story Behind China's Tainted Milk Scandal." *U.S. News & World Report*. October 9. http://www.usnews.com/news/world/articles/2008/10/09/the-story-behind-chinas-tainted-milk-scandal.

Mosher, Steven W. 1983. *Broken Earth: The Rural Chinese*. New York: Free Press.

Mount, Ferdinand. 1973. "Civility and Good Manners." *Encounter* 40, no. 1 (July): 31–43.

Mu, Eric. 2008. "Screw the Elderly, I'm Keeping My Bus Seat." Danwei. October 8. http://www.danwei.org/front_page_of_the_day/chinese_good_traditions.php.

Murdoch, Gillian. 2008. "Don't Ask Olympic Tourists' Age or Wage or . . . ." Reuters. July 23. http://www.reuters.com/article/2008/07/23/us-olympics-conversation-odd-idUSPEK32893420080723.

Murphy, Rachel. 2004. "Turning Peasants into Modern Chinese Citizens: 'Population Quality' Discourse, Demographic Transition and Primary Education." *China Quarterly* 177: 1–20.

Murthy, Sheela. 1983. "Deng's 'Civilized' China of 'Five Disciplines, Four Graces and Three Loves.'" *China Report* 19 (3): 3–11.

Muyard, Frank. 2014. "The Formation of Taiwan's New National Identity Since the End of the 1980s." In *Taiwan since Martial Law*, edited by David Blundell, 297–366. Taiwan: Shung Ye Museum of Formosan Aborigines; published by University of California Press and National Taiwan University Press.

NBSC (National Bureau of Statistics of China). Accessed May 14, 2014. http://www.quandl.com/STATCHINA/Q1819-Domestic-Tourism.

Nelson, Katie. 2013. "Asshole Tourists Throw Water Bottles at Lions in Shanghai Zoo." Shanghaiist. October 4. http://shanghaiist.com/2013/10/04/asshole_tourists_throw_water_bottles_at_shanghai_zoo_lions.php.

Nelson, Katie. 2014a. "Reluctant to Give Up Seat, Woman Jump-Kicks Old Man on Bus in Xiamen." Shanghaiist. April 24. http://shanghaiist.com/2014/04/24/woman-jump-kicks-old-man-on-bus.php.

Nelson, Katie. 2014b. "Trash Left by Visitors Kills Deer at Wildlife Park in Xiamen." Shanghaiist. February 23. http://shanghaiist.com/2014/02/23/trash_left_by_visitors_kills_deer_a.php.

Nelson, Katie. 2014c. "Woman Beaten with Brick by Tourist in Xiamen after Cutting in Line for Bathroom." Shanghaiist. October 10. http://shanghaiist.com/2014/10/10/woman-cut-in-line-beaten-with-brick-xiamen.php.

Nelson, Katie. 2015a. "Hangzhou Introduces 'Smart' Manhole Covers." Shanghaiist. March 20. http://shanghaiist.com/2015/03/20/hanghzou-smart-manhole-covers.php.

Nelson, Katie. 2015b. "Hundreds of Volunteers Donate Blood to Save New Mother amid Shortage in Jinan." Shanghaiist. August 7. http://shanghaiist.com/2015/08/07/hundreds-donate-blood-save-new-mother.php.

Nelson, Katie. 2015c. "Look: Baby Chicks Pour out of Overturned Truck on Shandong Roadside, Locals Scoop Them Up." Shanghaiist. August 26. http://shanghaiist.com/2015/08/26/chickies-truck.php.

Nelson, Katie. 2015d. "Mainland Family Kicked off Hong Kong-Bound Flight after Fight Erupts over Child's Seatbelt." Shanghaiist. February 26. http://shanghaiist.com/2015/02/26/mainland_family_kicked_off_hong_kon.php.

Nelson, Katie. 2015e. "Shandong District Issues Ban on Dogs, Threatens to Kill All Residents' Pets." Shanghaiist. September 11. http://shanghaiist.com/2015/09/11/shandong-village-issues-ban-dogs.php.

Ng, Grace. 2011. "Maoist Idol Turns into New-Age Hero." Singapore Straits Times. October 22. http://www.straitstimes.com/Asia/China/Story/STIStory_725976.html.

Ng, Joyce. 2015. "Zhengzhou Bus Passengers Stealing Emergency Hammers Walnut Crackers." Shanghaiist. June 25. http://shanghaiist.com/2015/06/25/zhengzhou-bus-passengers-stealing-emergency-hammers-walnut-crackers.php.

Ng, Mandy. 2013. "Why I Didn't Donate to Sichuan Earthquake Relief." South China Morning Post. April 30. http://www.scmp.com/comment/blogs/article/1226532/why-i-didnt-donate-sichuan-earthquake-relief.

Ni Tao. 2013. "Badly Behaved Chinese Tourists Just Doing What They Do at Home." Shanghai Daily. August 14. http://www.shanghaidaily.com/Opinion/shanghai-daily-columnists/Badly-behaved-Chinese-tourists-just-doing-what-they-do-at-home/shdaily.shtml.

Niu Hong. 1979. "野蠻與文明" [Barbarism and civilization]. People's Daily. June 5.

NPC (National People's Congress). 2011. "2011年最新交通法全文" [The complete text of most recent 2011 traffic laws].

OECD. 2011 "Society at a Glance, 2011, Pro- and Anti-social Behaviour." OECD Social Indicators. Accessed August 2, 2014. http://www.oecd.org/berlin/47570337.pdf.

Orwin, Clifford. 1991. "Citizenship and Civility as Components of Liberal Democracy." American Scholar 60, no. 4 (Autumn): 553–64.

Osnos, Evan. 2012. "Brother Wristwatch and Grandpa Wen: Chinese Kleptocracy." New Yorker. October 25. http://www.newyorker.com/news/daily-comment/brother-wristwatch-and-grandpa-wen-chinese-kleptocracy.

Oster, Shai. 2009. "China's Rich Youth Spark Bitter Divide." Wall Street Journal. September 22. http://online.wsj.com/article/SB125357000531429127.htm; story provided by author.

Page, Jeremy, and Noémie Bisserbe. 2013. "French Villa Linked to Fallen Leader." *Wall Street Journal*. August 6. http://www.wsj.com/articles/SB10001424127887323420604578650071253073626.

Pempel, T. J. 1999. *The Politics of the Asian Economic Crisis*. Ithaca, NY: Cornell University Press.

Peng Lianyi (彭漣漪). 2013. "台灣民眾最信任：家人，醫生，中小學老師" [The Taiwan public most trusts family members, doctors, and primary and middle school teachers]. *Yuanjian*. Accessed November 13, 2013. http://www.gvm.com.tw/Boardcontent_23562.html.

Peng Siqing (彭泗清). 2003. "我憑什麼信任你？——當前的信任危機與對策" [Why should I trust you? The present trust crisis and its countermeasures]. Beijing: Zhongguo chengshi chubanshe.

Peoplexz. 2008. "The Civility Slogan of the Time: Five Stresses, Four Beauties, Three Fervent Loves." Accessed August 17, 2009. http://gzhnfz.peoplexz.com/5831/20081001163232.htm.

Pew Research Center. 2012. "Pew Global Attitudes Project, 'Growing Concerns in China about Inequality, Corruption.'" October 16. http://www.pewglobal.org/2012/10/16/growing-concerns-in-china-about-inequality-corruption.

Phillips, Steven E. 2003. *Between Assimilation and Independence: The Taiwanese Encounter Nationalist China, 1945–1950*. Stanford: Stanford University Press.

Phillips, Tom. 2013. "Chinese Police Find Slaughterhouse Selling Cat Meat." *Telegraph*. October 31. http://www.telegraph.co.uk/news/worldnews/asia/china/10417032/Chinese-police-find-slaughterhouse-selling-cat-meat.html.

Pierson, David. 2010. "In China, Shift to Privatized Healthcare Brings Long Lines and Frustration." *Los Angeles Times*. February 11. http://articles.latimes.com/2010/feb/11/business/la-fi-china-hospital11-2010feb11.

Pinker, Steven. 2011. *The Better Angels of Our Nature: Why Violence Has Declined*. New York: Viking.

Pirbhai, Hasanali. 2015. "Look: Chinese Tourists Turn Qinghai Lake into a Garbage Dump after Golden Week." Shanghaiist. October 9. http://shanghaiist.com/2015/10/09/qinghai_lake_turned_garbage_dump.php.

Poston, Dudley L., and Wen-shan Yang. 2014. "Unbalanced Sex Ratios at Birth in Taiwan and China and Their Demographic and Societal Implications." In *The Family and Social Change in Chinese Societies*, edited by D. Poston, W. Yang, and D. Farris. Dordrecht: Springer.

Purves, Bill. 1991. *Barefoot in the Boardroom: Venture and Misadventure in the People's Republic of China*. Sydney: Allen and Unwin.

Quan, Isabel. 2013. "6-Year-Old Boy Who Can't Afford Alarm Clock Walks to School at Night." Shanghaiist. December 15. http://shanghaiist.com/2013/12/15/boy-walks-to-school-night.php.

Quan, Isabel. 2014a. "What Becomes of the Trains during the Spring Festival Holiday Rush?" Shanghaiist. January 24. http://shanghaiist.com/2014/01/24/trashy-trains-spring-festival.php.

Quan, Isabel. 2014b. "Shanghai Man Loses 22kg in Order to Donate Marrow to Stranger." Shanghaiist. February 28. http://shanghaiist.com/2014/02/28/shanghai-worker-loses-22-kg-donate-marrow.php.

Quan, Isabel. 2014c. "Sichuan's "Mine Mother" Raises 7 Children Including 4 Orphans." Shanghaiist. February 28. http://shanghaiist.com/2014/02/28/mine-mother-raises-7-children-including-4-orphans.php.

Rabson, Steve. 1996. "Assimilation Policy in Okinawa: Promotion, Resistance and 'Reconstruction.'" Japan Policy Research Institute (JPRI), Occasional Paper No. 8.

Rao Yinsha, Zhou Jiang, Tian Zhaobin, and Yang Xuanyin (饒印莎、周江、田兆斌、楊宜音). 2013. "城市居民社會信任狀況調查報告" [A report on social trust among urban dwellers]. In 中國社會心態研究報告 [Research report into the Chinese psyche], edited by Wang Junxiu and Yang Xuanyin (王俊秀與楊宜音主編), 71–93. Beijing: Social Science Press.

Rauhala, Emily. 2014. "Why China's Doctors Are Getting Beat Up?" Time. March 7. http://time.com/15185/chinas-doctors-overworked-underpaid-attacked.

Reuters. 2009. "Beijing Billionaires Wonder If Money Can Buy Love." December 23. http://www.reuters.com/article/2009/12/23/us-china-billionair.

Reuters. 2011. "Truck Kills Herder in China Inner Mongolia Protest: Group." October 24. http://www.reuters.com/article/2011/10/24/us-china-innermongolia-idUSTRE79N14L20111024.

Reuters. 2013a. "China Aims to Harness Religious Beliefs to Promote Harmony." November 26. http://www.reuters.com/article/2013/11/26/us-china-religion-idUSBRE9AP04420131126.

Reuters. 2013b. "China: 400 Million Cannot Speak Mandarin." New York Times. September 5. http://www.nytimes.com/2013/09/06/world/asia/china-400-million-cannot-speak-mandarin.html.

Reuters. 2013c. "Tourist Manners Worry Chinese." Reprinted in the Taipei Times. May 31. http://www.taipeitimes.com/News/world/archives/2013/05/31/2003563637.

Reuters. 2015. "Beijing Rolls Out Tough New Anti-smoking Laws." South China Morning Post, May 31. http://www.scmp.com/news/china/policies-politics/article/1814343/beijing-rolls-out-tough-anti-smoking-laws.

Rigger, Shelley. 2016. "The China Impact in Taiwan's Generational Politics." In Taiwan and the 'China Impact', edited by Gunter Schubert, 70–90. New York: Routledge.

Ringen, Stein. 2016. The Perfect Dictatorship: China in the 21st Century. Hong Kong: Hong Kong University Press.

RM. 2009. 品德與生活；品德與社會 [Moral character and life; moral character and society]. Beijing: People's Education Publishers.

RMP. 1988. 思想品德 [Thought and moral character]. Beijing: People's Education Publishers.

Roberts, Dexter. 2013. "Two-Thirds of Chinese Don't Trust Doctors, amid Rising Hospital Violence." Bloomberg. November 13. http://www.bloomberg.com/bw/articles/2013-11-13/two-thirds-of-chinese-dont-trust-doctors-amidst-rising-hospital-violence.

Roberts, Dexter. 2014. "400 Million Chinese Can't Speak Mandarin and Beijing Is Worried." Bloomberg. September 23. http://www.bloomberg.com/bw/articles/2014-09-23/say-that-in-mandarin-please.

Rorty, Amélie Oksenberg. 1997. "From Decency to Civility by Way of Economics: 'First Let's Eat and Then Talk of Right and Wrong.'" Social Research 64 (1): 112–30.

Rovnick, Naomi. 2012. "Educational Détente across Taiwan Strait." *New York Times*. July 26. http://www.nytimes.com/2012/07/26/world/asia/educational-detente-across-taiwan-strait.html.

Rowan, Ian. 2016. "The Geopolitics of Tourism: Mobilities, Territory, and Protest in China, Taiwan, and Hong Kong." *Annals of the American Association of Geographers* 106 (2): 385–93.

Roy, Denny. 2003. *Taiwan: A Political History*. Ithaca, NY: Cornell University Press.

Sant, Geoffrey. 2012. "In China, the Rich and Powerful Can Hire Body Doubles to Do Their Prison time for Them." *Slate*. August 2. http://www.slate.com/articles/news_and_politics/foreigners/2012/08/china_s_wealthy_and_influential_sometimes_hire_body_doubles_to_serve_their_prison_sentences.html.

Sant, Geoffrey. 2015. "Driven to Kill." *Slate*. September 4. http://www.slate.com/articles/news_and_politics/foreigners/2015/09/why_drivers_in_china_intentionally_kill_the_pedestrians_they_hit_china_s.html.

SCCR (Scottish Centre for China Research). 2013. "Performance Evaluations, Trust and Utilization of Health Care, Nationwide Survey in Mainland China, Fieldwork 1 November 2012–17 January 2013, N=3,680." Funded by UK Economic and Social Research Council Grant No. ES/J011487/1. Accessed October 30, 2013. http://www.gla.ac.uk/petu.

Schak, David C. 2009a. "Buddhism and Community in Taiwan." *Minsu Quyi* 163 (3): 161–92.

Schak, David C. 2009b. "The Development of Civility in Taiwan." *Pacific Affairs* 82 (3): 447–65.

Schak, David C. 2012. "Educational Modernisation across the Taiwan Straits: Pedagogical Transformation in Primary School Moral Education Textbooks in the PRC and Taiwan." *Protosociology: An International Journal of Interdisciplinary Research* 29: 143–58.

Schonsheck, Jonathan. 2004. "Rudeness, Rasp, and Repudiation." In *Civility and Its Discontents: Essays on Civic Virtue, Toleration, and Cultural Fragmentation*, edited by Christine T. Sistare, 169–85. Lawrence: University of Kansas Press.

Schoppa, R. Keith. 2000. *The Columbia Guide to Modern Chinese History*. New York: Columbia University Press.

SCMP. 2011. "Lack of Trust Blamed by Academics for Salt Rush." March 19. http://www.scmp.com/article/741360/lack-trust-blamed-academics-salt-rush.

SCMP. 2012. "Extend Spirit of Lei Feng to Religion." March 13. http://www.scmp.com/article/995302/extend-spirit-lei-feng-religion.

SCMP. 2016. "Charity Law Will Give Donors Greater Confidence." July 26. http://www.scmp.com/comment/insight-opinion/article/1994708/charity-law-will-give-donors-greater-confidence.

SEA (Social Ethics Association). n.d. Accessed August 12, 2014. http://www.sea.org.tw/cgi-bin/big5/k/37a2?q1=37a2v1&q65=2015111&q27=20130129113141&q35=&q12=1.

SEA (Social Ethics Association). 2013. "群我倫理促進會2013社會信任調查整理與說明" [Society to promote group-self ethics 2013 social trust survey collation and explanation]. Accessed November 22, 2013. http://www.sea.org.tw/20130625162401.doc.

Shanghaiist. 2015. "Tourists Have Been Forcing Their Way into This Giant Panda Reserve and Leaving Loads of Trash Behind." February 11. http://shanghaiist.com/2015/02/11/tourists_have_been_forcing_their_wa.php.

Shenzhen Daily. 2013. "Shenzhen Civility Law to Take Effect March 1." January 24. http://www.newsgd.com/news/gdnews/content/2013-01/24/content_62651053.htm.
Shils, Edward. 1991. "The Virtue of Civil Society." *Government and Opposition* 26 (4): 3–20.
Shils, Edward. 1992. "The Virtue of Civility." In *Civility and Citizenship in Liberal Democratic Societies*, edited by Edward Banfield, 1–15. New York: Paragon House.
Shils, Edward. 1996. "Reflections on Civil Society and Civility in the Chinese Intellectual Tradition." In *Confucian Traditions in East Asian Modernity: Moral Education and Economic Culture in Japan and the Four Mini-dragons*, edited by Wei-ming-Tu, 38–71. Cambridge, MA: Harvard University Press.
Shils, Edward. 1997a. "Civility and Civil Society." In *The Virtue of Civility: Selected Essays on Liberalism, Tradition, and Civil Society*, edited by Steven Grosby, 25–62. Indianapolis: Liberty Fund.
Shils, Edward. 1997b. "Ideology and Civility." In *The Virtue of Civility: Selected Essays on Liberalism, Tradition, and Civil Society*, edited by Steven Grosby, 63–102. Indianapolis: Liberty Fund.
Shils, Edward. 1997c. "Observations of Some Tribulations of Civility." In *The Virtue of Civility: Selected Essays on Liberalism, Tradition, and Civil Society*, edited by Steven Grosby, 3–24. Indianapolis: Liberty Fund.
Shu Xincheng, Yi Shen, Yanzhu Xu, and Xiang Zhang, eds. 1948. *Cihai Da Zidian*. Zhonghua Shuju.
Smith, Arthur, H. 1900. *Chinese Characteristics*. 5th ed. Edinburgh and London: Oliphant, Anderson and Ferrier.
Smith, Doug. 2006. "Public Spaces, Parks and Democratic Transition: A Case Study of Republican China." PhD diss., Department of International Business and Asian Studies, Griffith University.
Smith, Philip, Timothy L. Phillips, and Ryan D. King. 2010. *Incivility: The Rude Strange in Everyday Life*. Cambridge: Cambridge University Press.
Social Ethics Association (SEA). n.d. Accessed August 12, 2014. http://www.sea.org.tw/cgi-bin/big5/k/37a2?q1=37a2v1&q65=2015111&q27=20130129113141&q35=&q12=1.
Social Ethics Association (SEA). 2013. "群我倫理促進會2013社會信任調查整理與説明" [Society to promote group-self ethics 2013 social trust survey collation and explanation]. Accessed November 22, 2013. http://www.sea.org.tw/20130625162401.doc.
Sohu. 2014. "深圳近50億殘保金去哪裡了" [Where did the close to 5 billion Shenzhen Fund for the Disabled go]. Sohu. June 10. http://roll.sohu.com/20140610/n400668395.shtml.
Sonmez, Felicia. 2014. "China Is Forcing Its Biggest Cantonese-Speaking Region to Speak Mandarin." Business Insider. August 25. http://www.businessinsider.com/china-is-forcing-its-biggest-cantonese-speaking-region-to-speak-mandarin-2014-8.
Speare, Alden, Jr. 1992. "Taiwan's Rural Populace: Brought in or Left Out of the Economic Miracle." In *Taiwan: Beyond the Economic Miracle*, edited by Denis Simon and Michael Kau, 211–33. Armonk, NY: M. E. Sharpe.
Speare, Alden, Jr., Paul K. C. Liu, and Ching-lung Tsay. 1988. *Urbanization and Development: The Rural-Urban Transition in Taiwan*. Boulder, CO: Westview Press.
Spülbeck, Susanne. 1996. "Anti-Semitism and Fear of the Public Sphere in a Post-totalitarian Society: East Germany." In *Civil Society: Challenging Western Models*, edited by Chris Hann and Elizabeth Dunn, 64–78. London and New York: Routledge.

Stanton, Dan. 2013. "Chinese Drugmakers Still Suffering from Chromium Capsule Scandal." Accessed December 22, 2015. http://www.in-pharmatechnologist.com/Regulatory-Safety/Chinese-Drugmakers-Still Suffering-from-Chromium-Capsule-Scandal.

Stevens, Alex. 2014. "Rioting Crowd Severely Beats 5 Chengguan for Killing Civilian." Shanghaiist. April 21. http://shanghaiist.com/2014/04/21, rioting-crowd-beats-5-chengguan-for-killing-civillian.php.

Sullivan, Jon. 2014. "Taiwan's Identity Crisis." *National Interest*. August 18. http://nationalinterest.org/feature/taiwans-identity-crisis-11093.

Su Yining. 2011. "China's Elite Enjoy Untainted Fruits." Asia Times. July 7. http://www.atimes.com/atimes/China/MG07Ad02.html.

Su Yining. 2013. "Photos: Tourists Pose with Dying, Bleeding Dolphin in Hainan." Shanghaiist. June 20. http://shanghaiist.com/2013/06/20/photos_tourists_pose_with_dying_ble.php.

Swift, Ember. 2013. "Time to Bin Beijing's Litterbugs." China.org.cn. July 7. http://www.china.org.cn/opinion/2013-07/07/content_29334154.htm.

Sy, Angela. 2013. "Cyclist Dies While Being Ignored by Passersby for 50 Minutes." Shanghaiist. May 22. http://shanghaiist.com/2013/05/22/cyclist_dies_in_guangzhou_ignored_by_passersby_for_almost_an_hour.php.

Taipei Times. 2014. "Four Taiwanese Philanthropists on 'Forbes' list." *Taipei Times*. June 28. http://www.taipeitimes.com/News/taiwan/archives/2014/06/28/2003593869.

Taiwan Info. 2002. "Government Targets Community Development." Accessed September 14, 2015. http://taiwaninfo.nat.gov.tw/ct.asp?xItem=19745&CtNode=103&htx_TRCategory=&mp=4.

Tan, Kenneth. 2011. "Massive Steamed Bun Recall in Shanghai after Investigative CCTV Report." Shanghaiist. April 12. http://shanghaiist.com/2011/04/12/now_even_steamed_buns_arent_safe_en.php.

Tatlow, Didi Kirsten. 2013. "Li Tianyi Sentencing Is Small Step for Chinese Women." *New York Times*. October 8. http://www.nytimes.com/2013/10/09/world/asia/li-tianyi-sentencing-is-small-step-for-chinese-women.html.

Taylor, Jay. 2011. *The Generalissimo: Chiang Kai-shek and the Struggle for Modern China*. Cambridge: The Belknap Press.

TBSF (Taiwan Blood Services Foundation, 台灣血液基金會). 2017. "A Brief History of Blood Donation Services in Taiwan." Accessed August 25, 2017. http://www.blood.org.tw/Internet/english/docDetail.aspx?uid=7686&pid=7680&docid=36064.

TCG (Travel China Guide). n.d. "China Outbound Tourism in 2015." Accessed March 10, 2016. https://www.travelchinaguide.com/tourism/2015statistics/outbound.htm.

TEIC (Taiwan Environmental Information Center). 2007. "Four Large Environmental Tumors Created by the Lack of Civility." Excerpt from *Zhongguo Shibao*. August 29. Accessed August 2, 2014. http://e-info.org.tw/node/25992.

Telegraph. 2012. "Girl Rescued after Falling through Pavement." April 14. http://www.telegraph.co.uk/news/worldnews/asia/china/9222594/Girl-rescued-after-falling-through-pavement.html.

Tobin, Joseph J., David W. H. Wu, and Dana H. Davidson. 1989. *Preschool in Three Cultures: Japan, China and the United States*. New Haven: Yale University Press.

Tomba, Luigi. 2014. *The Government Next Door: Neighborhood Politics in Urban China*. Ithaca, NY: Cornell University Press.

Tozer, Warren. 1970. "Taiwan's 'Cultural Renaissance': A Preliminary View." *China Quarterly* 43: 81–99.
Tsai, Ming-Chang. 2011. "'Foreign Brides' Meet Ethnic Politics in Taiwan." *International Migration Review* 45 (2): 243–68.
Tseng, Wei-chen, and Jake Chung. 2015. "Professor Blogs about Bombing of Taipei." *Taipei Times*. June 2.
Tseng, Wei-chen, and Wei-han Chen. 2015. "'Taiwanese' Identity Hits Record Level." *Taipei Times*. January 26. http://www.taipeitimes.com/News/front/archives/2015/01/26/2003610092.
Tsoi, Grace. 2015. "Taiwan Has Its Own Textbook Controversy Brewing." *Foreign Policy*. July 21. http://foreignpolicy.com/2015/07/21/taiwan-textbook-controversy-china-independence-history.
Tsurumi, E. Patricia. 1977. *Japanese Colonial Education in Taiwan, 1895–1945*. Harvard East Asia Series, vol. 88. Cambridge: Harvard University Press.
Tuan, Yi-Fu. 1979. *Landscapes of Fear*. Minneapolis: University of Minnesota Press.
TVBS. 2016. "Public Opinion Research Center." January 19. Accessed May 15, 2016. http://www.tvbs.com.tw/export/sites/tvbs/file/other/poll-center/0501181.pdf.
TW. 2011. 綜合活動 [Comprehensive activities]. Taibei: Hanlin.
Twigden, Freya. 2015. "Easy Tiger! Nanjing Driver Tries to Run Woman Over after Line-Jumping Row." Shanghaiist. May 1. Accessed May 4, 2015. http://shanghaiist.com/2015/05/01/nanjing-driver-tries-to-run-woman-over-line-jumping-row.php.
TWP. 1970 生活與倫理 [Life and ethics]. Edited by the National Translation and Editing Office (國立編譯館). Taibei: Guoli bianshi guan.
UNDP (United Nations Development Program). 2015 "Human Development Report, China." Accessed March 20, 2016. http://hdr.undp.org/sites/all/themes/hdr_theme/country-notes/CHN.pdf.
Vogel, Ezra F. 1965. "From Friendship to Comradeship: The Change in Personal Relations in Communist China." *China Quarterly* 21: 46–60.
Wachman, Alan, M. 1994. *Taiwan: National Identity and Democratization*. Armonk, NY: M. E. Sharpe.
Wainwright, Oliver. 2014. "Inside Beijing's Airpocalypse—a City Made 'Almost Uninhabitable' by Pollution." *Guardian*. December 16. http://www.theguardian.com/cities/2014/dec/16/beijing-airpocalypse-city-almost-uninhabitable-pollution-china.
Walzer, Michael. 1974. "Civility and Civic Virtue in Contemporary America." *Social Research* 41: 593–611.
Wan, William. 2010. "China's Wealthy Ponder Whether to Help Others." *Washington Post*, September 17. http://www.washingtonpost.com/wp-dyn/content/article/2010/09/16/AR2010091607171_pf.html.
Wan, William. 2011. "China, Long Lax on Drunken Driving, Begins Crackdown after String of Fatal Crashes." *Washington Post*. June 3. http://www.washingtonpost.com/world/asia-pacific/china-long-lax-on-drunk-driving-begins-crackdown-after-string-of-fatal-crashes/2011/06/03/AGRFdjJH_story.html.
Wan, William. 2013. "In China, Anger Grows over Abuse of Street Vendors." *Washington Post*. March 31. http://www.washingtonpost.com/world/asia_pacific/in-china-anger-grows-over-abuse-of-street-vendors/2013/03/31/b9728ed6-984c-11e2-b68f-dc5c4b47e519_print.html.

Wang, Chris. 2013. "Ma's Approval Rating Plunges to 9.2 Percent." *Taipei Times*. September 16. http://www.taipeitimes.com/News/front/archives/2013/09/16/2003572243.

Wang, Dawn. 2013. "Weibo Blows Up after Famous Beijing Playboy Allegedly Assaults Reporter." Shanghaiist. May 17. http://shanghaiist.com/2013/05/17/wang_shuo_rich_beijing_playboy_fuerdai_allegedly_assaults_female_reporter_and_husband.php.

Wang, Fanfan, and Laurie Burkitt. 2016. "Chinese Vaccine Scandals Reveals System's Flaws." *Wall Street Journal*. March 25. http://www.wsj.com/articles/chinas-vaccine-scandal-reveals-systems-flaws-1458906255.

Wang Fei. 2011. "Fake Charity." *Global Times*. September 7. http://english.peopledaily.com.cn/102780/7590232.html.

Wang Feng. 2011. "The End of 'Growth with Equity'? Economic Growth and Income Inequality in East Asia." *Asia Pacific Issues* 101: 1.

Wang Fu-chang. 2005. "Why Bother about School Textbooks? An Analysis of the Origin of the Dispute over Renshi Taiwan Textbooks in 1997." In *Cultural, Ethnic, and Political Nationalism in Contemporary Taiwan: Bentuhua*, edited by John Makeham and A-chin Hsiau, 55–99. New York and Houndmills: Palgrave.

Wang Fu-chang. 2013. "A Prolonged Exile: National Imagination of the KMT Regime in Postwar Taiwan." *Oriens Extremus* 52: 137–72.

Wang Huazhong. 2010. "Drunken Driver Boasts Father Is a Police Official." *China Daily*, October 20. http://www.chinadaily.com.cn/china/2010-10/20/content_11431705.htm.

Wang, Jennhwan. 1988. "Political Movements against the State: The Transition of Taiwan's Authoritarian Rule." PhD diss., Department of Political Science, UCLA.

Wang Junqiu. 2008. 中國慈善與救濟 [Charity and relief in China]. Beijing: China Social Science Press.

Wang Shaoguang and Liu Xin (王紹光 and 劉欣). 2002. "信任的基礎：一種理性的解釋" [The foundation of trust: A rational explanation]. *Sociological Research* (社會學研究) 3: 23–39.

Wang, Xiaoying. 2002. "The Post-communist Personality: The Spectre of China's Capitalist Market Reforms." *The China Journal* 47: 1–18.

Wang Yifen. 2006. "寶島最值得忙的事：志願服務" [The most worthwhile busy-ness in Taiwan: Volunteer service]. *Yuanjian Zazhi* 241: 190–92.

WCT (Want China Times). 2011a. "Lavish Wedding Motorcade Draws Criticism." Accessed April 23, 2011. http://www.wantchinatimes.com/news-subclass-cnt.aspx?id=20110423000055&cid=1303.

WCT (Want China Times). 2011b. "Self Service: Zhejiang Officials Slammed for Exclusive Farms." Accessed September 21, 2011. http://www.wantchinatimes.com/news-subclass-cnt.aspx?id=20110920000008&cid=1303.

WCT (Want China Times). 2011c. "Vanity Case: Chinese Love to Flaunt Their Wealth." Accessed April 23, 2011. http://www.wantchinatimes.com/news-subclass-cnt.aspx?id=20110423000056&cid=1503.

WCT (Want China Times). 2013. "Man Caught Selling Poisonous Dyed Pork as Beef." April 22, 2013. http://www.wantchinatimes.com/news-subclass-cnt.aspx?id=20110422000038&cid=1103.

Washington, George. 1971. *Rules of Civility & Decent Behaviour in Company and Conversation: A Book of Etiquette*. Williamsburg, VA: Beaver Press.

Watts, Jonathan. 2008. "Sichuan Earthquake: Tragedy Brings New Mood of Unity." *Guardian*, October 6. http://www.theguardian.com/world/2008/jun/10/chinaearthquake.china.

WDIED (Worker's Daily Ideological Education Department). 1982. 五講四美一百題 [One hundred topics on "Five Stresses and Four Beauties"]. Beijing: Worker's Press.

Weller, Robert. 1999a. *Alternate Civilities: Democracy and Culture in China and Taiwan*. Boulder, CO: Westview Press.

Weller, Robert. 1999b. "Identity and Social Change in Taiwanese Religion." In *Taiwan: A New History*, edited by Murray Rubenstein, 339–65. New York: M. E. Sharpe.

Wenming ban (文明辦). n.d. "關於廣泛開展 '迎國慶講文明樹新風' 活動實施方案" [Regarding the broad launch of the Welcome National Day, Stress Civility, Adopt New Customs Activity]. Accessed July 1, 2014. http://wenku.baidu.com/view/198ff4a9d1f34693daef3e61.html.

WGI (World Giving Index). 2013 "A Global View of Giving Trends." Accessed August 6, 2014. https://www.cafonline.org/PDF/WorldGivingIndex2013_1374AWEB.pdf.

WHO. 2015. "Country Profiles, China." Accessed January 17, 2016. http://www.who.int/violence_injury_prevention/road_safety_status/2015/country_profiles/China.pdf.

WHO. 2016. "Tobacco in China." Accessed January 17, 2016. http://www.wpro.who.int/china/mediacentre/factsheets/tobacco/en.

Whyte, Martin King. 2010. *Myth of the Social Volcano: Perceptions of Inequality and Distributive Justice in Contemporary China*. Stanford: Stanford University Press.

Wikipedia. 2014a. "CCP Campaigns." Accessed January 20, 2014. http://en.wikipedia.org/wiki/List_of_campaigns_of_the_Communist_Party_of_China.

Wikipedia. 2014b. "Xinshenghuo Yundong" [新生活運動]. Accessed January 18, 2014. http://zh.wikipedia.org/wiki/新生活運動.

Williams, Jack F. 1992. "Environmentalism in Taiwan." In *Taiwan: Beyond the Economic Miracle*, edited by Denis Fred Simon and Michael Y. M. Kau, 187–210. Armonk, NY: M. E. Sharpe.

Wilkinson, Richard, and Kate Pickett. 2009. *The Spirit Level: Why More Equal Societies Almost Always Do Better*. UK: Allen Lane.

Wilson, Richard W. 1981. "Moral Behavior in Chinese Society: A Theoretical Perspective." In *Moral Behavior in Chinese Society*, edited by Richard W. Wilson, Sidney L. Greenblatt, and Amy Auerbacher Wilson, 1–20. New York: Praeger.

Winckler, Edwin A. 1994. "Cultural Policy on Postwar Taiwan." In *Cultural Change in Postwar Taiwan*, Stevan Harrell, and Chun-chieh Huang, 22–46. Boulder, CO: Westview Press.

Wines, Michael. 2009. "Civic-Minded Chinese Find a Voice Online." *New York Times*. June 17. http://www.nytimes.com/2009/06/17/world/asia/17china.html.

Wines, Michael. 2010. "China's Censors Misfire in Abuse-of-Power Case." *New York Times*. November 17. http://www.nytimes.com/2010/11/18/world/asia/18li.html.

Wines, Michael. 2011a. "Bystanders' Neglect of Injured Toddler Sets Off Soul-Searching on Web Sites in China." *New York Times*. October 18. http://www.nytimes.com/2011/10/19/world/asia/toddlers-accident-sets-off-soul-searching-in-china.html.

Wines, Michael. 2011b. "Execution in a Killing That Fanned Class Rancor." *New York Times*. June 7. http://www.nytimes.com/2011/06/08/world/asia/08china.html.

Wines, Michael, and Ian Johnson. 2011. "After a Horrific Crash, a Stark Depiction of Injustice in China." *New York Times*. November 19. http://www.nytimes.com/2011/11/19/world/asia/a-horrific-crash-sets-off-online-anger-in-china.html.

Wong, Cai. 2016. "Wukan Stirs Again." *Diplomat*. June 30. http://thediplomat.com/2016/07/wukan-stirs-again.

Wong, Chun Han. 2014. "Death of Elderly Man Denied a Bus Seat Sets Off Introspection in China." *Wall Street Journal*. September 15. http://blogs.wsj.com/chinarealtime/2014/09/15/death-of-elderly-man-denied-a-bus-seat-sets-off-introspection-in-china.

Wong, Edward. 2011. "An Online Scandal Underscores Chinese Distrust of State Charities." *New York Times*. July 4. http://www.nytimes.com/2011/07/04/world/asia/04china.html.

Wong, Edward. 2013. "Survey in China Shows a Wide Gap in Income." *New York Times*. July 20. http://www.nytimes.com/2013/07/20/world/asia/survey-in-china-shows-wide-income-gap.html.

Worldlifeexpectancy. 2015. "World Health Rankings, Road Traffic Accidents." Accessed January 17, 2016. http://www.worldlifeexpectancy.com/cause-of-death/road-traffic-accidents/by-country/.

Woronov, Terry Ellen. 2003. "Transforming the Future: 'Quality' Children and the Chinese Nation, Volume One." PhD diss., Department of Anthropology, University of Chicago.

Wu, Bin. 2012. "Coping with an Extreme Rainstorm in Beijing on 21st July 2012: Some Observations and Reflections." *China Policy Institute: Analysis* (blog). July 24. http://blogs.nottingham.ac.uk/chinapolicyinstitute/2012/07/24/coping-with-an-extreme-rainstorm-in-beijing-on-21st-july-2012-some-observations-and-reflections.

Wu Haixia. 2012. "關於魯迅小說對 '看客文化' 的批判" [A critique of the treatment of the "gawker mentality" in Lu Xun's short stories]. Accessed July 21, 2014. http://big.hi138.com/wenxueyishu/dangdaiwenxue/201211/428584.asp#.U8yFmFblfwI.

Wu Jiawen, and Han Xiaorong. 2012. "Catalogue of Crisis." *Chinadialogue*. May 28. http://www.chinadialogue.net/article/show/single/en/4946-Catalogue-of-a-crisis?utm_source=Chinadialogue+Update&utm_campaign=8116891ee9-newsletter+22+May+2012&utm_medium=email.

Wu, Nai-teh. 2015. "歷史記憶中的模糊與位置：二二八死難人數的爭論" [The confusion and the unknown in historical memory: The controversy over the number of dead in Two-Two-Eight]. *Sixiang* 21 (5): 179–94.

Wu Yixue. 2014. "The Elderly Should Not Tell Others to Vacate Seats." *China Daily*. September 16. http://www.chinadaily.com.cn/opinion/2014-09/17/content_18610917.htm.

Wu Yiyao. 2009. "Rich Getting Richer, but Poor Becoming Resentful." *China Daily*. December 10. http://www.chinadaily.com.cn/china/2009-12/10/content_9151067.htm.

Xiang Yang (向陽). 2005. "從「當家」到「作主」：二十年後重讀龍應台《野火集》有感" [From household manager to decision maker: Feelings upon rereading Lung Ying-tai's *Wildfire Collection* twenty years later]. Accessed April 8, 2015. http://tns.ndhu.edu.tw/~xiangyang/crib_18.htm.

Xichengdudao. 2006. "'八榮八恥' 是非明" [In "Eight Honor, Eight Shame" right and wrong are clear]. Accessed February 19, 2014. http://xichengdudao.bokee.com/60828091.html.

Xie, Chuanjiao. 2009. "Cook's Death Sparks Protests in Hubei." *China Daily*, June 22. http://www.chinadaily.com.cn/china/2009-06/22/content_8306649.htm.

Xing, Yu (邢瑜). 2013. "政策變遷對社區意涵的影響：台灣一九九四至二〇一二年的社區總體營造政策" [The effect of government policy toward community meaning: Community construction policy in Taiwan from 1994 to 2012]. *Chinese Public Administration Review* 19 (4): 1–2.

Xinhua News Agency. 2003. "Lei Feng Remains National Icon Despite Social Changes." China.org.cn. March 4. http://www.china.org.cn/archive/2003-03/04/content_1057322.htm.

Xinhua News Agency. 2008. "45 Years on, Lei Feng Still a Selfless Model?" China.org.cn. March 5. http://www.china.org.cn/culture/2008-03/05/content_11691456.htm.

Xinhua News Agency. 2011. "China City to Award Uruguayan Woman for 'Good Samaritan' Deed." *People's Daily*. November 3. http://english.peopledaily.com.cn/90882/7634493.html.

Xinhua News Agency. 2012. "China's Drunk Driving Cases Drop 40 Pct Following New Law." Accessed June 18, 2014. http://news.xinhuanet.com/english/china/2012-05/23/c_131605916.htm.

Xinhua News Agency. 2014. "China Receives Surging Charitable Donations in 2013." Accessed August 6, 2014. http://news.xinhuanet.com/english/china/2014-06/18/c_133417316.htm.

Xinhua News Agency. 2015. "China Encourages Square Dancing with More Management." *New China*. September 6. http://news.xinhuanet.com/english/2015-09/06/c_134595443.htm.

Xu Lin. 2009. "中國的宗教與5.12地震發生後的抗震救災活動" [Chinese religion and the rescue activities following the 5/12 earthquake]. Paper delivered at the Sixth Symposium of the Social Scientific Study of Religion in China: Globalization and Localization of Religion, Wuxi, Jiangsu, July 7–8.

Yan, Alice. 2012. "'Beautiful Teacher' Becomes New Hero." *South China Morning Post*. May 28. http://www.scmp.com/article/1002243/beautiful-teacher-becomes-new-hero.

Yan, Alice. 2015. China's Airports and Airlines Lead the World in Flight Delays: US Survey." *South China Morning Post*. March 21. http://www.scmp.com/news/china/article/1743637/chinas-airports-and-airlines-lead-world-flight-delays-us-survey.

Yan Yunxiang. 2009. *The Individualization of Chinese Society*. Oxford: Berg.

Yan Yunxiang. 2011. "The Changing Moral Landscape." In *Deep China: The Moral Life of the Person, What Anthropology and Psychiatry Tell Us about China Today*, by Arthur Kleinman, Yunxiang Yan, Jing Jun, Sing Lee, Everett Zhang, Tianshu Pan, Wu Fei, Guo Jinhua, 36–77. Berkeley, Los Angeles, and London: University of California Press.

Yan, Zu (晏祖). 1972. "人情味與公德：青年自覺運動專輯" [The human touch and public morality: The youth self-awareness movement special edition]. Taibei: Wuzhou.

Yang Ailing, and Song Xuemei. 2006. "威海市農民無償獻血者的招募" [The recruitment of unpaid farmer blood donors in Weihai city]. *J Clin Transfus Lab Med* 9 (4): 346–49.

Yang Fan. 2006. "福州市民文明禮儀手冊" [A handbook of civilized etiquette for Fuzhou citizens]. Fuzhou: People's Press.

Yang, Guobin. 2009. *The Power of the internet in China: Citizen Activism Online*. New York: Columbia University Press.

Yang, Guobin, and Craig Calhoun. 2007. "Media, Civil Society, and the Rise of a Green Public Sphere in China." *China Information* 21 (2): 211–36.

Yang, Martin M. C. 1945. *A Chinese Village: Taitou, Shantung Province*. New York: Columbia University Press.

Yang, Xiao-jun. 2010. "Taiwanese Give Most to Charity in Greater China Area." WCT. December 23. http://www.wantchinatimes.com/news-subclass-cnt.aspx?cid=1103&MainCatID=11&id=20101223000009.

Yau, Sea-Wain. n.d. "Tobacco Control in Taiwan: A Taiwanese NGO Perspective." Accessed September 11, 2015. http://www.ehfg.org/intranet/app/webroot/uploads/presentations/files/uploads/16e166010ac3a3ca7939107faf9be1.pdf.

Ye, Josh. 2017. "Beijingers Exercise Collective Ownership of Public Toilet Paper." Shanghaiist. March 2. http://www.scmp.com/news/china/society/article/2075431/beijingers-exercise-collective-ownership-public-toilet-paper.

Ye Xiaofan. 2007. "我國無償獻血者人群構成現狀" [The structure of China's unpaid blood donors]. *Jiangsu Weisheng Shiye Guanli* 2 (18): 71–73.

Yen Chen-shen. 2005. "Taiwan's Foreign Brides Deserve Respect." *Taiwan Info*. January 14. http://taiwaninfo.nat.gov.tw/ct.asp?xItem=21101&CtNode=103&htx_TRCategory=&mp=4.

YouTube. 2015. https://www.youtube.com/watch?v=hfipcI0tq44.

Yu, Rose. 2015. "China Road Rage Cases Top 17 Million So Far in 2015." *Wall Street Journal*. December 2. http://blogs.wsj.com/chinarealtime/2015/12/02/china-road-rage-cases-top-17-million-so-far-in-2015.

Yu, Sophie. 2014. "Charitable Venture Valued at US$3b Will Focus on Environment, Health and Education." *South China Morning Post*. April 26. http://www.scmp.com/business/china-business/article/1497224/alibaba-founders-give-back-charitable-trust-worth-us3b.

Yung, Chester. 2014. "State Media Advises Chinese tourists in Hong Kong: Don't Talk So Loud." *Wall Street Journal*. May 12. http://blogs.wsj.com/chinarealtime/2014/05/12/state-media-advises-chinese-tourists-in-hong-kong-dont-talk-so-loud.

Zang, Xiaowei. 2008. "Market Transition, Wealth and Status Claims." In *The New Rich in China: Future Rulers, Present Lives*, edited by David S. G. Goodman, 53–70. London and New York: Routledge.

Zeng, Shaojun. 2009. "Searching for the Disappearance of Trust in the Context of W. F. Tang's Chinese Public Opinion and Civil Society." *China NPO Critique* (July): 221–33.

Zhang Congzhi, Sheng Menglu, and Li Rongde. 2017. "Chinese Billionaires Donate Record Sum in 2016, Report Shows." Caixin. January 13. http://www.caixinglobal.com/2017-01-13/101043725.html.

Zhang Han, and Beibei Ji. 2011. "Experts Dispute 'Trust' Survey." *Global Times*. January 27. Accessed March 15, 2015. http://china.globaltimes.cn/chinanews/2011-01/617326.html.

Zhang Liande. 2011. "農民社會信任危機的生成原因與對策探討——基於皖北D縣調查" [The root cause of and countermeasures for migrant worker crisis of social trust based on a survey in D county]. *Northwest Population* 5 (32): 90–94.

Zhang, Mei. 1999. "From Lei Feng to Zhang Haidi: Changing Images of Model Youth in the Post-Mao Reform Era." In *Civic Discourse, Civil Society & Chinese Communities*, edited by Randy Kluver and John H. Powers, 111–24. Stamford, CO: Ablex.

Zhang Rui. 2013. "New Twist in Li Tianyi Rape Case." China.org.cn. August 8. Accessed July 24, 2014. http://china.org.cn/china/2013-08/08/content_29659252.htm.

Zhang Xujun, Yao Hongyan, Hu Guoqing, Cui Mengjing, Gu Yue, and Xiang Huiyuan. 2013. "Basic Characteristics of Road Traffic Deaths in China." *Iran Journal of Public Health* 42 (1): 7–15. http://www.ncbi.nlm.nih.gov/pmc/articles/PMC3595633.

Zhang Yiqian. 2014. "As Population Ages, Young Square Off against Old in Public Spaces." *Global Times*. September 21. http://www.globaltimes.cn/content/882590.shtml.

Zhao Lixin (趙立新). 2005. "社會資本與當今農村社會信任──基於一項調查的社會學研究" [Social capital and present-day village social trust—based on a sociological survey]. *Inner Mongolia Social Science* (內蒙古社會科學) 26 (2): 118–22.

Zheng, Guoshen, Lianyi Li, Xialing Fu, and Shumin Zheng. 2012. "高職學生生態文明素質現狀及其提升研究──基於福建省四所告知院校的調查" [On the current situation and the enhancement of the ecological civilization quality of vocational college students: A case study of the survey on four higher vocational colleges in Fujian Province]. *Journal of Chengdu University: Educational Sciences Edition* 26 (6): 86–92.

Zhongguowang (中國網). 2013. Accessed January 18, 2013. http://www.china.com.cn/zhibo/2013-01/18/content_27692231.htm.

Zhu, Changjun. 2015. "四川傷醫事件調查：9分鐘到現場家屬說來太晚" [Investigation of an injured doctor case in Sichuan: Relatives say that 9 minutes to the site was too long]. Accessed January 10, 2016. http://www.chinanews.com/sh/2016/01-06/7704228.shtml.

Zhu Hong (朱虹). 2010. "社會信任與和諧社會建設" [Social trust and the construction of a harmonious society]. *Hunan Normal University Journal of Social Science* (湖南師範大學社會科學學報) 5: 72–74.

Zhu Hong (朱虹). 2011. "轉型時期社會信任的狀況與特徵" [Characteristics and conditions of social trust in an era of change]. *Guizhou Journal of Social Science* (貴州社會科學) 262 (10): 118–23.

Zhuang, Pinghui. 2013. "Migrant Workers Feel Like Outsiders in Mainland Cities, Says Survey." *South China Morning Post*. May 3. http://www.scmp.com/news/china/article/1170903/migrant-workers-feel-outsiders-mainland-cities-says-survey.

Zijue Yundong (自覺運動). n.d. Wikipedia. Accessed December 18, 2013. http://zh.wikipedia.org/wiki.

Zuo, Mandy. 2013. "Nanjing Teenager Exposed as Perpetrator of Temple of Luxor Graffiti Attack." *South China Morning Post*, May 27. http://www.scmp/news/china/article/1246892/nanjing-teenager-exposed-perpetrator-temple-luxor-graffiti-attack.

Index

Allito, Guy, 20
Almond, Gabriel, and Sidney Verba, 19
Anderson, Benedict, 16

be civilized (*jiang wenming*), 54–60
Becker, Marvin, 13
Beijing Playboys (*jingcheng sishao*) 108–9
blood donations, 100, 114
bogus products, 58, 105–6
Brother Watch, 110

Caldwell, Mark, 14
Calhoun, Cheshire, 13, 14
Carter, Stephen, 14
Chang, Hao, 26–27
Chen Ruoshui, 8, 22, 24, 25–26, 27, 128
Chen Shui-bian, 40–41, 112, 158
Chen Wen-cheng, 126
Chiang Ching-kuo (CCK), 40, 61, 124, 125, 126, 130–31
Chiang Kai-shek, 36, 37, 38, 39, 124
China-Taiwan differences and similarities, 5, 10, 29–30, 34–36, chapter 3, 136–47; divergence, 30–31, 33–36; ethnic makeup, 30; history, 30; socioeconomic development, 30, 33–35, 121–22, 137–38; teaching civility in, 60–69
China Youth Self-Awareness Promotion Movement, 3
Chinese Communist Party (CCP), 7
Chinese Cultural Renaissance Movement, 3, 9, 39–40

civility, vii, chapter 2; and civil society, 6; and democratization 5; development in Europe, 7, 9, 11–14; and court behavior 11–13; and democracy, 153–54, 157–58; and government, vii, 7, 18, 40–41; and public space, 7; and self-expression values 153–54; and tourism, 18; and trust, 17, 18, 144–48; and values, 153–54; Chinese acceptance of, 7; conditions facilitating, 17–18, 148–50; conditions hindering, 18–19, 150–53; defined, 4, 6–7, 8, 13–17, 55–56, 57; civility in dynastic China, 11, 19–20, 21–24, 25–26
civility, Taiwan and China compared 115–16, 117
civility in China, 10, improvements in, 73, 111; structural and social impediments, 136–47
civility in Taiwan, 1–5, 6, 10, 17, 35, 39–42, 117, 118; as seen by Chinese, 116–17; by foreigners, 115–16; by Taiwanese, 115; at present, 112–14, 117–35; development of, 121–35; in the past 4–5, 17, 117; political events, 124–26
civilizing campaigns, 10, 36; China, 10, 42–60; ROC/Taiwan, 10, 36–30, 40–42. *See also* specific campaigns
cixu geju (differential modes of association), 21
condescension, 88, 101–2
Confucian "Golden Rule," 7
Confucius, Confucianism, 20, 95
considering others, 65–67, 113

Index

Cultural Renaissance Movement, 3, 39–40, 137
customer service, 57–58, 88–89

Davetian, Benet, 12, 13
democracy/democratization, 34, 130, 157–58
Democrat Progressive Party (DPP), 112, 130
Deng Xiaoping, 46
Deng Yujiao, 110–11
Dirlik, Arif, 37, 38, 45, 46, 47, 50, 51
disregarding rules, 64, 65, 94–96
disturbing others, 64, 65, 84–86; by children, 84–85n20–21
Don Baron (Di Renhua), 1, 3
Dongcheng be civilized campaign, 56–60
dynastic China, 19, 19–20

Elias, Norbert, 11, 12, 13, 14
environment, 63–64, 149–50
Erasmus, 12
Erbaugh, Mary S., 48

face (*mianzi*), 7
February 28 Incident, 33
Fei Xiaotong, 21
five polite phrases, 48
five stresses, four beauties, three fervent loves, 45–48, 95, 158
Formosa/*Meilidao* incident, 124, 125
Fukuzawa Yūkichi, 24, 27

Gold, Thomas, 34
gongdexin. See public morality
good Samaritan actions, 23, 74–78; cheat good Samaritans, 75–76, 78
governance, China, 142–43, 148–49, 152, 158; Taiwan, 33–34, 117–18, 119–20, 123–26, 130, 137, 142–43, 149, 153
guiju (rules) vs *limao* (manners), 19–20

Habermas, Jürgen 16
Hakka, 17, 30, 118, 130, 131, 155
Hall, John A., 11, 13, 19
Han, in Taiwan 30, 137, 155

Harrell, Stevan, 35
hawkers, 2–3
helping others, 65, 88–89
Hessler, Peter, 27, 80
Hoklo, 17, 30, 118, 130, 155
Hsiao, Hsin-huang Michael, 128, 129
Hsiao, Kung-chuan, 20, 21
Hu Bin, 106–7

identity, 124, 132–35
ignoring rules, 73, 82, 94–96
incivility in Taiwan, vi, 1–2, 114–15, 129
inequality, China, 101–4, 106, 138, 140–42; Taiwan, 138
Inglehart, Ronald and Christian Welzel, 153–54
in-group, out-group, 18–19

Jacobs, J. Bruce, 125
Japan and Taiwan, 30–32, 117; assimilation of Taiwanese, 31–32; *kōminka*, 31, Nipponization, 31–32, 33
jiang wenming (be civilized) 54–55
jinzi, 20
Jones, Susan Mann, 24

Keane, John, 12, 13
Kesler, Charles R., 15
Kim, Sungmoon, 20
Kipnis, Andrew, 49, 51

Lee Teng-hui, 131, 142
Lei Feng, learning from, 42–45, 46, 60, 75n5
Levenson, Joseph, 26
li (ceremonious behavior/etiquette), 19–20, 95
Liang Qichao, 17, 24, 128
Li Kwoh-ting, 128, 145; sixth relationship, 128, 145
Lin, Qinghong (Delia), 50, 51
Lin Yutang, 23
Li Qiming, 107
Li Tianyi, 108
littering, 5, 18, 61–62, 63, 91–94
Little Yueyue, 74, 75, 76, 78
Liu, Henry, 126

Lung Ying-tai, 129–30, 158
Lu Xun, 27

Mainlanders, 5, 17, 33, 118–19, 131; attitudes toward Taiwan/Taiwanese, 119
Mao Zedong, 5, 29, 124
Margalit, Avishai, 15
Marxism, 9
McGregor, Joan, 15
methodology and data sources, vii, 4, 5–6, 8–9, 112
Mount, Ferdinand, 14
Murthy, Sheela, 46, 47, 48, 51

New Life Movement, 3, 7, 9, 37–39, 95, 158
noise, 66, 85–86

Orwin, Clifford, 15

pa chikui, 80
Peng Yu, 75, 75n5–7, 76
philanthropy, 97–101, 113–14, 122–23, 131–32; government role in, 97, 99–100, scandals, 98–99
Phillips, Steven, 33
Pinker, Stephen, 11, 12, 18
privileged vs. the rest 101–10, 139–40
public (*gong*), 16, 24–28
public morality (*gongdexin*), vi, 1, 6; lack of in Taiwan, 1–3, 4. *See also* civility
public space and facilities, 25–28, 61–63, 94
public transport behavior, 90–91, 113
Purves, Bill, 27

quality (*suzhi*) 49–51
queuing, 3, 5, 7, 17, 64, 89–90, 113

religion and civility, 13–14, 113, 122–23, 131, 157–58
renqingwei (the human touch), vi, 1
resentment toward the rich and powerful, 104–5, 106, 109
road behavior, vi, 2, 5, 17–18, 40, 70, 79–82, 112–13, 128, 149
Rorty, Amélie Oksenberg, 15, 17, 18

Schonsheck, Jonathan, 15
Shils, Edward, 14–15, 17, 19
Smith, Arthur, 25
Smith, Douglas, 16
smoking, vi, 1–2, 5, 8, 70, 86–88, 113, 115
social movements, 127–31; consumer, 127; environmental, 127–28
social unity/nationalism, 138–42, 151, 155–57
society for itself, 10, 16, 120, 154–57; Taiwan's transformation to, 121–35, 155–56
special supply (*tegong*), 106
spitting, 62, 112, 115
Spülbeck, Susanne, 18
strangers, 1, 7, 27, 64, 74–84; assist in distress, 76–78; ignore, 2, 64, 74–75; interactions with, 7, 18, 82–84, 88
suzhi (human quality), 45, 49–51
Sun Yat-sen, 17, 36–37

Taiwan nativist literature movement (*xiangtu wenxue*), 39, 123–24
Taiwanese, 5, 33; ethnic makeup, 29–30; identity, 132–33, 133–35
Taiwanese-Mainlander relationship, 33, 119–20
teaching civility, 9, 10, 29, 60–69, 136–47
toilet behavior, 70, 71, 73
tourists/tourism, 18, 70–73, 93, 95, 116–17
trust, 18, 144–47, 151
Tuan, Yi-fu, 11, 19

uncivil, 82–84
Uncle House, 110
urban managers (*chengguan*), 74, 152

violence, 11, 74, 86–87, 90–91, 152
Vogel, Ezra, 18
volunteering, 63, 113–14; in disasters, 78

Walzer, Michael, 14, 15
Washington, George, 14
Welcome National Day (Dongcheng campaign), 56–59
Welcome the Olympics, 55–56

Weller, Robert, 6, 131
wenming, 6–7, 45, 55
Whyte, Martin King, 103–4
Wilkenson, Richard, and Kate Pickett, vii
Wilson, Richard, 22
Wu, Haixia, 27

xiangyue (village compact), 20–21
Xiao Heba Village campaign, 52–54
Xu Xitu, 3, 4

Yan, Yunxiang, 35
Yang, Guobin, and Craig Calhoun, 16
Yao Jiaxin, 107–8

zhan pianyi (benefiting at others' expense), 71, 75, 94
zhengqian konghou (wanting to be first), 80, 83
zijiren (insiders), 17

About the Author

David Schak is currently an adjunct associate professor in the Department of International Business and Asian Studies at Griffith University, Australia. He earned a PhD in anthropology from the University of California, Berkeley, in 1973 and was an associate professor of Asian studies at Griffith University before his retirement. He is the author of *A Chinese Beggars' Den: Poverty and Mobility in an Underclass Community* and coeditor of *Civil Society in Asia*.